GRAPHIS PUBLICATION 1

THE INTERNATIONAL SURVEY OF EDITORIAL DESIGN

EDITED BY: B. MARTIN PEDERSEN

PUBLISHER AND CREATIVE DIRECTOR: B. MARTIN PEDERSEN

EDITOR: JOY AQUILINO

ART DIRECTOR: ADRIAN PULFER

DESIGNERS: MARY JANE CALLISTER, ERIC GILLETT, ADRIAN PULFER

GRAPHIS PRESS CORP., ZÜRICH, SWITZERLAND

Contents

CONTRIBUTORS...6

PREFACE...8

INTRODUCTION: A HISTORICAL OVERVIEW OF EDITORIAL DESIGN [BY ALVIN GROSSMAN].........9

1 MAGAZINE COVERS [BY DANA ANDREW JENNINGS]................21

2 THE GRID [BY MASSIMO VIGNELLI]..........................33

3 NEW TECHNOLOGY: COMPUTERS IN DESIGN [BY MICHAEL KAPLAN]....45

4 PICTURES ON THE PAGE: EDITORIAL ILLUSTRATION & PHOTOGRAPHY [BY JILL BOSSERT]......59

5 THE EDITOR/DESIGNER RELATIONSHIP [BY TOM BENTKOWSKI]........79

6 UNITY AND DIVERSITY: A CROSSREAD OF EUROPEAN MAGAZINES [BY HERBERT LECHNER]......91

CASE STUDIES: THE MAGAZINES

   VOGUE ITALIA [BY NICOLE VIAUD]........................103

   INDUSTRIAL LAUNDERER [BY PEGGY ROALF]..................117

   BUSINESS WEEK [BY MICHAEL McTWIGAN]....................123

   FMR [BY HERBERT LECHNER].............................129

   VOGUE [BY VÉRONIQUE VIENNE]..........................137

   FAZ MAGAZIN [BY HERBERT LECHNER].....................145

   ROLLING STONE [BY MICHAEL McTWIGAN]...................155

CASE STUDIES: THE ART DIRECTORS

   FRANK ZACHARY [BY VÉRONIQUE VIENNE].....................165

   FABIEN BARON [BY VÉRONIQUE VIENNE]......................175

   WALTER BERNARD & MILTON GLASER [BY VÉRONIQUE VIENNE]......185

   ROBERT PRIEST [BY VÉRONIQUE VIENNE].....................191

RETROSPECTIVE: A SELECTION OF INFLUENTIAL EDITORIAL DESIGN........................203

INDEX..243

ACKNOWLEDGMENTS..256

CONTRIBUTORS

TOM BENTKOWSKI, design director of *Life* magazine since 1987, has worked on such notable publications as *New York*, *New West*, *L'Express*, the *Saturday Review*, *The New York Times*, and various special issues, supplements, and prototypes. His work has been cited by the American Institute of Graphic Arts (AIGA) and the Society of Publication Designers (SPD). ■ JILL BOSSERT, formerly associate publisher at Madison Square Press, is at work on a novel. She has curated exhibitions for and managed a variety of award-winning design and illustration annuals. ■ Former art director of *American Home*, *Family Circle*, and *McCall's* magazines, ALVIN GROSSMAN has designed magazines, books, and corporate identity programs, and lectured on editorial design at The Parsons School of Design, Pratt Institute, and The School of Visual Arts. His design work has been featured in *Idea* and *Communication Arts* magazine. ■ DANA ANDREW JENNINGS is a journalist, novelist, and corporate communications specialist. His articles have appeared in *The Wall Street Journal*, *Esquire*, *New England Monthly*, *Graphis*, and many other publications. His first novel, *Mosquito Games*, was published in 1989, and his second, *Women of Granite*, is scheduled for publication in the spring of 1992. ■ MICHAEL KAPLAN is a New York–based journalist who writes for *GQ*, *American Photo*, and *Spy*. ■ HERBERT LECHNER was editor-in-chief of *Graphik Visuelles Marketing* magazine for five years. Since 1986, he has worked as a freelance journalist, frequently writing about "visual culture." He is currently at work on a series of books on movements and trends in modern graphic design for Graphis Press. He is also a partner in Basse & Lechner, a small publishing firm specializing in limited editions. ■ MICHAEL McTWIGAN is the founding editor of *American Ceramics* magazine, a former editor of *ID (Industrial Design)*, and currently the features editor of *VARBUSINESS*, a magazine covering the computer industry. His articles on art and design have appeared in numerous publications and exhibition catalogs, and he is a frequent lecturer at museums and universities. He was awarded an Art Critic's Fellowship by the National Endowment for the Arts in 1981. ■ Former art director PEGGY ROALF is writing a series of art books for young readers entitled *Looking at Paintings*. The first four in the series will be published in the spring of 1992 by Hyperion Books for Children, a Disney Company imprint. ■ NICOLE VIAUD studied graphic arts in Paris and graduated from the University of Zurich with a degree in Art History. She works as an illustrator and lives in Como, Italy. ■ A writer, creative director, and editorial designer, VÉRONIQUE VIENNE has art directed numerous magazines, including *Self*, *Parenting*, *Image*, *West*, *San Francisco*, and *Interiors*. She is currently director of business development for Yves Saint Laurent Parfums Corp., New York. ■ An award-winning designer of publications, corporate identity programs, architectural graphics, and exhibition, interior, furniture, and consumer product designs, MASSIMO VIGNELLI'S work has been published and exhibited throughout the world and entered in the permanent collections of several museums. He is also the recipient of many awards and honors, including honorary doctorates from Pratt Institute and the Rhode Island School of Design, and has served as president of the Alliance Graphique Internationale and the AIGA. ■

TOM BENTKOWSKI

JILL BOSSERT

ALVIN GROSSMAN

DANA ANDREW
JENNINGS

MICHAEL KAPLAN

HERBERT LECHNER

MICHAEL McTWIGAN

PEGGY ROALF

NICOLE VIAUD

VÉRONIQUE VIENNE

WE EXTEND OUR
HEARTFELT THANKS
TO CONTRIBUTORS
THROUGHOUT THE
WORLD WHO HAVE
MADE IT POSSIBLE
FOR US TO PUBLISH
A WIDE SPECTRUM
OF OUTSTANDING
WORK IN THIS FIELD

MASSIMO VIGNELLI

PREFACE

This book describes and illustrates through the words and work of professionals the process of editorial design. The various settings that affect magazine design are addressed, with each acknowledged as having a significant impact on the development and continuing evolution of a publication's identity. □ In the first part of the book, each of six chapters covers a different aspect of the magazine: its historical context, the commercial prerequisites of "successful" covers, the basic principles of magazine design, the impact of new technology, the execution of art and photography, the relationship of the editor and designer, and the latest trends in international publication design. □ The second part is comprised of case studies in which the work and circumstances of individual magazines and art directors are reviewed and discussed. □ Finally, the Retrospective is a selection of influential work, where innovative approaches to design, photography, and illustration point toward the future of the profession. □ The purpose of this book is to provide insight into a range of successful editorial design procedures and solutions. Style is not merely the way in which materials are chosen and arranged in order to effectively convey an idea, but is also the definition of the work, its audience, and of the magazine itself. ■

INTRODUCTION

A HISTORICAL OVERVIEW OF EDITORIAL DESIGN

[ALVIN GROSSMAN]

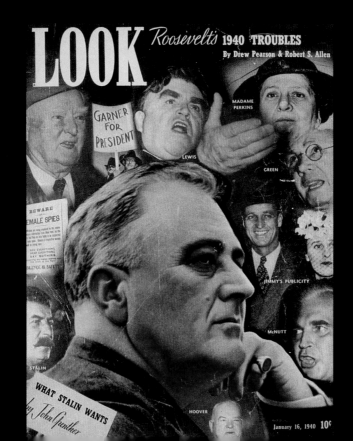

LOOK

Roosevelt's 1940 TROUBLES

By Drew Pearson & Robert S. Allen

GARNER FOR PRESIDENT

MADAME PERKINS

LEWIS

GREEN

BEWARE
EMALE SPIES

JIMMY'S PUBLICITY

McNUTT

STALIN

WHAT STALIN WANTS

by John Gunther

HOOVER

January 16, 1940 10¢

INTRODUCTION

Publication design is not a decorative art. Its function has always been to take words and ideas and to combine them with images to reflect, reinforce, and enhance a point of view. □ *Long before there was a sizable literate populace, there were visual communicators who could influence, persuade, teach, stimulate thinking, disseminate information, and entertain. Written language is about five thousand years old. For at least 3,500 of those years human culture was recorded and transmitted on papyrus, clay, stone, or vellum. The readership was small and exclusive, consisting chiefly of priests, scholars, and the literate nobility. What the Western Everyman knew depended solely on what he had witnessed and heard.* □ *Papermaking, block printing, and moveable type are all Chinese inventions that, with their introduction to the West, produced a revolution in communications. Before Gutenberg there were a few thousand manuscripts for a European population of one hundred million. By 1480, it was possible to produce about one hundred printed copies of any given work. During the seventeenth century twenty times that number could be produced in a single printing. Reading became part of popular culture, and the market for the world's knowledge had been expanded infinitely.* □ *By* the time printing became practical and widespread, the basic tools of the graphic communicator were already in use. The monastic regimen of the Benedictines, for example, dating from the sixth century A.D., required that monks read at least two hours a day and that they copy manuscripts and lend them to other monasteries and to the public. Their copying room, or scriptorium, was an "art department" consisting of scribes, calligraphers, rubricators, and binders. ■ In the eighth century, Charlemagne and the English monk Alcuin joined forces to reorganize the written language. Alcuin's school of calligraphy permanently altered the monastic writing system. Until this time, calligraphers had copied the Latin capital letters exclusively, which had derived from the use of the chisel in stone or marble. Now, working with the pen on vellum or parchment, the calligraphers were able to refine and control the thick and thin elements and the angles of their strokes, but as before they still wrote only in capitals. To conserve the use of the writing surface (a single book required the hides of some two hundred sheep), the monks experimented in accommodating more words on a page by using smaller letters and ultimately developed a minuscule or hand that departs from the traditional capitals. Alcuin studied Roman monuments for the most attractive and easily read and written letterforms. He standardized the smaller letters and created the highly legible Carolingian alphabet, the precursor of all roman type fonts. ■ Medieval scribes had solved many of the perennial problems of editorial design: legibility, maximizing available space, and capturing and holding the reader's attention. They did so through effective use of margins and white space, strong initial letters, inventive use of narrow column measure, casure, color illustrations, and dimensional effects that surprise the eye. Much may be learned about com-

(PREVIOUS SPREAD, LEFT) *LOOK*, DATE: JANUARY 16, 1940 ■ (ABOVE) *ROYAL AMER-ICAN MAGAZINE*, DATE: 1774

(BELOW) PUBLICATION: *HARPER'S WEEKLY*, SEPTEMBER 20, 1862

pelling, functional graphics by studying the pages produced by these mostly anonymous artists and designers. ■ As Alcuin's alphabet laid the foundation for modern typography, so the introduction of paper, the printing press, and moveable type revolutionized the format of the book. In England, William Caxton created the first table of contents in 1480. Aldus Manutius produced the first paginated book in 1499. Then came a title page crediting both author and publisher. In France, Claude Garamond (1480–1561) and Robert Granjon (d. 1579) created their classic typefaces. Christopher Plantin (1514–1589) used these and other new faces to produce over two thousand books. Plantin used copperplate engravings for his decorative title pages, a practice that was imitated throughout Europe and eventually in America. Type design was furthered in England by William Caslon (1692–1766), John Baskerville (1706–1753), and William Bulmer (1757–1830); in Italy by Giambattista Bodoni (1740–1813); in France by Pierre and Firmin Didot (1761–1853; 1764–1836). These designers, printers, and publishers established a standard of excellence for the printed page that is influential still. ■ A magazine, as defined by the dictionary, is "a periodical publication containing stories, sketches, essays and often illustrations." At the beginning of the eighteenth century, there were many such periodicals, but it was not until 1731 that the term magazine was applied to the title of a publication: *The Gentleman's Magazine*, published by Edward Cave. The general magazine, meant both to inform and to entertain, had come into being. ■ Ten years later, the first two American magazines were published, both in Philadelphia. Andrew Bradford's *American Magazine* and Benjamin Franklin's *General Magazine* were launched only three days apart in 1741. These publications attempted to mirror the look of their successful English counterparts. Covers resembled the title page of an eighteenth-century book. The cover of the *American* included its table of contents. Franklin used a woodcut of the coronet of the Prince of Wales on his cover, and Bradford reproduced in copperplate a representation of the "Enlightenment of America"—the first examples of American magazine cover art. The *General*, it appears, also carried the first magazine advertisement. It describes a ferry service across the Potomac from Annapolis, Maryland to Williamsburg, Virginia. The *General Magazine* lasted six months; the *American Magazine* only three. The reasons are not unfamiliar 250 years later: poor circulation, high production costs, and delinquent subscribers. ■ It wasn't until forty-five years later that the *American Museum* (1787–1792) was launched, the first American magazine that proved a more long-term success. Included in the preface to the fifth volume was an endorsement from George Washington: "I consider such easy vehicles of knowledge as more highly calculated than any other to preserve the liberty, stimulate the industry and meliorate the morals of an enlightened free people." Popular magazines have ever since been discussed as disseminators of mass culture and reflective of the social history of their times. ■ In the early years of American magazine publication, visual creativity was limited by technology. Type, presses, and paper were imported from England. In general, printing and reproduction of illustrations were of poor quality. Copperplate eventually replaced woodcuts, and the *Royal American Magazine* (1774–1775) became the first American publication to use illustrations regularly. In its fifteen issues it produced twenty-two engravings, Paul Revere's political cartoons among the most notable. It marked the beginning of illustration as an integral element of

PUBLICATION: *LADIES' HOME JOURNAL*, CIRCA 1900–1910

PUBLICATION: *WOMAN'S HOME COMPANION*, JANUARY 1908

the magazine. ■ During the first half of the nineteenth century, two magazines were noteworthy for their use of illustration: *Graham's Magazine* (1826–1858) and *Godey's Lady's Book* (1836–1898). *Graham's* commissioned new art and engraving plates for each issue, rather than following the common practice of reusing impressions from existing plates. Often, more was spent on illustration than on writing. Artists might be better paid than even such noteworthy contributors as Poe and Longfellow. Portraits, landscapes, and representations of contemporary events relieved long stretches of text. *Godey's Lady's Book*, with its circulation of 150,000, was an extraordinary success. Contributing to its popularity were its unusual fashion illustrations. The foldout fashion plates were hand-colored by what Louis A. Godey described as "our corps of one hundred and fifty female colorers"—a far cry from the Benedictine scriptorium, but within its creative lineage. Yet little consideration was given to legibility. Type was jammed into small, closely printed columns with tight margins. Often a new story would begin where the last broke off. There was little typographic variety to relieve the monotony. Advertising, if accepted, was relegated to inside covers or special back-of-the-book inserts, often on different stock. ■ In the 1860s *Harper's Weekly* documented the Civil War with engravings by Thomas Nast and Winslow Homer. The reporting artist foreshadowed the documentary photographer. Although the camera was already in use, battle scenes could not be photographed because of the technical limitations of film. ■ The Industrial Revolution accelerated change in the printing industry. Stereotyping, the process of making papier-mâché matrices of entire type pages, and more uniform machine-manufactured paper, made high-speed printing possible. The old method of typesetting was replaced by Ottmar Merganthaler's "Linotype" machine, which composed and cast type at the same time. As the century came to a close, faster photographic film was perfected, and photojournalism became another graphic resource for the publication designer. In 1910, *National Geographic* published the first color photograph in a magazine. The introduction of photography in magazines was helped by the invention of photogravure and then cylinder, or rotogravure, printing. The process was completed with the development of coated paper. All the elements of modern publication design were now in place. ■ At the same time magazines were benefitting from a new, wider readership, born of a population explosion, the widening of literacy, and an increase in leisure time. By the turn of the century, covers took on increased importance, as publishers competed for the public's attention. Will Bradley, a poster artist and publisher of his own magazine, changed cover illustrations with each issue, a practice soon widely copied. The combination of art-nouveau typography and the adaptation of rapidly developing poster art resulted in boldly illustrated covers with strong logotypes that provided instant recognition and product identification. ■ The technology of the 1910s and 1920s sparked an international explosion of creativity in publication design. Picabia, Picasso, and Braque in France; Malevitch, Tatlin, and Altman in Russia; Marinetti, Boccioni, and Severini in Italy; Klee, Bill, and Schwitters in Switzerland; Albers in Germany; Nicholson in England; and Vasarely in Hungary were among the many artists experimenting with new graphic elements in their work. Chiaroscuro and perspective were abandoned in favor of abstract geometric forms. Letter symbols and printed matter were transformed into elements of texture, pattern, or design; color juxtapositions toyed with the response

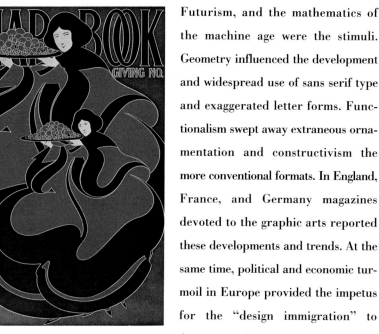

WILL BRADLEY'S *CHAP BOOK*, THANKSGIVING

of the eye. The effects of superimposition were explored in collage. Type was used playfully and expressionistically, stressing design over meaning. ■ This artistic iconoclasm continued with Walter Gropius's establishment of the Bauhaus school in Germany. The impact of his new "language of vision" had a profound effect on the design of publications. Laszlo Moholy-Nagy from Hungary and Herbert Matter from Switzerland collaborated with Gropius to develop a design aesthetic that would reflect the new technological world, one not bound by tradition. Dadaism, Cubism, Futurism, and the mathematics of the machine age were the stimuli. Geometry influenced the development and widespread use of sans serif type and exaggerated letter forms. Functionalism swept away extraneous ornamentation and constructivism the more conventional formats. In England, France, and Germany magazines devoted to the graphic arts reported these developments and trends. At the same time, political and economic turmoil in Europe provided the impetus for the "design immigration" to America. ■ Among the first arrivals were Mehemed Fehmy Agha (1929) and Alexey Brodovitch (1930), who must be considered the founding fathers of the American movement. Both were born and had their early education in Russia. Both experienced the artistic excitement of Paris in the 1920s. Agha worked for Condé Nast publications from 1929 to 1943, where he was art director of *Vogue* until 1942 and the designer of *Vanity Fair* and *House and Garden*. Brodovitch was art director of *Harper's Bazaar* from 1934 to 1958. ■ Both men brought distinctive energy and originality to their publications. Their use of photographers Edward Steichen, Man Ray, Cecil Beton, Martin Munkcasci, Henri Cartier-Bresson, Irving Penn, and Richard Avedon pioneered new forms of visual expression.

Layout was liberated by the introduction of extensive color photography, bleed pages, montage, and innovative typography. Photographs were cropped for dramatic effect. The sequence of editorial pages became an important element of overall makeup and design. ■ In the next decade many leaders of European design would follow these talented emigres. Herbert Matter arrived in 1936 and took photographs for *Vogue, Harper's Bazaar*, and other Condé Nast publications before turning to advertising, where he was widely influential. In 1937, the Hungarians Gyorgy Kepes and Laszlo Moholy-Nagy brought their traditions and talent. Moholy-Nagy's *New Vision* (1932) and *Vision in Motion* (1947), along with Kepes's *Language of Vision* (1944), could be found in every designer's library. ■ From Germany came Will Burtin and Herbert Bayer in 1938. Burtin was art director of *Architectural Record*, and then brought his Bauhaus training to *Fortune*, from 1945 to 1949. Bayer, who shaped the typographic look of Bauhaus publications, spread the gospel through his lectures and writings. A 1939 emigre was Dutch-born Leo Lionni, an abstract painter and student of the futurist F. T. Marinetti. Experienced in advertising, he spent his first ten years in the United States working for the Container Corporation of America. Appointed art director of *Fortune* in 1949, Lionni moved Burtin's design in a new direction. He decided to tell the story of industry by combining journalism, photography, and illustration with a cinematographer's sense of pacing. The result softened the Bauhaus look and brought further distinction to *Fortune*'s editorial image. ■ One of the last of this generation of influential emigres was Alexander Liberman, who arrived in 1940. A magazine art director in Paris, he was hired by Condé Nast to work at American *Vogue* as an assistant to Agha. In 1942 he became art director, and he brought his European training, sense of style, and a distinctive elegance that was the hallmark of the magazine through the 1960s. Liberman is now the editorial director of all Condé Nast publications. ■ During the years of the design immigration, a core of homegrown talent was developing in the United States. Paul Rand, at New York's Pratt Institute, became aware of the Bauhaus and the European avant-garde early in his career. Those influences are discernable in his design solutions for corporate clients. In 1937 he was art director of *Esquire* and *Apparel Arts* magazines. William Goldin worked for Agha at Condé Nast publications before going to CBS in 1937. In the late 1930s Bradbury Thompson was editor and designer of *Westvaco Inspirations*, a publication of the West Virginia Paper and Pulp Company. His visual creativity for Westvaco remains an inspirational example of graphic experimentation. He blended tradition artfully with avant-garde thinking to produce beautiful designs for postage stamps, books, posters, and dozens of publications. Thompson later art directed *Mademoiselle* and *Art News*. ■ Two related publications of the period greatly enlarged the creative potential of publication design. In 1936, Henry R. Luce brought out *Life* magazine. Picture magazines were not entirely new; they had been published in the United States, England, and France. But the scale was new, and Luce encouraged the development of technology to match his expansive vision. R. R. Donnelly, who was to print the new publication, developed paper and inks that could accommodate the unprecedented circulation of up to one million per week. The magazine would also exploit new photographic technology. The 35-millimeter camera was produced by Leica in Germany. Its fast lens, as used for visual "eavesdropping" by Erich Salomon in Berlin, gave birth to "candid" photography. Thus a new era in photojournalism began. When the prototype for *Life* was circulated, an unsolicited criticism was sent to Luce by Paul Hollister, an advertising executive at Macy's. Hollister was hired and gave the magazine its basic format. It's worth noting his advice to Luce on hiring an art director: "Put tape over his mouth, show him the dummy, feed him the photographs, and make sure he doesn't stray from the format." ■ The following year Gardner and John Cowles began publishing *Look* magazine. *Life* and *Look* made stars of photojournalists by devoting an extravagant

VOGUE

INCORPORATING VANITY FAIR

HOT WEATHER
HOLIDAYS
JULY 1, 1938
PRICE 35c

  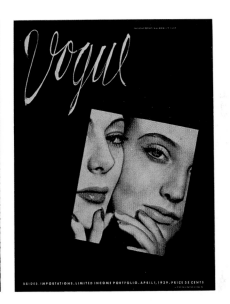

(OPPOSITE) PUBLICATION: *VOGUE* MAGAZINE   DATE: JULY 1938 ■ (ABOVE) PUBLICATION: *VOGUE* MAGAZINE   DATE: 1939 ART DIRECTORS: M. F. AGHA, CIPÉ PINELES ■ (ABOVE, LEFT TO RIGHT) PHOTOGRAPHERS: VOGUE STUDIOS; ANDRÉ DE DIENES; HORST

number of large-format pages to picture stories. Art director, picture editor, and story producer worked as a team to select and present striking visual material against unnervingly short deadlines. Their images of people and events had an indelible impact on the public consciousness. ■ In the 1940s the talents and energies of the design community were directed toward a new consumer market. Norman Rockwell was at the peak of his career illustrating the lives of ordinary folk for the covers of *The Saturday Evening Post*. *Holiday*, a travel magazine, appeared in 1946, reflecting the world for the sophisticated traveler. Women's magazines, such as *McCall's, Ladies Home Journal, Redbook* and *Good Housekeeping*, flourished. These offered the housewife, along with romantically illustrated fiction, still-life photo illustrations of delectable food in gracious settings. Designers now engaged specialists to prop and style an idealized household with theatrical flair. ■ By the early 1950s, changes were in the making that would dramatically affect publications and their design. Women were entering the workplace in increasing numbers. Television was delivering information instantaneously in the home, and the printed page had to compete with the television screen for the consumer's attention. Magazine publishers and editors sought to retain their share of the marketplace. They turned to the art director. The talent in place at magazines in 1953 reads like an Art Directors' Hall of Fame: Henry Wolf at *Esquire*, Allen Hurlburt at *Look*, Otto Storch at *McCall's*, Alexey Brodovith at *Harper's Bazaar*, Alexander Liberman at *Vogue*, Art Kane at *Seventeen*, Arthur Paul at *Playboy*, Bradbury Thompson at *Mademoiselle*, and Frank Zachary at *Holiday*. ■ At *Esquire*, Henry Wolf's conceptual use of photography and illustration to convey content created a distinctive look for the magazine's covers. The images now functioned as visual cover lines. ■ Allen Hurlburt at *Look* raised the picture story to a fine art. He used photography and illustration to create visual paradoxes and comment on popular culture and social and political events. For example, he assigned Norman Rockwell to cover the first integra-

tion of a public school in the South, and he took Irving Penn away from the world of high fashion to photograph Hell's Angels. ■ Frank Zachary, before going to *Holiday*, had produced with Alexey Brodovitch three memorable issues of *Portfolio*, a 1947 magazine devoted to the visual arts, one with unparalleled visual and editorial freedom. ■ Otto Storch's 1958 redesign of *McCall's* was instrumental in giving the art director a greater role in shaping the total look of the magazine. Storch and his staff presented the conventional women's service material in an unconventional way. To emphasize the effect of street noise, he assembled a helicopter, a police car, and a motorcycle in the same photograph. For an article about arson, a photograph of a house of matches aflame succinctly conveyed the idea. A caption was playfully kicked by a model to give verve to a fashion page, and a food spread titled "A La Carte Dinners on Ice" pictured an ice skater in white tie and tails carrying a silver tray of food. ■ The magazine market reflected the changes toward conceptual visual thinking. As the creative aspects of editing and art directing became more closely intergrated, distinct magazine identities and images began to emerge. Logotypes were redesigned for maximum newsstand recognition and impact. Photographs became increasingly dramatic; sentimental illustration became a thing of the past. Bold expressionistic typography, conceptual photography, and innovative use of white space to gain attention for the message on the page are notable design elements of the period. *Town, Nova, Vogue, Queen, Harper's Bazaar* in England, *Twen* in Germany, and *Elle, Marie Claire*, and *Jardin des Modes* in France were among the many magazines that embodied these exciting developments. This "golden age" of the publication art director continued through the early 1970s. ■ The same consumers who responded enthusiastically to the new visual approach were now also responding in ever greater numbers to television. The page was no match for the screen. Television could deliver information and entertainment faster. As magazine revenues started to decline, publishers explored ways to

PUBLICATION: McCALL'S ART DIRECTOR: OTTO STORCH

recoup. Page size and editorial space were reduced, and more advertising was placed within the main section of the magazine. Art directors now had to make the editorial content visually distinct from the ads. ■ Along with these changes came the rise of the special-interest magazine. Notable work, characterized by effective use of conceptual photography, illustration, and typography, was done by Robert Kingsbury at *Rolling Stone*, Milton Glaser and Walter Bernard at *New York* magazine, Robert Hallock at *Lithopinion*, and Dugald Stermer at *Ramparts*. ■ Herb Lubalin added a new graphic dimension to typographic communication with his knowledge and understanding of letterforms. He was one of the first to use the touching, joining, and overlapping of letters and words to create greater visual impact for logotypes and trademarks. His work for *Eros, Fact,* and *Avant-Garde* magazines includes oustanding examples of his innovative approach to typographic design. ■ Few magazines now had the luxury of space they once enjoyed, and the need for a standardized format gave rise to the dominance of the "grid," previously essential only to publications whose content was primarily text. The use of the grid is not new. The specification of type faces and sizes and column widths for various editorial elements has been part of magazine design since Benjamin Franklin's day. Uniformity of page makeup made it easy for editors to fit copy to space, a particular virtue for literary magazines,

such as *The New Yorker*, and short-deadline news or business weeklies. Now, economic constraints gave it renewed importance for other types of publications. Sidebars and rules, uniformity of title, blurb type, and body text are characteristics of these changes, as is the "retro" look of the page design. In order to appeal to the greatest number of readers, editors increased the number of cover lines. Art directors had to find ways to use cover art to effectively compete with quantities of type. ■ And now, another new technology has affected the appearance of publications: the computer. Electronics have added another capability to the publication designer's repertoire. The computer screen has replaced the layout page, offering typographic and design options that are instantaneous and infinite, and that make the collaboration between editor and designer easier. As a production tool, computer graphics can take much of the uncertainty out of editorial decision making, but the computer's creative capabilities have barely been tapped. The programming of a "grid" and the specification of typefaces and page formats should not mean the reduction of design solutions to formula. ■ Technology provides options, it does not make decisions. Design history has always found a place for publication designers who can articulate their ideas, demonstrate a mastery of their craft, and create pages where form and content coincide in exciting ways to communicate meaning. ■ *With special thanks to Derek Ungless.* ■

1

Foraging at a newsstand is not unlike those first awkward moments at a dinner party, after the host's hand has been heartily shaken and the hostess' cheek daintily pecked, when one covertly assesses the room and determines who's worth talking to and who isn't. At the newsstand, we want to know what's worth reading, what isn't. ▢ With magazines, sans host to grease the skids of cordiality, we depend on covers to assume that introductory role. Thus we take in the chisel-cheeked anorectics of the fashion journals; the civility of The New Yorker; *the cul-de-sac of topicality faced by the news weeklies; the (well, you know) of* Playboy *and* Penthouse; *the erudition of* Atlantic *and* Harper's *(they should be sold shrink-wrapped with pipes); and the manias, obsessions, and peccadilloes of the special-interest magazines: pecs and lats tanned and oiled to the shade of a perfectly browned Thanksgiving turkey; impossibly fast cars (sailboats, bicycles, skiers, and runners); impossibly fast women; impossibly chic homes, pied-a-terres, and love nests; orgiastic PCs. ▢ And celebrities. Big names, little names, big-little names, little-big names. Hey there, Harrison Ford! You again, Tom Cruise? Why, helll-lllooo, Madonna! So many of the smiling and smirking famous and near-famous that* even allegedly serious magazines seem to have regressed to those Rockwellian days of the pulpy, fan-club rags that dreamy bobby-soxers once mooned over in Topeka, Montpelier, Sauk City, and the like. ■ So many covers. So many magazines. In general, a (perfectbound) collection of polite, well-turned-out creatures without a brain in their dear heads—the Finishing-School School of cover design. ■ But the bigger question is: Is this so bad? ■ "What is the designer's obligation?" asks graphic designer Paula Scher. "To sell the magazine? Or to create an environment where the magazine can get better?" ■ The integrity of the image and the demands of the marketplace collide on a magazine cover, and the cover designer is forced to straddle the fault line of art and commerce. This always has been the case in the magazine world. But that tension between the pure image and "the sell" has been aggravated in recent years by fiercer competition on the newsstand, the increased bottom-line orientation of all media, and, as we start the 1990s, a nearly across-the-board slump in advertising linage in the magazine industry. ■ I recently talked with a range of graphic designers and magazine art directors about the state (and future) of magazine covers. Many bemoaned the frail health of the "idea cover" as perfected by George Lois at *Esquire* in the 1960s and 1970s (for an interview with Lois, see page 28), while objecting to the glut of "celebrity covers," an approach perhaps perfected and personified by *People* magazine. (For an interview with *People* managing editor Landon Y. Jones, see page 31.) But what became most clear is that the choices aren't clear. But then again, they never are when art and commerce grapple. ■ Paula Scher, who has served as a cover consultant to *Business Week*, *Time*, and other publica-

(PREVIOUS SPREAD, LEFT) PUBLICATION: *ESQUIRE*, MAY 1969 ART DIRECTOR: GEORGE LOIS (ABOVE) PUBLICATION: *BUSINESS WEEK* ART DIRECTOR: PAULA SCHER

PUBLICATION: *PEOPLE* MAGAZINE, ART DIRECTOR: ROBERT ESSMAN PHOTOGRAPHER: JACK MITCHELL/*NEW YORK TIMES*

tions, seeks content in a magazine cover over the sell. "A cover shouldn't necessarily please people," she says. "The public can't like what it doesn't know yet. You take a leap of faith that they will like it. But even if they don't, maybe it lays the groundwork for something they will like next year. The problem is convincing magazine publishers and editors to do that." ■ Scher is disappointed by the current state of cover design. "The actual designs and the use of type are getting snazzier," she says. "But there's no content in the images. There's not one thought. Editors aren't willing to risk that." ■ One symptom of editors' risk aversion is the celebrity cover, a glitzy species that in recent years has become the kudzu of the magazine racks (one wonders whether Sean Connery won't pop up on the cover of *Foreign Affairs* one of these star-struck days) while providing a safe haven for wary editors and designers. ■ "The audience for your magazine kind of tells you what to put on the covers," says Walter Bernard, who has been art director at *New York* and *Time* magazines and has redesigned many other publications. "If you live and die by the cover, the audience shapes it for you. And these days the audience wants stars and celebrities. ■ "Celebrity covers can be done very well and beautifully. But you don't have to work as hard. It's very difficult today to sell a magazine based on provocative ideas." ■ While many cover designers are, at best, ambivalent about celebrity covers, Robert Priest, art director of *Gentleman's Quarterly*, likes them. ■ "In a way, you can't fight the audience," says Priest, who also has been art director at *Esquire*, *Newsweek*, and *Us*. "It's the easiest, most effective way to get to the reader on the newsstand. It is a business, after all. We're here to sell copies to

1

MAGAZINE COVERS

[DANA ANDREW JENNINGS]

MAY 1969
PRICE $1

THE MAGAZINE FOR MEN

**The final decline and total collapse
of the American avant-garde.**

See page 142

MACUSER 76
MACWORLD 52, 76
MADEMOISELLE 15, 18, 213
MAGYAR 94
MANHATTAN INC. 125, 186, 187
MARIE CLAIRE 18
MAX 98
MCCALL'S 18, 19
METROPOLIS 212, 219, 240
METROPOLITAN HOME 87, 89, 208
MONEY 31

THE NATION 186
NATIONAL GEOGRAPHIC 14, 228
NATION'S BUSINESS 123
NEOCON 206
NEWSWEEK 24, 48, 124, 191
NEW WEST 186
NEW YORK 19, 24, 62, 65,
. . . . 86, 87, 185, 186, 188, 210
THE NEW YORKER 23, 26, 27, 87, 165, 185
THE NEW YORK TIMES 89, 186, 227
THE NEW YORK TIMES MAGAZINE 75, 232
NEW YORK WOMAN 175
NOVA 18
NOVITA 103

OMNI 95
OPTION 98

PACIFIC 224
PARIS MATCH 186
PENTHOUSE 23
PEOPLE 24, 25, 30, 31
PHILADELPHIA INQUIRER 62, 70
PLAYBOY 18, 23
PORTFOLIO 165, 166
PRINT 117
PROGRESSIVE ARCHITECTURE 208

QUEEN 18

RAMPARTS 19
REDBOOK 18
REGARDIE'S 62, 224
REVU 98
ROLLING STONE 19, 62, 66, 76, 155–163, 215, 221

RÖMER 98
ROYAL AMERICAN MAGAZINE 12, 13

SAN FRANCISCO CHRONICLE 89
SAN FRANCISCO FOCUS 212
THE SATURDAY EVENING POST 18, 185
SATURDAY REVIEW 124
SAVVY 215
SCHOLASTIC ACTION 212
SCHÖNER WOHNEN 98
SELF 175
SEVENTEEN 18
SHOW 36
SMART 46–52
THE SOPHISTICATED TRAVELER 188
SPLICE 240
SPORTS AFIELD 47
SPY 70, 224, 236
STATUS 166
SÜDDEUTSCHE ZEITUNG 99

TAGES ANZEIGER MAGAZIN 99
TAXI 213
TEMPO 94, 98
TEXAS MONTHLY 62, 232
TIME 24, 62, 65, 70, 87, 157, 185–188, 213, 227
TOWN 18
TOWN & COUNTRY 165
TWEN 18, 36

US 24, 157, 191, 192
U.S. NEWS & WORLD REPORT 123, 186, 188

V 206
VOGUE 15, 17, 18, 103–105, 137–143
VOGUE ITALIA 103–105, 175, 176, 180, 228, 239
VANITY FAIR 15
THE VILLAGE VOICE 186
VU 83

THE WALL STREET JOURNAL 123, 156, 186
THE WASHINGTON POST 186
THE WASHINGTON POST MAGAZINE 188
WEEKEND MAGAZINE 191
WIENERIN 98
WIGWAG 62, 69, 208
WOMAN'S HOME COMPANION 13

SUBSCRIBE TO GRAPHIS: USA AND CANADA

MAGAZINE	USA	CANADA
☐ NEW ☐ RENEW		
☐ TWO YEARS (12 ISSUES)	US$149	US $166
☐ ONE YEAR (6 ISSUES)	US $79	US $88

☐ 25% DISCOUNT FOR STUDENTS WITH COPY OF VALID,
DATED STUDENT ID AND PAYMENT WITH ORDER
FOR CREDIT CARD PAYMENT:
☐ VISA ☐ MASTERCARD

ACCT. NO   EXP. DATE

SIGNATURE

☐ CHECK ENCLOSED   ☐ BILL ME
CHECK THE LANGUAGE VERSION DESIRED:
☐ ENGLISH ☐ GERMAN ☐ FRENCH

PLEASE PRINT

NAME   DATE

TITLE

COMPANY

ADDRESS

CITY   POSTAL CODE

COUNTRY

SEND ORDER FORM AND MAKE CHECK PAYABLE TO:
GRAPHIS US, INC.,
P.O. BOX 3063 SOUTHEASTERN, PA 19398-3063
SERVICE WILL BEGIN WITH ISSUE THAT IS CURRENT
WHEN ORDER IS PROCESSED. (PUBLICATION 1)

REQUEST FOR CALL FOR ENTRIES
PLEASE PUT ME ON THE "CALL FOR ENTRIES" LIST FOR THE
FOLLOWING TITLES:

☐ GRAPHIS DESIGN   ☐ GRAPHIS ANNUAL REPORTS
☐ GRAPHIS DIAGRAM   ☐ GRAPHIS CORPORATE IDENTITY
☐ GRAPHIS POSTER   ☐ GRAPHIS PACKAGING
☐ GRAPHIS PHOTO   ☐ GRAPHIS LETTERHEAD
☐ GRAPHIS LOGO   ☐ GRAPHIS TYPOGRAPHY

SUBMITTING MATERIAL TO ANY OF THE ABOVE TITLES QUALIFIES SENDER
FOR A 25% DISCOUNT TOWARD PURCHASE OF THAT TITLE.

SUBSCRIBE TO GRAPHIS: EUROPE AND WORLD

MAGAZINE	BRD	WORLD	U.K.
☐ NEW ☐ RENEW			
☐ TWO YEARS (12 ISSUES)	DM305,-	SFR262.-	£102.00
☐ ONE YEAR (6 ISSUES)	DM162,-	SFR140.-	£54.00

☐ 25% DISCOUNT FOR STUDENTS WITH COPY OF VALID,
DATED STUDENT ID AND PAYMENT WITH ORDER
SUBSCRIPTION FEES INCLUDE POSTAGE TO ANY PART OF THE
WORLD. AIRMAIL AVAILABLE EVERYWHERE EXCEPT EUROPE AND
NORTH AMERICA
FOR CREDIT CARD PAYMENT:
(ALL CARDS DEBITED IN SWISS FRANCS):
☐ AMERICAN EXPRESS ☐ DINER'S CLUB ☐ EURO/MASTERCARD
☐ VISA/BARCLAY/CARTE BLEUE

ACCT. NO   EXP. DATE

SIGNATURE

☐ CHECK ENCLOSED   ☐ BILL ME
CHECK THE LANGUAGE VERSION DESIRED:
☐ ENGLISH ☐ GERMAN ☐ FRENCH

PLEASE PRINT

NAME   DATE

TITLE

COMPANY

ADDRESS

CITY   POSTAL CODE

COUNTRY

SEND ORDER FORM AND MAKE CHECK PAYABLE TO:
GRAPHIS PRESS CORP.,
DUFOURSTRASSE 107 CH-8008 ZÜRICH, SWITZERLAND
SERVICE WILL BEGIN WITH ISSUE THAT IS CURRENT
WHEN ORDER IS PROCESSED. (PUBLICATION 1)

REQUEST FOR CALL FOR ENTRIES
PLEASE PUT ME ON THE "CALL FOR ENTRIES" LIST FOR THE
FOLLOWING TITLES:

☐ GRAPHIS DESIGN   ☐ GRAPHIS ANNUAL REPORTS
☐ GRAPHIS DIAGRAM   ☐ GRAPHIS CORPORATE IDENTITY
☐ GRAPHIS POSTER   ☐ GRAPHIS PACKAGING
☐ GRAPHIS PHOTO   ☐ GRAPHIS LETTERHEAD
☐ GRAPHIS LOGO   ☐ GRAPHIS TYPOGRAPHY

SUBMITTING MATERIAL TO ANY OF THE ABOVE TITLES QUALIFIES SENDER
FOR A 25% DISCOUNT TOWARD PURCHASE OF THAT TITLE.

■ **GRAPHIS** THE INTERNATIONAL BIMONTHLY JOURNAL OF VISUAL COMMUNICATION ■ **GRAPHIS DESIGN** THE INTERNATIONAL ANNUAL OF DESIGN AND ILLUSTRATION ■ **GRAPHIS PUBLICATION** THE INTERNATIONAL SURVEY OF EDITORIAL DESIGN ■ **THE GRAPHIC DESIGNER'S GREEN BOOK** ENVIRONMENTAL CONCERNS OF THE DESIGN AND PRINT INDUSTRIES, BY ANN CHICK ■ **THE ILLUSTRATOR AND THE ENVIRONMENT: ART FOR SURVIVAL** THE CATALOGUE FOR AN EXHIBITION SPONSORED BY THE UNITED NATIONS ENVIRONMENTAL PROGRAMME IN COOPERATION WITH EARTH ISLAND INSTITUTE AND THE SOCIETY OF ILLUSTRATORS, INC. ■ **GRAPHIS LETTERHEAD** THE INTERNATIONAL SURVEY OF LETTERHEAD DESIGN ■ **GRAPHIS LOGO** THE INTERNATIONAL SURVEY OF LOGO DESIGN ■ **GRAPHIS PHOTO** THE INTERNATIONAL ANNUAL OF PHOTOGRAPHY ■ **GRAPHIS POSTER** THE INTERNATIONAL ANNUAL OF POSTER ART ■ **GRAPHIS PACKAGING** AN INTERNATIONAL SURVEY OF PACKAGING DESIGN ■ **GRAPHIS DIAGRAM** THE GRAPHIC VISUALIZATION OF ABSTRACT, TECHNICAL, AND STATISTICAL FACTS AND FUNCTIONS ■ **GRAPHIS ANNUAL REPORTS** AN INTERNATIONAL COMPILATION OF THE BEST DESIGNED ANNUAL REPORTS ■ **GRAPHIS CORPORATE IDENTITY** AN INTERNATIONAL COMPILATION OF THE BEST IN CORPORATE IDENTITY DESIGN ■ **42 YEARS OF GRAPHIS COVERS** ANTHOLOGY OF ALL GRAPHIS COVERS FROM 1944–86, WITH SHORT ARTISTS' BIOGRAPHIES AND INDEXES OF ALL GRAPHIS ISSUES ■ **POSTERS MADE POSSIBLE BY A GRANT FROM MOBIL** A COLLECTION OF 250 INTERNATIONAL POSTERS COMMISSIONED BY MOBIL AND SELECTED BY THE POSTER SOCIETY ■

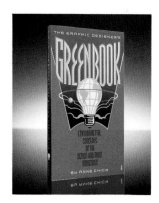

BOOKS	USA	CANADA
☐ GRAPHIS PHOTO 91	US$69	US $94
☐ GRAPHIS POSTER 91	US$69	US $94
☐ GRAPHIS DESIGN 91	US$69	US $94
☐ GRAPHIS LETTERHEAD 1	US$69	US $94
☐ GRAPHIS LOGO 1	US$50	US $70
☐ THE GRAPHIC DESIGNER'S		
GREEN BOOK	US$25	US $41
☐ GRAPHIS PUBLICATION 1	US$75	US$100
☐ GRAPHIS ANNUAL REPORTS 3	US$75	US$100
☐ ART FOR SURVIVAL: THE ILLUSTRATOR		
AND THE ENVIRONMENT	US$40	US $60
☐ GRAPHIS PHOTO 90	US$69	US $94
☐ GRAPHIS POSTER 90	US$69	US $94
☐ GRAPHIS CORPORATE IDENTITY 1	US$75	US$100
☐ GRAPHIS PACKAGING 5	US$75	US$100
☐ GRAPHIS DIAGRAM 1	US$65	US $91

☐ CHECK ENCLOSED (GRAPHIS AGREES TO PAY MAILING COSTS)
☐ BILL ME (MAILING COSTS IN ADDITION TO ABOVE BOOK PRICE WILL
BE CHARGED, BOOK(S) WILL BE SENT WHEN PAYMENT IS RECEIVED)

PLEASE PRINT

NAME _____ DATE _____

TITLE _____

COMPANY _____

ADDRESS _____

CITY _____ POSTAL CODE _____

COUNTRY _____

SEND ORDER FORM AND MAKE CHECK PAYABLE TO:
GRAPHIS US, INC.,
141 LEXINGTON AVENUE,
NEW YORK, NY 10016, USA

REQUEST FOR CALL FOR ENTRIES
PLEASE PUT ME ON YOUR "CALL FOR ENTRIES" LIST FOR THE
FOLLOWING TITLES:

☐ GRAPHIS DESIGN	☐ GRAPHIS ANNUAL REPORTS
☐ GRAPHIS DIAGRAM	☐ GRAPHIS CORPORATE IDENTITY
☐ GRAPHIS POSTER	☐ GRAPHIS PACKAGING
☐ GRAPHIS PHOTO	☐ GRAPHIS LETTERHEAD
☐ GRAPHIS LOGO	☐ GRAPHIS TYPOGRAPHY

SUBMITTING MATERIAL TO ANY OF THE ABOVE TITLES QUALIFIES SENDER
FOR A 25% DISCOUNT TOWARD PURCHASE OF THAT TITLE.

BOOKS	BRD	WORLD	U.K.
☐ GRAPHIS PHOTO 91	DM149,-	SFR.123.-	£49.00
☐ GRAPHIS POSTER 91	DM149,-	SFR.123.-	£49.00
☐ GRAPHIS DESIGN 91	DM149,-	SFR.123.-	£49.00
☐ GRAPHIS LETTERHEAD 1	DM149,-	SFR.123.-	£49.00
☐ GRAPHIS LOGO 1	DM108,-	SFR. 92.-	£36.00
☐ THE GRAPHIC DESIGNER'S			
GREEN BOOK	DM 54,-	SFR. 46.-	£18.00
☐ GRAPHIS PUBLICATION 1	DM162,-	SFR.137.-	£52.00
☐ GRAPHIS ANNUAL REPORTS 3	DM162,-	SFR.137.-	£52.00
☐ ART FOR SURVIVAL: THE ILLUSTRATOR			
AND THE ENVIRONMENT	DM 86,-	SFR. 73.-	£28.00
☐ GRAPHIS PHOTO 90	DM149,-	SFR.123.-	£49.00
☐ GRAPHIS POSTER 90	DM149,-	SFR.123.-	£49.00
☐ GRAPHIS CORPORATE IDENTITY 1	DM160,-	SFR.132.-	£48.00
☐ GRAPHIS PACKAGING 5	DM160,-	SFR.132.-	£48.00
☐ GRAPHIS DIAGRAM 1	DM138,-	SFR.112.-	£45.00

☐ CHECK ENCLOSED (FOR EUROPE, PLEASE MAKE SFR, CHECKS
PAYABLE TO A SWISS BANK)
☐ AMOUNT PAID INTO GRAPHIS ACCOUNT AT THE UNION BANK OF
SWITZERLAND, ACCT NO 3620063 IN ZÜRICH.
☐ AMOUNT PAID TO POSTAL CHEQUE ACCOUNT ZÜRICH 80-23071-9
(THROUGH YOUR LOCAL POST OFFICE)
☐ PLEASE BILL ME (MAILING COSTS IN ADDITION TO ABOVE BOOK
PRICE WILL BE CHARGED, BOOK(S) WILL BE SENT WHEN PAYMENT IS
RECEIVED)

PLEASE PRINT

NAME _____ DATE _____

TITLE _____

COMPANY _____

ADDRESS _____

CITY _____ POSTAL CODE _____

COUNTRY _____

SEND ORDER FORM AND MAKE CHECK PAYABLE TO:
GRAPHIS PRESS CORP.,
DUFOURSTRASSE 107, CH-8008
ZÜRICH, SWITZERLAND

REQUEST FOR CALL FOR ENTRIES
PLEASE PUT ME ON YOUR "CALL FOR ENTRIES" LIST FOR THE
FOLLOWING TITLES:

☐ GRAPHIS DESIGN	☐ GRAPHIS ANNUAL REPORTS
☐ GRAPHIS DIAGRAM	☐ GRAPHIS CORPORATE IDENTITY
☐ GRAPHIS POSTER	☐ GRAPHIS PACKAGING
☐ GRAPHIS PHOTO	☐ GRAPHIS LETTERHEAD
☐ GRAPHIS LOGO	☐ GRAPHIS TYPOGRAPHY

SUBMITTING MATERIAL TO ANY OF THE ABOVE TITLES QUALIFIES SENDER
FOR A 25% DISCOUNT TOWARD PURCHASE OF THAT TITLE.

ACKNOWLEDGMENTS

SPECIAL THANKS TO BRIDE WHELAN, EXECUTIVE DIRECTOR OF

THE SOCIETY OF PUBLICATION DESIGNERS, WHOSE SUPPORT WAS UNEQUALED, AND TO

LITA TALARICO, WHO DID A GREAT DEAL OF THE PRELIMINARY WORK ON THE BOOK,

ACQUIRED ARTWORK, AND HELPED COORDINATE EVERYTHING. THANKS ALSO TO:

MICHAEL BROCK OF *L.A. STYLE*, NANCY COHEN AT *METROPOLIS*,

DIANA EDKINS AT CONDÉ NAST, INGRID SISCHY OF *INTERVIEW* MAGAZINE,

MALCOLM FROUMAN AT *BUSINESS WEEK*,

BARBARA GENOVA OF VIGNELLI ASSOCIATES, CHARLES HESS AT *BUZZ* MAGAZINE,

JERALDINE HESSLER AND CLAUDINE GUERGUERIAN OF *ROLLING STONE*,

WILL HOPKINS AND JANE MCFADDEN OF HOPKINS/BAUMAN,

DOROTHY KALINS OF *METROPOLITAN HOME* MAGAZINE,

GEORGE LOIS, FORMERLY OF *ESQUIRE*, LEE LORENZ AT *THE NEW YORKER*,

GAYLE MARSH AT PENTAGRAM, MARY RILEY OF *PEOPLE* MAGAZINE,

RHONDA RUBENSTEIN FOR HER MATERIAL ON *SMART* MAGAZINE,

PROFESSOR VIRGINIA SMITH OF BARUCH COLLEGE, OTTO STORCH,

RUDY VANDERLANS AT *EMIGRE* MAGAZINE, SHERRY WINSTON AND MARIA MORETTI AT *VOGUE*,

HENRY WOLF AT THE NEW YORK PUBLIC LIBRARY PICTURE COLLECTION,

KELLY WORT AT *THE FACE* MAGAZINE, AND ALL THE ARTISTS, PHOTOGRAPHERS

AND WRITERS WHO PARTICIPATED IN THE PRODUCTION OF THIS BOOK.

the readers, then we can show the reader that the magazine is more than they think. ■ "Strong sales give you the leeway to do the magazine that you want. You just can't make mistakes right now in this [tight] magazine market." ■ Agreed. But today's steady, too-sweet diet of celebrity covers still makes some designers wince: "Not having Tom Cruise on a cover is a victory," says Paula Scher. ■ Graphic design veterans Bernard and Scher say that one thing that has gone awry with cover design is that the art director's role has been diminished. ■ "On magazines devoted to popular culture, the art director has taken his lumps," Bernard says. "Many covers aren't even art directed. The art director has been compromised by the marketplace, even as the magazine editor has been compromised." ■ Adds Scher: "In the late fifties, the sixties, and early seventies, art directors were literate and worked hand in hand with the editor of a magazine. Somewhere along the way, that partnership fell apart and the art director became subservient to the editor. The art director became a stylist rather than a thinker. There's rarely any thought now of letting an art director create true ideas for a publication." ■ Mary K. Baumann, a partner with Hopkins/Baumann and currently a cover consultant for *People* magazine, has given a lot of thought to the tension between creating a compelling cover image and selling a magazine. ■ First of all, she says, a cover has to work for three constituents: the subscriber, the newsstand

PUBLICATION: *GENTLEMEN'S QUARTERLY*, JULY 1989 ART DIRECTOR: ROBERT PRIEST PHOTOGRAPHER: HERB RITTS

buyer, and the advertiser. And, she adds, "a cover should provide a clear identity for the magazine. *GQ*, for example, is consistent from issue to issue. You want to show that you're the same product from month to month." ■ But Baumann insists that this consistency should be a jumping-off point for the magazine, not an end in itself. "One of the things I've learned," she says, "is that most editors and art directors don't understand that you need to make money, that what you need to do is make a bridge between aesthetics and the sell. I don't think that's going on in magazines. We need to do something creatively that brings standards to a higher level. ■ "I don't think covers have kept up with the times. I don't see that there is a lot of innovation going on. There is a lack of risk. Cover designers need to learn the demands of the market, and then apply that knowledge aesthetically." ■ The magazine industry's advertising slump may be the nudge art directors need to take cover design in that direction, to mint a design vocabulary for the 1990s. Most designers interviewed agreed the economic squeeze will have an impact one way or another. Some magazines will become even more cautious, they say, while others will be forced to abandon the current, tired formulas. ■ Walter Bernard summed it up best: "I think cover design will be liberated as magazines become more and more desperate. You'll see more provocative covers—some good, some bad. The marketplace is totally confused now, and I think you'll see magazines throwing out the marketing surveys as they experiment and try to figure out what will sell."■

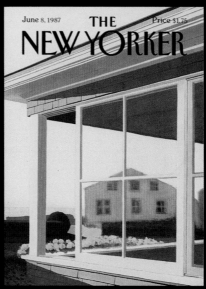

THE NEW YORKER AMID THE JOSTLE AND TUSSLE OF THE NEWSSTAND, NOT UNLIKE A STEAMY MANHATTAN SUBWAY PLATFORM AT RUSH HOUR, *THE NEW YORKER* STANDS TO ONE SIDE OF THE FRAY: THE DISTINGUISHED-LOOKING FELLOW, TEMPLES GRAYING, SPORTING THE CHICLY SHABBY TWEED BLAZER AND READING HENRY JAMES. □ WHIPPED INTO A FRENZY BY "THE SELL," MOST OTHER MAGAZINES CAN BE FOUND GRUBBING AND GRABBING FOR THE SAME SLEEK CELEBS AND MASS-MARKET EPHEMERA IN THE SAME BARGAIN-BASEMENTS OF POP CULTURE. □ WHILE THOSE OTHER MAGAZINES ARE ABOUT AS STABLE AS A NEUROTIC IN AUGUST, *THE NEW YORKER* SINCE 1925 CALMLY HAS GONE ABOUT CARVING ITS IDENTITY AS A HOME TO SERIOUS FICTION, POETRY, AND JOURNALISM (AND DON'T FORGET THE CARTOONS). ITS COVERS ARE EMBLEMATIC OF THAT IDENTITY: THE CLEAN LINES AND PURE LIGHT OF GRETCHEN DOW SIMPSON, THE WHIMSY OF WILLIAM STEIG, THE AMUSED ELEGANCE OF SEMPE. □ "THE COVERS ARE THE DIRECT EXPRESSIONS OF THE ARTISTS," SAYS LEE LORENZ, *THE NEW YORKER*'S ART EDITOR SINCE 1973. "THEY AREN'T COMMISSIONED. WE TRY TO BRING TOGETHER DISTINCTIVE STYLES AND POINTS OF VIEW. □ "TO BE HONEST, WE'RE MORE INTERESTED IN THE ARTIST THAN THE PIECE OF ART. AND THE PERSONAL QUALITY OF THE COVER DOES SAY SOMETHING ABOUT THE MAGAZINE. THE COVER SAYS THIS IS A MAGAZINE THAT GROWS OUT OF THE EDITORIAL TALENTS OF THE PEOPLE WHO PUT IT TOGETHER." □ AT *THE NEW YORKER*, "THE SELL" IS BESIDE THE POINT, EVEN THOUGH, IRONICALLY, THE MAGAZINE OFTEN STANDS OUT ON THE NEWSSTAND MORE VIVIDLY THAN OTHER PUBLICATIONS. "WE'VE BEEN FORTUNATE THAT WE HAVEN'T HAD TO CHASE OUR AUDIENCE, LIKE OTHER MAGAZINES," LORENZ SAYS. "THE MAGAZINE AND ITS COVERS HAVE A CERTAIN TIMELESSNESS." □ FOR EVERY COVER THE MAGAZINE RUNS, LORENZ LOOKS AT AT LEAST 100 CONTENDERS. HE TRIES TO NURTURE ARTISTS THE WAY OTHER EDITORS BRING ALONG WRITERS. □ "ARTISTS HAVE THE OPPORTUNITY TO DEVELOP WHILE WORKING WITH US," LORENZ SAYS. "AND IT'S IMPORTANT TO US THAT THEY CONTINUE TO GROW. AS FOR THE ART ITSELF, WE WANT A PIECE THAT WEARS WELL. SOMETHING YOU CAN LOOK AT OVER AND OVER AGAIN." □ HAVE THERE BEEN CHANGES IN *NEW YORKER* COVERS IN RECENT YEARS? "WELL," LORENZ OFFERS, "[EDITOR] BOB GOTTLIEB DOES LIKE HUMOR ON THE COVER MORE THAN [FORMER EDITOR] WILLIAM SHAWN DID." □

(OPPOSITE) PUBLICATION: *THE NEW YORKER* ■ (TOP) ILLUSTRATOR: PETER ARNO DATE: JANUARY, 1940 ■ (CENTER) ILLUSTRATOR: GRETCHEN DOW SIMPSON ART DIRECTOR: LEE LORENZ DATE: JUNE, 1987 ■ (BOTTOM) DATE: FEBRUARY, 1979 ILLUSTRATOR: SAUL STEINBERG

GEORGE LOIS & ESQUIRE MAGAZINES, REPORTEDLY, DID HAVE COVERS BEFORE *ESQUIRE* GOT A HOLD OF GEORGE LOIS (AND VICE VERSA) IN 1962. SOMETIMES YOU WONDER, THOUGH. TALK SHOP WITH A COVER DESIGNER AND, GENERALLY, IT TAKES LESS THAN A MINUTE FOR THE DESIGNER TO LAPSE INTO A REVERENT HUSH AND BRING UP THE SUBJECT OF LOIS AND THE STRIKING COVERS HE CREATED FOR *ESQUIRE* IN THE 1960S AND EARLY 1970S. □ THAT'S BECAUSE EVEN TODAY, TWENTY TO TWENTY-FIVE YEARS LATER, LOIS'S IMAGES STILL RESONATE: ANDY WARHOL DROWNING IN A CAN OF CAMPBELL'S SOUP, BOXER SONNY LISTON DECKED OUT AS A BLACK SANTA (THIS, WHEN MUCH OF AMERICA WASN'T REAL KEEN ON A BLACK ANYTHING), LIEUTENANT WILLIAM CALLEY SURROUNDED BY BEAMING VIETNAMESE CHILDREN. □ "THE REASON I GOT AWAY WITH THOSE COVERS WAS BECAUSE I HAD A GREAT EDITOR [HAROLD HAYES] AND I HAD TOTAL FREEDOM; IT WAS MY STATEMENT," SAYS LOIS, HIS VOICE A PROFANE RASP. "IF I HAD HAD TO WORK THROUGH ALL THE GARBAGE WITH THE EDITORS AND THE ADVERTISING SALES PEOPLE, I WOULD'VE THROWN SOMEBODY OUT THE WINDOW." □ LOIS SAYS HIS COVERS WERE THE DESIGN EQUIVALENT OF THE NEW JOURNALISM BLOSSOMING IN THE MAGAZINE: "GAY TALESE HAD HIS POINT OF VIEW. TOM WOLFE HAD HIS POINT OF VIEW. AND I HAD MY POINT OF VIEW." □ HE ADDS: "WITH THOSE COVERS, I TRIED TO NAIL DOWN WHAT WAS HAPPENING IN THE CULTURE. I ALWAYS WANTED TO COME UP WITH A PURE, CRYSTAL-CLEAR IMAGE THAT'D KNOCK YOU ON YOUR ASS AND HAYES HAD THE GUTS AND TALENT TO LET ME DO IT." □ WHAT LENT POWER TO HIS COVERS, LOIS SAYS, IS THAT THEY WERE DRIVEN BY IDEAS: "A GREAT IDEA SHOULD SINK YOU TO YOUR KNEES. YOU SHOULD DO A COVER, AND PEOPLE SHOULD FAINT. THEIR EYEBALLS SHOULD FALL OUT. DESIGN SHOULD REFLECT AN IDEA. □ "A SOLID PROBLEM WITH COVER DESIGN TODAY IS THAT TYPE IS BEING USED AS DECORATION. THERE'S DECORATION ON COVERS AND PAGES RATHER THAN POWERFUL IMAGES. THE TYPE, IT'S LIKE CONFETTI. NEWER DESIGNERS DON'T UNDERSTAND THAT EVERYTHING SHOULD HAVE AN IDEA." □ LOIS HASN'T DONE ANY MAGAZINE WORK SINCE HIS *ESQUIRE* DAYS, THOUGH, HE SAYS, HE GETS REQUESTS ALL THE TIME. □ "THERE'S ONLY ONE WAY TO DO GREAT COVERS," HE SAYS, "AND THAT'S TO ASSIGN THEM THE WAY YOU DO ARTICLES—YOU ASSIGN ONE PERSON TO DO IT. AND I SAY THAT TO THESE GUYS ASKING ME TO DO COVERS. □ "BUT WHEN YOU GIVE THEM A POWERFUL IDEA, THEY LOOK AT YOU LIKE YOU'RE CRAZY, LIKE YOU'RE NUTS. □ "THEY'RE JUST TOO CHICKEN."□

(OPPOSITE) PUBLICATION: *ESQUIRE* MAGAZINE ART DIRECTOR: GEORGE LOIS PHOTOGRAPHER: CARL FISCHER DATE: DECEMBER, 1963

1963. Price One Dollar

squire

azine for Men

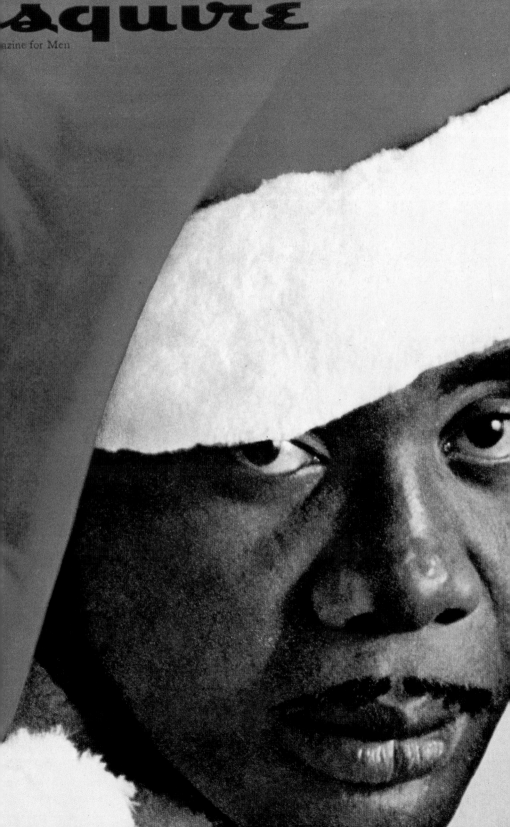

DURAN DURAN: A romp with the idol rich

People
weekly

JULY 22, 1964 • $1.25

MALICE in the **PALACE**

orget shy Di!
Behind this facade
is a willful
woman who has
family servants
on the run and
who's dancing
the night away—
sometimes
without Charles

Jeopardy's Alex Trebek joins the newlywed game

JULY 30, 1990 • $2.25

People
weekly

AIDS:
A Woman's
Story

Her date came
with champagne,
roses . . . and AIDS.
Eight years later,
ALI GERTZ, 24,
is fighting for her life
and warning women
that, yes, it can
happen to you.
Inside: Her story and
those of six other
women living with the
deadly disease

People
weekly

SEPTEMBER 27, 1982 • $1.25

PRINCESS
GRACE
1929-1982
A TRIBUTE

Camelot's Caroline: A Wedding Album

People
weekly

AUGUST 5, 1985 • $1.50

NICE WORK, LUV

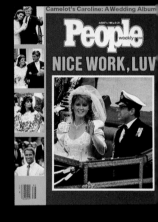

A terrifying murder rocks Boston

People
weekly

NOVEMBER 27, 1989 • $1.95

Look who's back
John Travolta

TV's JANE PAULEY
KISS
TODAY
GOODBYE

She doesn't blame
DEBORAH NORVILLE, but here's
how NBC's bungling created
their embarrassing 'rivalry.'
'I felt awkward,' says Jane.
'I cried buckets,' says Deborah.

People
weekly

AUGUST 3, 1981 • $1.25

The Mob moves in
on Wayne Newton
Beverly Hills Diet:
Can it kill you?
Brazil gags Baez

GOOD
SHOW!

Behind the pageantry
a handful of loyal subjects
gives a magic touch
to the fairy-tale
wedding

P E O P L E "THE GOAL OF A *PEOPLE* MAGAZINE COVER IS TO MOVE ISSUES. WE DON'T TALK MUCH ABOUT AESTHETICS. WE TALK ABOUT WHETHER A COVER WORKED." □ THAT'S LANDON Y. JONES, *PEOPLE*'S MANAGING EDITOR, TALKING. JONES GETS THE FINAL CALL EACH WEEK ON THE MAGAZINE'S COVER. IT'S A DECISION, HE SAYS, THAT CAN MEAN A SWING OF ONE MILLION (UP OR DOWN) IN NEWSSTAND SALES, WHICH ACCOUNT FOR ABOUT HALF OF THE MAGAZINE'S 3.1 MILLION CIRCULATION. □ "THE COVER IS A CRITICALLY IMPORTANT ASPECT OF THE MAGAZINE," SAYS JONES, A FORMER EDITOR OF *MONEY* MAGAZINE. □ IT'S SO IMPORTANT, IN FACT, THAT *PEOPLE* OFTEN TESTS PROPOSED COVERS WITH SUBSCRIBERS. "COVER TESTING IS A FORMER OF DISASTER PREVENTION," JONES SAYS. "YOU HAVE TO HIT FOR AVERAGE IN THIS BUSINESS." □ ONCE A COVER IMAGE IS CHOSEN—WITH JONES WORKING CLOSELY WITH THE ART DIRECTOR—THE NEXT CRUCIAL DECISION IS WHAT TO WRITE ON THE COVER. "COVER LANGUAGE NEEDS SOME BUZZ, SOME ENERGY, SOME EXCITEMENT," JONES SAYS. "IT NEEDS SOME POP, SOMETHING EXTRA." HE CITES "MALICE IN THE PALACE," ON LIFE WITH BRITAIN'S ROYAL FAMILY, AS A BLURB THAT PACKED SOME *PEOPLE*-STYLE PUNCH. □ SUBJECTS THAT TEND TO DO WELL ON *PEOPLE*'S COVERS ARE: □ A WOMAN TALKING ABOUT HER PROBLEMS. JONES POINTS OUT THAT MOST OF THE MAGAZINE'S READERS ARE WOMEN. □SOMEONE IN THE NEWS WHO PEOPLE ARE CURIOUS ABOUT, BUT DON'T KNOW MUCH ABOUT. DONALD TRUMP'S FORMER AMANTE, MARLA MAPLES, IS A GOOD EXAMPLE. □ ROYALTY. □ AND THE DEATHS OF PROMINENT AND BELOVED ENTERTAINERS, SUCH AS LUCILLE BALL, SAMMY DAVIS JR., AND JIM HENSON. □ BUT IT STILL IS A SLIPPERY BUSINESS, JONES CAUTIONS: "JUST WHEN YOU THINK YOU HAVE A SURE SELLER, THE GROUND SHIFTS." □ OF COURSE, WHEN THAT HAPPENS, ONE CAN ALWAYS FALL BACK ON STOLLEY'S LAW, NAMED AFTER A FORMER *PEOPLE* EDITOR, DICK STOLLEY. ACCORDING TO JONES, STOLLEY'S LAW PLAYS SOMETHING LIKE THIS: □ TV SELLS BETTER THAN MOVIES, WHICH SELLS BETTER THAN MUSIC, WHICH SELLS BETTER THAN SPORTS—AND EVERYTHING SELLS BETTER THAN POLITICS. □

(OPPOSITE, LEFT TO RIGHT IN DESCENDING ORDER) PUBLICATION: *PEOPLE* MAGAZINE ■ ART DIRECTOR: SANAE YAMAZAKI PHOTOGRAPHERS: (COVER) LORD SNOWDON/CAMERA PRESS (INSET) BRIAN ARIS/OUTLINE DATE: 1985 ■ ART DIRECTOR: JOHN SHECUT JR. PHOTOGRAPHERS: (COVER) PETER SERLING (INSET) MARK SENNET/ONYX DATE: 1980 ■ ART DIRECTOR: SANAE YAMASAKI PHOTOGRAPHER: HARRY BENSON DATE: 1982 ■ ART DIRECTOR: SANAE YAMAZAKI PHOTOGRAPHERS: GAMMA-LIAISON (INSETS, TOP TO BOTTOM) MIKE FULLER, SOBOL/VILLARD/SIPA, SPECIAL FEATURES DATE: 1986 ■ ART DIRECTOR: T. COURTNEY BROWN PHOTOGRAPHERS: CHRISTOPHER LITTLE (INSETS) BILL BERNSTEIN/OUTLINE, ADAM SCULL/GLOBE PHOTOS DATE: 1989 ■ ART DIRECTOR: ROBERT N. ESSMAN PHOTOGRAPHER: LORD SNOWDON/GAMMA-LIAISON DATE: 1981

THE GRID

[MASSIMO VIGNELLI]

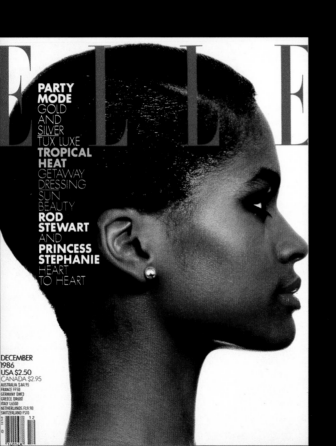

ELLE

**PARTY
MODE**
GOLD
AND
SILVER
TUX LUXE
**TROPICAL
HEAT**
GETAWAY
DRESSING
SUN
BEAUTY
**ROD
STEWART**
AND
**PRINCESS
STEPHANIE**
HEART
TO HEART

DECEMBER
1986
USA $2.50
CANADA $2.95
AUSTRALIA $A4.95
FRANCE FF50
GERMANY DM13
GREECE DRA600
ITALY L6500
NETHERLANDS FL9.90
SWITZERLAND FS70

1 2

2

Since the 1930s magazine design has been one of the most lively and imaginative areas of the graphic arts. Some of this liveliness is, of course, a reflection of the nature of the magazine. As contrasted with the book, with its aspirations of permanence, the magazine is ephemeral and thus rather naturally reflects the inspiration of the moment. Too often, though, this liveliness has degenerated into trendiness and excessiveness. □ But magazines can acquire a kind of permanence. A newspaper is quintessentially ephemeral. The following day, it is all over. A magazine has a longer life; its content becomes reference material. Ephemeral images find their immortality in magazines. The transient becomes permanent. Unfortunately, too often, in the effort to enliven a magazine, we see too much color, too many gratuitous devices, too many tint backgrounds, too many rules, too much of everything. Generally, typography for magazines benefits from restraint, and those magazines that use two or three typefaces are far much better than those that use the whole typebook. Typographical restraint adds to the magazine's presence, helps the reader, and strengthens the magazine's identity. The issue of identity and diversity is of great significance in magazine design. Too much identity becomes gratuitous, too much diversity obliterates the magazine. It is not a question of balance as much as appropriateness. ■ In designing a magazine, one of the most important tasks is to find a way to express the content that will be specific to that magazine. That means creating a "voice," one that can be recognized, identified among the others. The solution lies in the nature of the material itself, not in some current trend. The task is to provide a framework within which to articulate the content in such a way that the "voice" becomes clear. Also essential is that the framework allows other designers enough freedom to articulate their solutions without destroying the format or losing the magazine's identity. Some do's and don'ts are set up. Grids are designed and typeface specifications established. Basically, a manual of guidelines is devised for every section of the magazine, showing all possible alternatives within the program, and those preferred as well, to stress the magazine's identity. A magazine format represents the "voice," which needs to be articulated, but not changed too often or fragmented too much, lest identity be lost. The look of a magazine could easily last twenty, thirty years before being updated. There is certainly no need to change it sooner, if it is properly and imaginatively designed. Forced obsolescence is a waste of time, money, and energies. ■ Type stacked up in a meaningless way, decorative borders, or silly shapes tinted and sprinkled all over the spread: Why all this? Simply to be different, to hype the publication. I find this type of magazine design very demeaning to our profession. Why resort to so much decoration when so much could be done with the real thing? There are so many things one can do with typography that are exciting, appropriate, and readable, and that produce forceful, memorable, beautiful images. ■ Everyone responds to certain codes. Big, small; col-

(OPENING SPREAD, LEFT) PUBLICATION: *ELLE* MAGAZINE ■ (ABOVE) PUBLICATION: *INTERVIEW*, ART DIRECTOR: FABIEN BARON

PUBLICATION: *METROPOLIS* MAGAZINE, ART DIRECTOR: HELENE SILVERMAN

ors or black and white; close-ups or long fields—all these contrasts have particular connotations that we decipher in one way or another according to our exposure to them. The discipline of semiotics deals with the meaning of images, situations, and things. It is indeed the discipline of our profession and is concerned with every aspect of communication. A magazine by its nature is a highly semiotic media, where every detail acquires a specific meaning and, therefore, can be manipulated to provoke a specific response. This subliminal operation aimed at reaching the reader is called a "code." ■ Looking at a magazine, the reader should immediately understand its codes. The reader should be able to easily determine the hierarchy of the contents and its sequence, either by the scale of the titles or that of the images. The reader should be able to understand by breaking the code and tuning himself in to it. ■ The issue of establishing a code that can be broken by a certain reader or category of readers is extremely important in designing a magazine. A mistake could cost the magazine its audience. The set of connotations set up by a particular code builds up the reader's identification with the magazine. It becomes a personal relationship, a subtle, morbid passion. ■ Magazines are a very sensorial experience, and I have memories of the feelings evoked from throughout my life. I remember when I was anxiously waiting for the new issues of *Esquire*, *Bazaar* or *Show* to see the imaginative layout and the exquisite design by Henry Wolf, or for the new issue of *Twen*, designed by Willy Fleckhaus, with photo details blown up to full-spread impact, which gave me incredible emotions. *Twen* was the banner of a lifestyle. ■ Structure is the key word in designing a new magazine. Everything is related to the structure; everything is part of it. Structure, not type, is what we first per-

THE BLACK OUT

In a season with such a rich
variety of shapes, textures, moods,
nothing quite gets the message across
so clearly, so simply, as black—with an
exclamation of white.
On these eight pages, glimpses of the
most graphic color couple now....

BODY DRESSING NOW...

New reason to consider a black
jersey dress: contour-ability. The
understated elegance of Michael
Kor's wool jersey turtleneck
(right) can dress up as easily as
dress down. About $250, at Bar-
ney's, NYC; Ultimo, Chicago; Neiman Marcus, Dallas, Frost Broth-
ers, San Antonio. Sachiko for La
Crasia Gloves, $30. At Bergdorf
Goodman, NYC. For details and
stores, see Shopping Guide.

PUBLICATION: *ELLE* PUBLICATION DIRECTOR: RÉGIS PAGNIEZ ART DIRECTOR: PHYLLIS SCHEFER PHOTOGRAPHER: GILLES BENSIMON

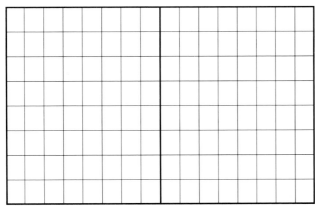 

(ALL IMAGES THIS SPREAD) PUBLICATION: *ELLE* MAGAZINE PUBLICATION DIRECTOR: REGAS PAGNIEZ ART DIRECTOR: OLIVIA BADRUTT-GIRON PHOTOGRAPHER: PIERRE BERDOY DESCRIPTION: *ELLE* MAGAZINE GRID AND A SAMPLE FEATURE SPREADS

ceive in a magazine layout. ■ Magazines are divided into parts: contents page, front matter, "editorial well," where most of the stories are, and back matter, where jumps and features are. The covers are a separate issue, discussed elsewhere in this book. (See Chapter 1, "Magazine Covers") ■ The contents page is to a magazine what a window is to a department store. Much more than simply a show of contents, it is an opportunity to announce the character and the tone of the publication. Words and images compete to attract the reader's attention. ■ The front matter is usually a pretext to sell advertising pages. Few magazines have yet discovered a way to handle this section in an exciting way. The fragmentation and the competition from the facing ads is usually a disaster and makes the solution to the problem very difficult. ■ One common idea is that "something" should face advertising in order to make it more readable. This is not true; all this does is make the text fragmented and out of place. Hold advertising all together, and it would be a service to the reader, keeping text with the magazine so that it makes sense. Selling advertising facing text is a lie invented by salesmen to make their lives easier, and magazines worse. ■ The "editorial well" is where the magazine really happens. It is crucial that every story signals its presence; therefore, the title page requires a strong solution that will stand out in context. Usually, a double page will do it, or a strong typographical handling of the title or an impactive picture that will clearly signify the beginning of a new story.

In the following pages, scale, sequence and drama will help to engage the reader's attention. Spectacular images, intriguing illustrations, out-of-scale manipulations of the content are just a few of an endless line of exciting solutions. My favorite sequence is a white page with pictures in the center, facing a full page followed by a spread image, followed by another one, followed by a full page facing a white page with a picture in the center grid position. A simple format made very effective by the scale of the images and their sequence. Naturally, this is only one of the ways to layout stories. Actually, every story has its right way, "the way it wants to be." Just listen to it, the solution is there. . . . ■ The back matter is a collection of leftovers, or special sections ranging from horoscopes to society columns. It requires some somber typography and it's all over. Making too much of it is definitely out of place. ■ To visually organize all its contents, a magazine has a "grid." The grid is a series of reference points on a spread, with which one could decide the width and number of columns of text and the size and position of the illustrations in such a way that there would be consistency and identity from story to story. Every magazine, according to the kind of material at hand, will have a grid designed to handle the material in the most appropriate way. There is no such thing as a grid for all kinds of magazines, although there are some basic ones that may be more recurrent. We often use a grid of 3 and 2 columns subdivided into 6 or 12 horizontal modules per column, because it

offers great flexibility of use. However, there are endless ways to do grids. Ultimately, though, one way should be better than the others for that particular magazine. ■ The main purpose of the grid, we said, is to provide reference and continuity. However, it is very important to learn when to use it and when to break away from it. The grid is a very useful tool, but just a tool. Without the grid a magazine will look loose, unstructured, noisy, illiterate. Some think that a grid stifles the contents, freezes the magazine. This is only true if the designer doesn't know how to use it. The grid is like grammar. Can you do without it? The grid relates to the format or size of a magazine. The format relates to the content and expresses it visually. A small-sized magazine is more like a journal and implies serious reading. A standard size (9 x 12 or 9 x 10 ⅞ inches) is for a standard, high volume magazine, good for everything. (One ad fits them all. . . .) Hype magazines are tabloid size, their connotation is news, fashion, lifestyle, youth, trendiness, energy. Deciding on the size is crucial; it reflects the character of the publication and its audience. Size is a code to be read. ■ In reviewing magazine design today, worldwide, the obvious exciting trend is brought forward by the tabloid size, 11 x 17 inches, printed in web on uncoated paper, with large-scale photographs, sequences of full-bleed spreads, duotone, black and white or full color, simple, not visible layout. . . . a very tangible, sensorial experience, a nonsleek texture of unconventional refinement. ■ Magazines like *Life* essentially created photojournalism. Memorable images that became icons of mankind's situations were shot for magazine. Our visual memory bank is full of them. We remember the images more than the way they were laid out in the magazines, and that is because the layout was so good that it receded and allowed the picture to talk. I think the intelligence of the magazine designer is in understanding the nature of the material at hand, within the scope of the magazine. Too often, instead, we see magazines designed by art directors whose egos prevail over the content and offer a miserable display of ignorance, shallowness, and irresponsibility. Too often, the art director's message is "Look at me," rather than "Look at the content." ■ Eventually, television commercials killed photojournalism by killing such great magazines as *Life* and *Look*, which couldn't reach a comparable audience with their ads. Indeed, advertising killed photojournalism by depriving magazines of their main source of income. ■ I think a magazine should stand on its own feet financially, by relying on its subscribers rather than having an inflated prosperity created by advertising revenues, which could be lost at any time. ■ Looking back at magazines designed by the great Brodovitch, Lubalin, Fleckhaus, Hulburt, and so forth, it becomes indeed apparent that the brilliance of the design solution resides in the content itself and the intelligence of the designer to bring it forward, simply, strongly, beautifully. And that is all there is to magazine design. ■

Published by
Art Center College of Design

Spring Issue, May 1989
Volume 2, Number 1

ArtCenter

REVIEW 5

Exploring the
territory of ideas
and images
defined by the
worlds of design
education and
the design
professions.

2

Notes of celebration:
corporate support
and plans for a
north wing.

12

Robert Peat wins
the second
annual Don Kubly
Professional
Attainment
award.

4 A richly varied bag of recently
completed student work.

10

Excerpts from an
informal question
and answer session
with the reader
of graphic design.

9

Survey out? Vesper's
on the results of
the first Art Center
alumni survey.

Paul Rand's first visit to Art Center.

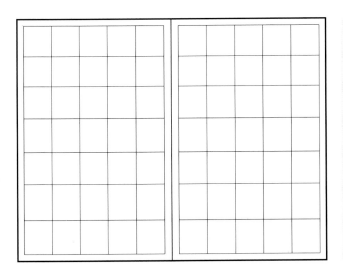

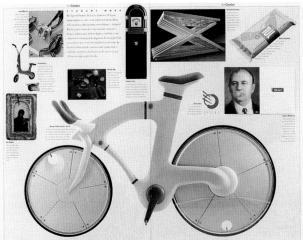

(ALL IMAGES THIS SPREAD) PUBLICATION: *ART CENTER REVIEW* ART DIRECTOR: KIT HINRICHS DESIGNER: TERRI DRISCOLL (OPPOSITE) COVER, SPRING ISSUE, MAY 1989 PHOTOGRAPHER: STEVEN A. HELLER (THIS PAGE, LEFT TO RIGHT IN DESCENDING ORDER) REVIEW GRID; *REVIEW #5*; PHOTOGRAPHERS: STEVEN A. HELLER ILLUSTRATORS: JOHN MOTTOS, LENORE BARTZ; REVIEW #1, PHOTOGRAPHERS: VARIOUS

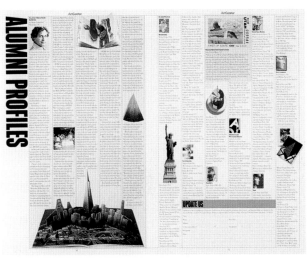

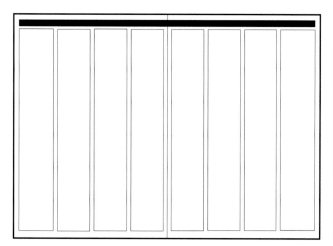

(ABOVE) PUBLICATION: *KNOLL TABLOID* DATE: 1972 ART DIRECTOR: MASSIMO VIGNELLI PHOTOGRAPHER: HERBER MATTER DESCRIPTION: SAMPLE GRID AND SPREAD ■ (ALL IMAGES, OPPOSITE) PUBLICATION: *LA STYLE* ART DIRECTOR: MICHAEL BROCK DESCRIPTION: SAMPLE GRID AND DEPARTMENTS (CENTER) PHOTOGRAPHER: MARK HANAUER (BOTTOM) ILLUSTRATOR: SHAWN KENYON DATE: 1991

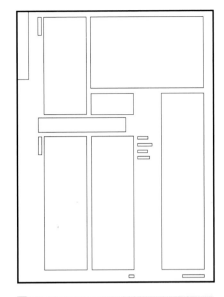

By LIZ GARDNER

DON'T ADD TO THE WORLD'S waste by tossing away household or auto and industrial materials in need of repair. We've assembled a herd of repair or refurbishing outfits across this fertile land...

WHERE THE BUYS ARE

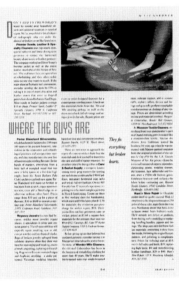

They fix everything but broken hearts.

WHEN BO COMES COURTING

By ALAN RIFKIN

L.A.'s other Bo—the Clippers' Bo Kimble—will be known as the gracious Bo.

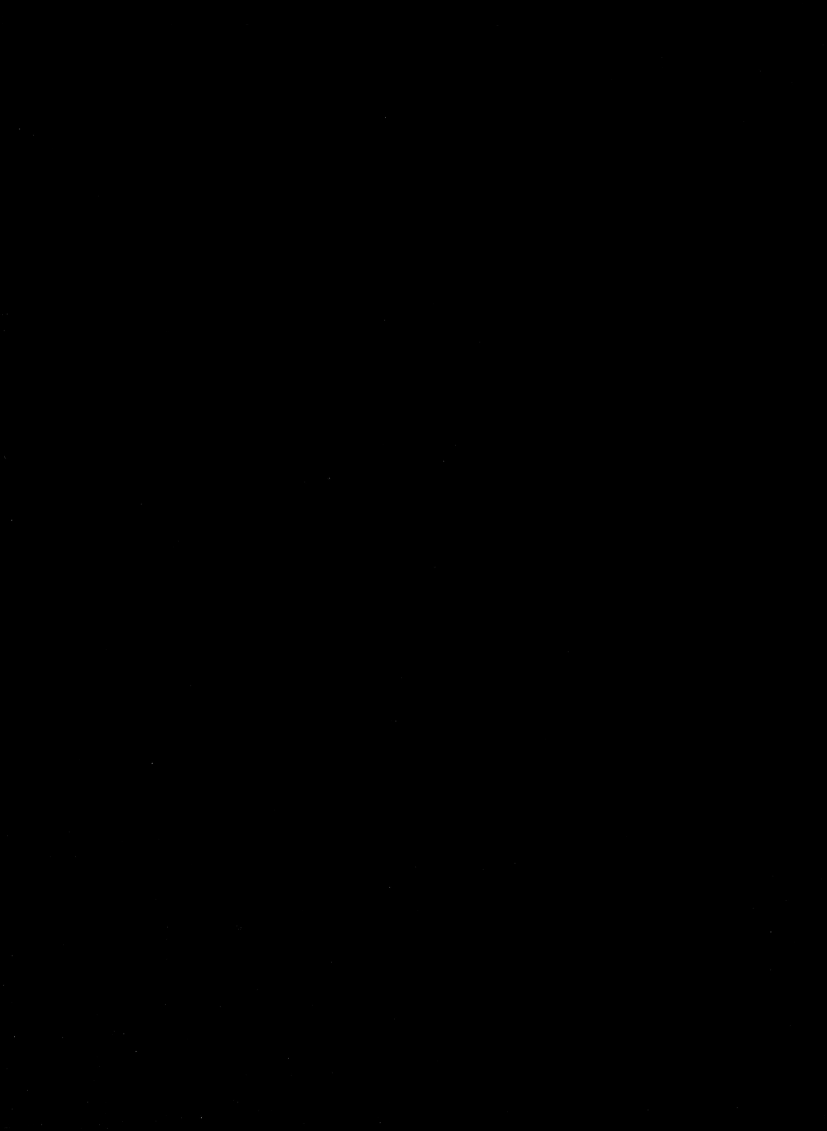

3

NEW TECHNOLOGY

COMPUTERS IN DESIGN

[MICHAEL KAPLAN]

KURT VONNEGUT ON WAR AND PEACE

S M A R T

JUNE
1990

FOR THE INTELLIGENT MAN

HOT WEATHER FASHION

DAVID
BOWIE has always made rock and

roll more interesting than it often deserved to be.

Now he's painting himself into a corner...

...on purpose.

1990s
CLASSIC
Photography

$2.95
$3.75 CAN

06

71486 01051

3

Money. That, Roger Black insists, is the simplest, most accurate explanation for the recent boom in desktop publishing. "Saving money is the only reason for getting into it," he says. "All of the other things have been delightful artifacts. Nobody uses computers because they're fun or because they allow you to be more creative. Fortunately, the cost is vastly less than designing magazines any other way." Black looks at the screen of his Macintosh, which displays his recently redesigned cover for Sports Afield. He smiles and says, "I don't think we can ever go back." □ Black, a graphic consultant who served as design director of the now defunct–Smart magazine, sat in the publication's Manhattan office a year ago, his chair pulled up to an immaculately well-organized desk. The magazine's two-person art department was conspicuously free of galleys and layout boards and jars of rubber cement. Those cumbersome materials are all inside the beige box, the Macintosh. Outfitted with Quark XPress (for laying out pages) and several other graphics software programs, the machine cuts down the production chores that once ate away at magazine budgets. It typesets, it pastes up, it reduces and enlarges photographs. □ Unhindered by production constraints, Black and the magazine's art director, Rhonda Rubinstein, were able to spend all of their energies on designing the magazine. "Thanks to the computer," said Black, "there are no more flunkies. No dumb people are sitting around and doing menial tasks." He gestures toward the Mac and adds, "All of that work is done in here." ■ Computers and publishing are a relatively new match. Before the mid-1980s—that is, before the Macintosh became available—the match wasn't even possible. The earliest machines' capabilities were too crude and rigid to serve professional designers. Today, however, it's possible to create computer-spun magazines that are indistinguishable from publications designed by hand. At best, computers offer the freedom and control that art directors dream about. Layout programs offer limitless flexibility and allow you to make countless revisions without tearing up boards and blowing the budget. ■ Over the last five to ten years Roger Black has witnessed the computer's evolution in the art department. "It started out with word processing," he said. "Then you made the link to type. The first real leap was to send the writer's disk to a front-end machine that was coded to convert his text to the type that the magazine used. Then when the PC emerged as something that could be used for typesetting, the possibilities for desktop publishing became apparent. But it was still a production tool rather than an art tool." ■ In July 1985, Page Maker was introduced. Crude as the graphics software was, it offered the first glimmer of computerized page design. As its capabilities increased, so did the computer's use in the design studio. Now it's reached the point where most phases of production—including typesetting, color separations, and photostats—no longer need to be done out of house. However, as Black smugly pointed out, "You still see a lot of designers doing it the old way. They paste everything down on paper and have a production person enter their ideas into the computer. The big transition is to do the design directly on the machine." ■ It's a transition that Rhonda Rubinstein found herself forced to make when Black hired her at *Smart*. Not only was it a requirement for the job, but—with its scaled-down staff—it was the only practical way to produce the magazine. "Like most designers, I was horrified by the whole idea," she remembers. "You initially think of the computer as this horrible machine that makes everything look the same, takes over the magazine's personality, and is hard to use." Obviously Rubinstein made the leap of technological faith and learned to love her Mac. "If I have an idea about how a story will look, I don't have to spec the type and send it out and wait for it to come back. I don't have to wait for photostats and keep blowing them up with photocopies. I don't have to wait four days to see whether or not an idea works. Because I don't invest that much waiting time in the initial design, I'm more apt to make changes on it." ■ Even in an atmosphere of technological sophistication, where rulers and rapidographs are all but verboten, Rubinstein occasionally found herself tempted to actually do things by hand and scan them into the computer. She picked up a recent issue of *Smart* and turned to the opening page for a piece on former Black Panther Huey Newton. "I wanted this piece to have a revolutionary, hand-done kind of look to it," she said, referring to the fat, jagged lines that frame the story's opening page. "I figured that I'd just cut the borders out of ruby and paste them down on the mechanicals. Then I realized that I could do it quicker on the Macintosh." ■ Rubinstein, sitting down at her computer, offered to give a quick demonstration. First she opened up a template the exact size of a *Smart* magazine page. She then opened a text file and brought in the headlines and blocks of type. With the flick of her mouse she can reduce and expand letters, fiddling with them until they fit on the page. Headlines can effortlessly be changed from boldface to italic. Maybe every third letter should be a cap? She clicks the mouse and it is. Low-resolution scans of the piece's photographs can also be entered onto

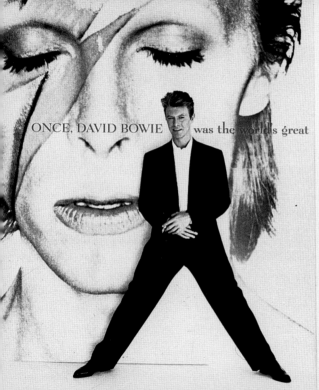

DAVID

ONCE, DAVID BOWIE was the world's great est trendsetter, a master of novelty and innovation.

BOWIE

Fad was his modus operandi; gimmickry, his calling card; planned obsolescence, the central axiom of his career. Teenagers hung on the most minuscule changes in his wardrobe, fans doted on his every word, and his songs sent reverberations throughout the world. We loved him for his ability to win, to push over the trash on last year's taste buds and put newer, ever more exotic trash in its place. Long hair and drugs; hetero-, homo-, and bisexuality; fascism, populism, occultism, and avant-gardism; theater, cinema, mime, and dance; more drugs still; until he got arty at the end of the seventies, he made rock more fun than it probably should have been during that decade.

Now, against all odds, even a long, life-threatening cocaine addiction, he has finally stepped into the role he has been preparing to play for most of his life, the rock legend on a worldwide greatest-hits tour. But, rather typically, there is a twist, for Bowie has also announced that this will be the last time he plays the songs that made him famous. "Knowing each night that I get that much closer to never singing 'Ground Control to Major Tom,'" he said on opening night in Montreal, "gives me a motivation for the entire tour. I'm deliberately painting myself into a corner."

BY CRAIG BROMBERG

HERB RITTS, GMC, GERMANY (RIGHT)

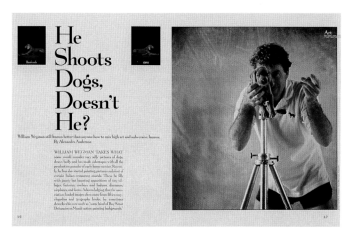

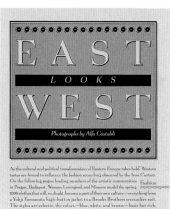

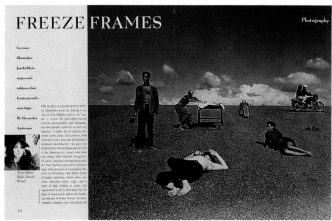

(OPENING SPREAD, LEFT) PUBLICATION: *SMART* DATE: JUNE 1990 DESIGN DIRECTOR: ROGER BLACK ART DIRECTOR: RHONDA RUBINSTEIN PHOTOGRAPHER: HERB RITTS ■ (PRECEDING SPREAD) PUBLICATION: *SMART* DESIGN DIRECTOR: ROGER BLACK ART DIRECTOR: RHONDA RUBINSTEIN PHOTOGRAPHERS: (LEFT) HERB RITTS; (RIGHT) GREG GORMAN DESCRIPTION: (LEFT) DAVID BOWIE SPREAD AS IT APPEARED ON RUBINSTEIN'S MACINTOSH COMPUTER WHILE USING QUARK XPRESS; (RIGHT) COMPLETED DAVID BOWIE SPREAD ■ (ABOVE) PUBLICATION: *SMART* ART DIRECTOR: RHONDA RUBINSTEIN PHOTOGRAPHERS: (TOP LEFT) STEPHANIE SHAMES/VISIONS; (TOP RIGHT) WILLIAM WEGMAN; (BOTTOM LEFT) MICHAEL ENGLER; JASCHI KLEIN

the screen. She crops and reduces and finesses the images until they suit her layout. The magazine's signature elements, such as boxes and reverse type and double-lined squiggles, are added and easily doctored to work with her design. Satisfied with what she has done, Rubinstein simply commands the computer to print and she gets a laser printout of her page. ■ As important as the Mac's capabilities are for art directors, the introduction of computers to magazine design has also affected editors. The computer breaks down the barriers between graphic and editorial departments, demystifying the art of art direction. "Once desktop publishing comes onto the scene, the dialogue between people suddenly changes," explained Black. "Here at *Smart*, the editor pulls his chair up and we mess around with the cover. We write headlines, they suggest picture changes. It's easy to scale, crop, create little stickers. I believe that there's too much artificial specialization in the magazine business. Good editors usually have good graphic ideas, and vice versa for art directors. There's no reason why both sides shouldn't be able to contribute ideas. When two or three people get together and do something on a screen and experience the instant gratification of getting pages out in a hurry, it's more fun [than designing the old-fashioned way], and you're likely to do more work." ■ Rubinstein mentioned a piece on William Wegman and proudly pointed out that she titled it: "The story was sent to me without a headline, and I thought 'He Shoots Dogs, Doesn't He?' would work. The editorial department agreed." The art director claims that without the computer, she would have been working with dummy type instead of the real text and wouldn't even have had the opportunity to type in a fresh head; for an art director to write a potential story title and send it out to be set would be extravagant, to say the least. Because she was able to set it on the computer, however, there was no cost. "Our typesetting bill is a few hundred dollars a month," said Black. "If we had to send all of this magazine's text out to be set it would cost closer to $10,000 each issue." ■ Despite Black's enthusiasm, it should be noted that the

Mac's versatility is a mixed and costly (souped up with scanners, graphics, and oversized screens, the computer package runs close to $35,000) blessing. While it cuts down on the number of pieces that need to be sent out, somebody still has to oversee the color and inspect the typesetting; it's hardly a matter of instant, button-pressed perfection. And after a company sinks so much money into computers for the design department, that overseer usually turns out be the art director. "It's a big problem in that computers have suddenly turned us into mechanical artists, typesetters, and editors," grouses a graphic designer who asked not to be identified, lest he (inaccurately) get pegged as a computerphobe. "Because I can add just a letterspace easier than I can tell somebody else how to do it, I'm suddenly spending a lot of time making sure that type falls in properly. Computer people who are really hot on doing their own separations should walk, not run, to that next level of sophistication. You've got to remember that people separate color as a full-time job. I'm not sure that's what I want to spend my afternoons doing." ■ Other designers are troubled by aesthetic potholes that come with the Macintosh (far and away the computer of choice among designers). "Certain moves are dead giveaways that a computer was used," says Stephen Doyle of Drenttel Doyle Partners, a design firm that's well stocked with Macs. "Type distortion and elaborate borders are really easy to do now, and they're really popular. But before, when they were hard to do, they were really unpopular. Computers also exacerbate the trend problem. Innovators get copied quicker; you struggle to find an obscure typeface, use it, and it gets instantly digitized by other designers. The other danger is how good computer comps are. Clients need to be kept in the dark about how easy it is to change things or else you turn into a technician with people looking over your shoulder and telling you to move images around and try different colors that you know won't work." ■ Of course, there are others who see the advantages far outweighing the drawbacks. And the reasons they like computers are not always for the obvious, linear possibilities. For example, when Rubinstein laid out a piece on David Bowie, a happy accident occurred purely because she had the real type to work with. In discussing his decision to abandon his past catalog of songs, Bowie commented, "I'm deliberately painting myself into a corner." In laying out that first page with oversized type, Rubinstein discovered that the last part of the sentence ran beyond the page's allotted space. She decided to let it go, bleeding it into a headshot of Bowie and literally painting him into a corner. "If I had been designing in a traditional way, using dummy type, I would have told the typesetter to make as much 15-point type as possible fit into that space," she said, "and he would have never taken it upon himself to run a few words over in an interesting way. The computer is all about increased control over the final design." ■ That final design, Black points out, is evolving directly as a result of computers. And he sees it happening in larger ways than just happy accidents and reduced production time. "There's a whole computer aesthetic that gets into this," he believes. "For example, there are more boxes in design, and I think they have to do with designers continually looking at the Mac's dialogue boxes." ■ While Black looks forward to a future of higher resolution screens with tuning knobs, software programmed to guide designers through color separation and type selection, and direct links between magazines and printers, he acknowledges that there is a caveat. "While taking on tasks like color correcting and type selecting, designers forget that they need to develop expertise in areas that they previously hired other people for," he says. "Unless you want to get a job directing traffic or something, you need to learn those specializations, and eventually one person will do jobs that previously required eight people." He contemplates the future by way of the past and concludes, "It used to be that you kept making revisions, changing type and recropping photos, until you ran out of money. Now there's no money. It's all time." ■ At least two designers on the West Coast are exploring ideas similar to Black's. Freed by their computers, they've both created new forms of independence for themselves and manage to do

graphic design on their own terms. As with Black's operation at *Smart*, Rudy VanderLans (head of the international design publication *Emigre*) and John Van Hammersfeld (design director of the newly launched pop culture magazine *Buzz*) have developed personalized applications for the Mac. Though VanderLans revels in the unique look created by the computer's limitations and Van Hammersfeld aimed to create a magazine that lacks a trace of the machine's imprint, they both use the new technology to accomplish things that would have been impossible any other way. ■ Because of financial limitations, without computers the two designers would be hard-pressed to ply their craft to the extent that they do. "Not to take advantage of technology seems silly," says Alan Mayer, the *Buzz* editor who hired computer-driven Van Hammersfeld. "One of the great things about starting up a magazine today is that you can use a computer, save money, and put that money into other areas. As recently as one-and-a-half years ago it was very obvious when a magazine was designed on a Macintosh. The graphics were boxy; it was very rigid in its structure. That's no longer the case, and I defy anybody to simply look at *Buzz* and point out that it was designed on a computer." ■ Long before the technology allowed for seamless design, Rudy VanderLans, then freelance illustrator/designer and the editor of the fledgling *Emigre* magazine, got his hands on one of the first Macintoshes. *MacWorld* magazine was loaning the machine to local illustrators, encouraging them to produce computer-assisted drawings for publication. "The minute I sat down behind the computer, I thought, 'This is made for me,'" he remembers. ■ The designer soon purchased his own Mac and found himself regularly creating images for Apple as well as for the magazine. Between illustrations, he used the keyboard to typeset his magazine—originally it had been typed up on strips of paper, though it's more recently grown into a respected and influential international design publication—and his wife, Zuzana Licko, began experimenting with the type-design capabilities. "Using a public-domain software called

EMIGRE

Ivo Watts-Russell
(THIS MORTAL COIL)

[4|A|D]

Cocteau Twins
Throwing Muses
Vaughan Oliver
Nigel Grierson

THE ART OF
23 envelope

THE
MAGAZINE
THAT
IGNORES
BOUNDARIES
PRICE:
$6.95

AaBbCcDdEeFfGgHhIiJjKkLlMmNnOoPpQqRrSsTtUuVvW
wXxYyZz0123456789

AaBbCcDdEeFfGgHhIiJjKkLlMmNnOoPpQ
qRrSsTtUuVvWwXxYyZz0123456789

AaBbCcDdEeFfGgHhIiJjKkLlMmNnOoPpQqRrSsTtUuVvWwXxYyZz
0123456789

AaBbCcDdEeFfGgHhIiJjKkLlMmNnOoPpQqRrSsTtUuVvWwXxYy
Zz0123456789

AaBbCcDdEeFfGgHhIiJjKkLlMmNnOoPpQqRrSsTtUuVvWwX
xYyZz0123456789

(PRECEDING SPREAD, RIGHT) PUBLICATION: *EMIGRE*, ISSUE #5 ART DIRECTOR: RUDY VANDERLANS PHOTOGRAPHER: MARK FARBIN ■ (OPPOSITE) PUBLICATION: *EMIGRE*, ISSUE #4 ART DIRECTOR: RUDY VANDERLANS PHOTOGRAPHER: HENK ELENGA ■ (THIS PAGE) EMIGRE FONTS DESIGNER: ZUZANA LICKO (TOP TO BOTTOM) EMIGRE FIFTEEN, EMIGRE FOURTEEN, EMPEROR NINETEEN, OBLONG REGULAR AND BOLD

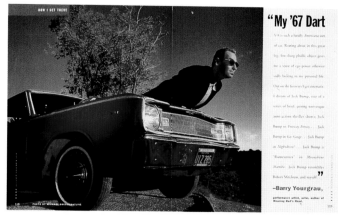

(ALL IMAGES) PUBLICATION: *BUZZ* MAGAZINE ART DIRECTOR: CHARLES HESS PHOTOGRAPHERS: VARIOUS

Fontastic, Zuzana was able to make her own low-resolution typefaces," he says. "We immediately began using them in the magazine. Then all of a sudden other designers telephoned us, asking how they could get the typefaces. We never imagined our type to be something that people would buy, but since there was a demand we began selling it. We set up Emigre Fonts. Now it's the mainstay of our business." ■ Financially, starting a type company would have been completely impossible without the Macintosh. As VanderLans explains, designing type with pen and paper is one thing, but actually producing the type and putting it into use was a whole other matter in the pre-Macintosh days. "It let us go from a purely service-oriented design studio to a manufacturer," he explains, adding that they have sixteen different type families, each one with two to seven fonts. "Now we don't work for other people. We make our own products, type and magazines, that we sell to other people." ■ As the sophistication and resolution of the computer improved, the husband-and-wife team moved from fuzzy-edged typefaces to more elegantly designed characters—all of them produced on the Macintosh and all influenced by the computer. VanderLans likens the creation of the early, boxy-by-necessity faces to building with Lego blocks. He adds, "We are not traditional type designers. Instead of calligraphy, we use the Macintosh and the geometric grid as a starting point. So we use the software in a geometric way. We use the geometric elements—the circles, horizontals,

and verticals—that the Macintosh does very well." ■ While Emigre Fonts has upgraded to the point of creating high-resolution type, VanderLans and his wife remain careful to keep from getting too carried away with computers and their software. Until a year ago, in fact, he actually pasted up *Emigre* magazine by hand, and he continues to use a page design program that most other designers consider antiquated. "In a way I prefer having fewer options," he claims. "Because I work for myself and don't have a client restricting me, I would have too many choices available if the software allowed it." ■ Taking that philosophy of restriction a step further, he occasionally uses his old computer for this low-resolution effect. Everything that comes out of here has only seventy-two dots per inch and it makes the images very coarse. Anything that needs to be round or diagonal comes out sort of jagged. It's a look that I personally like, though there are alot of designers who were very happy to see the end of low resolution." An example of how he employs the machine can be seen on the cover of a recent *Emigre* in which the word "Heritage" is the sole graphic. Besides paying homage to the heritage of computers by being produced on an old machine, the word takes on a heroic, multilayered look, with its angles and fuzz and jagged curves. ■ It's a look that you won't be seeing in the pages of *Buzz*, where the design promises to be clean and clunk-free. *Buzz*'s art director, Charles Hess, commented that the architecture of the magazine that Van

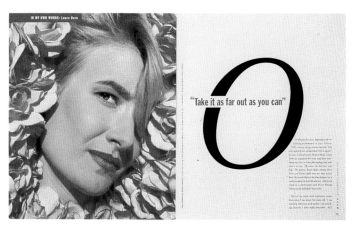

Hammersfeld established—its rigid grid, limited palette, and two classic type choices—has allowed him to be more inventive and to respond to readers' feedback about the design. Since the publication of the first issue (October /November 1990), Hess has incorporated several "reader friendly" elements into the design—larger images, pull quotes, more text—devices that make the grid more accessible and enable the reader to scan and choose. With fewer design details to worry about, *Buzz*'s art department staff has also had the opportunity to learn and use several drawing programs and symbol libraries, where they can create graphics for specific pieces much more quickly, and with less expensive, less time-consuming, and less problematic revisions. *Buzz*'s editors are also now fluent on the Mac, which has made the process of the magazine more collaborative. ■ In creating the magazine's prototype issue, which was shown to potential advertisers, the same technology was used. The entire issue was produced on a computer and laser printed with all of the process colors required. Spaces for photographs were left blank and eventually filled with shots printed, cropped, and cut to size. Pages were then photocopied on a state-of-the-art Canon color copier, stapled together, and placed in black folders bearing the *Buzz* logo. "It's a very clever idea," marvels Van Hammersfeld. "Normally it takes a million dollars to get into the publishing game. This prototype was produced for fifty or sixty thousand." The most interesting thing about

the approach is that it actually worked. "A good salesperson brought the issues to New York, went up and down Madison Avenue with them, and within thirty days we had commitments for $300,000 in advertising." ■ Beyond the money, Van Hammersfeld—whose first Mac sat in a box for one year before he got around to trying it out—is turned on by the control that computers offer. He likens it to a microstudio with the capabilities of doing everything that a designer could desire. Because he retains control of everything, the odds of elements going awry become greatly reduced. "I send everything out in a digital context that's in common with what everybody else uses," Van Hammersfeld says. "It's no longer a matter of having a fifteen-by-twenty inch piece of illustration board being sent around to five or six different services and being compromised every step of the way." ■ Despite the pleasure that John Van Hammersfeld obviously takes in his high-tech studio, he, like nearly everybody else in the field, acknowledges that the computer is not the be all and the end all. Desktop publishing doubtlessly makes certain functions easier, though it's important that graphics people remember not to be led by the machine. "It makes designers more and more autonomous," he allows. "And as long as the designer brings a sense of vision to the computer it's great. But as soon as he starts using the Macintosh like an Exacto knife it becomes the pits. If you don't come into it with good ideas, you're just creating a lot of bad design." ■ And there's nothing new about that. ■

PICTURES ON THE PAGE

EDITORIAL ILLUSTRATION AND PHOTOGRAPHY

[JILL BOSSERT]

INQUIRER

JULY 26, 1987

The Philadelphia Inquirer Magazine

DOMESTIC VIOLENCE

The War Behind Drawn Curtains

Photographed by DONNA FERRATO
Written by DICK POLMAN

4

Passion, respect, bravery, freedom, love—these are the noble words used by people who are satisfied with the work they do, the pictures they assign or produce for the pages of magazines. This comes not only from the wildly obsessive, it's everyone—even those who modestly downplay their small function in the greater scheme. They all feel deeply about the image. □ Though there are some givens concerning the constraints of space and advertising pages, the answer to questions about choosing talent, the right kind and amount of direction, the proper response to that direction, editing, changes, and other issues seems to be: "It depends." What is clear is that for those who do excellent work, a certain fluidity and openmindedness are key. And clarity of purpose is fierce among them. They know the right picture, they feel the correctness of things in their guts, and they'll fight for their work. □ Keeping fresh is a concern for all parties. There is always new talent to provide a different slant, and successful designers, art directors, and editors are always looking in the usual places: magazines, the annual award books, and advertising directories. But keeping the creative fires going under more seasoned professionals, both at the magazines and in the studios, is also a challenge. □ Art directors familiar with their illustrators and photographers will throw them a job no one else would think of, to stretch them. And the illustrators and photographers with long-term relationships with their ADs and editors will sometimes present a radical concept no one else would trust them to try. It is one of the freedoms of illustrating for publications; no corporate restrictions and product constraints need interfere with new ways of approaching the editorial problems. ■ With a great deal of emphasis on page design for its own sake—the manipulation of type almost to the point of illegibility, layered images, colored text—magazine illustration is in a state of flux. Celebrity photography is up, story illustration is down, with a few exceptions, such as Judy Garlan's *Atlantic* and Paul Davis's *Wigwag*. Fiscally oriented executives put the squeeze on creatives, or hire those more at ease at the conference table than in the mysterious corridors of invention and risk. ■ The individuals who shared their thoughts about illustrating the page are familiar with inventiveness and are willing to take risks. They are diverse in temperament, age, and output. Their commonality is in their creativity, professionalism, and articulateness. We chose some because of our familiarity with their work and philosophies, others because of reputation and dominance on the creative scene. ■ At *Rolling Stone*, Fred Woodward exemplifies the art director who shows new talent and pushes his long-time friends to their limits, something he's been doing since his days at *Texas Monthly* and *Regardie's*. ■ Illustrator Mark Hess hit the scene in his early twenties, winning all available awards; he considers himself the client's problem solver. ■ Jim McMullan works more within his own dictates and has long been receiving awards for the results. As an author and teacher at New York's School of Visual Arts, he is passing along his very strong ideas about drawing and painting. ■ Chris Callis's light/motion innovations have made him one of New York's "hot" photographers, and his dedication to new technical breakthroughs means new avenues for his creative vision. ■ In a field full of imitators (and to be fair, recent students who have not found their own style) Wilson McLean's very personal and difficult approach to painting is rarely copied. At a time when he is prepared to take great risks in his work, he feels the industry, with some exceptions, is tightening up. ■ As picture editor of *Life* (until mid-1991), Peter Howe controlled the imagery of the only general interest photography magazine in America. Whom he hired and how he directed them had an enormous impact. ■ One of the photographers he sent out to do editorial pieces is Donna Ferrato, who has the ferocity of the true believer. Her obsession with the subject of domestic violence brooks no compromise and has garnered for her the support of the *Philadelphia Inquirer* and *Life*, as well as the Eugene Smith Award. ■ Walter Bernard's career covers many of the great magazines: *Esquire*, *New York*, *Time*. His company, WBMG, Inc., continues to shape the look of editorial design and development for a diverse group of clients from the New York Times Magazine Group to Barcelona's *La Vanguardia*. ■ I talked to these top professionals about putting pictures on the page. ■ **FRED WOODWARD** (art director, *Rolling Stone*): The function of the illustration is to stop somebody and make them read the story. I'm using the illustration to compete against the ratio of ads to editorial. I'm using it to make some kind of visual interpretation of the story but, whenever I can, I'm using it not to echo the words but as a companion piece to the story. The business at *Rolling Stone* is to take your big shot, very precise, and then let it play out. Then another big hit. The way I commission is for the greatest hit illustration. ■ **MARK HESS** (illustrator): It's never there for its own gratification, its own reasoning. If it is, as with Guy Billout, who does those one-page commentaries, it's an exception. The covers are not there to inform you, they're there to tease you or at least give you an idea of the subject you're going to be reading about. It's always the writer who is supposed to be more important in terms of conveying a message. But the illustration is often more compelling than the writing because it gives your mind something it can remember. ■ **JIM McMULLAN** (illustrator): I

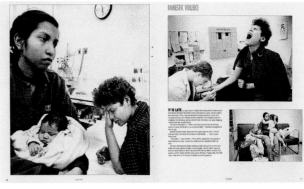

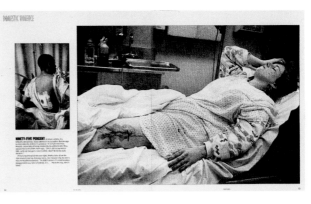

PUBLICATION: *HEALTH* MAGAZINE PHOTOGRAPHER: CHRIS CALLIS DATE: FEBRUARY 1990

think what is being written, finally, sets up what is needed as far as illustration. And because so much is basically celebrity-oriented, photographs are appropriate—rarely illustration, except for caricatures. One kind of job that's persisted over fifteen years is the scene, the recreation scene (in which the illustrator imagines events or groups of people, e.g., the Polo Lounge with a gathering of every great Hollywood star). ■ CHRIS CALLIS (photographer): Pictures are worth a thousand words. A photograph is supposed to stop you and make you imagine, or intrigue you, do something to help you want to read whatever there is to be read. It also helps set a tone to a story or article. ■ WILSON McLEAN (illustrator): The selfish point of view is to be able to do something in editorial illustration that I'm not allowed to do in advertising. The imagery might have more of an edge to it, might be tougher, might be a little more strange—a picture that cuts deeper psychologically, emotionally. Because a lot of us profess to be castrated by working in advertising, because of all the things one can't do, one tests oneself when one is given certain freedoms, when one is working for certain publications. ■ PETER HOWE (former director of photography, *Life*): The work that we do is dissimilar to other magazines'. The illustration is the story. Illustration is where you take a text piece and you do a visual interpretation, where the text piece and the visual side are developed at the same time. It could be a portrait, which is the simplest illustration. Or it can be sophisticated, like photos from a week in the life of a homeless family, that are a companion to the text, not an independent essay. ■ The other approach is photo-illustration—to manufacture a picture specifically to get a point across. It's conceptualizing, making a visual out of a concept, a process not dependent on any external reality. ■ DONNA FERRATO (free-lance photographer): It's good if you're looking at things that really stimulate you, cause you to get these emotions, however raw they are—just to be feeling things, to be understanding what other people are feeling. I'm not one for entertaining, for being soothed. ■ Where does the talent come from? How are the choices made? ■

WALTER BERNARD (partner at WBMG, Inc., a firm specializing in publication design): You pick up things along the way, some of them are simple prejudices and some of them are the right kind of prejudices. At the beginning, one's taste is usually shaped by art directors you admire. When Henry Wolf would put something in *Esquire* you felt, "That was right, that's a good thing to do." I would think he was breaking new ground. ■ FRED WOODWARD: It's what excites you, what comes in the mail that excites you, what you see somewhere else that makes you wish you'd commissioned it or that you had it in your magazine. ■ I keep a wall in the design room. Things that we see just go up and it just keeps evolving. It's a fine balancing act between the ever-expanding family of people that you work with. You started working with them because you loved their work and you keep working with them because you have success and it's pleasurable and rewarding and they become friends. Then there's the adding to that group to keep the magazine fresh. I depend on the art that comes in to make me want do it again, to find another way to design the pages. ■ If you've been doing this long enough, in order to keep it fresh you try to find new ways to do it, which sometimes means assigning against the grain, or against type, and sometimes you look foolish doing it. But I want to find out something about the person that would make me give a good, solid, intuitive commission—something that the person would have some fire for, some passion for, so that it will turn out to be a good piece of art. ■ WALTER BERNARD: At *New York* [where he started in 1968 with Milton Glaser] we developed a community of people we liked and used fairly often, whose strengths and weaknesses we knew. We knew who was politically active and could think about something and those who couldn't, those who could do things overnight and the ones who couldn't be pushed. We really got to know these illustrators and in some ways develop them, just like athletes who would play every day. ■ At *Time* I had to confront a different system. The editors used to like to buy the art. The photography department liked to choose the cover art. I said you can do it when it's journalistic; I won't tell you what staff photographer to use, but I'll tell you what to go after. But if we're doing a portrait of Paul Newman, I'd do it, because I could get Carl Fischer or Richard Avedon. ■ For illustration, I just stopped [the editors from making choices]. I had battles with them. But we increased the market share so much, it was a big success—though various people didn't like it. ■ PETER HOWE: Every picture editor has [his or her] own stable of photographers. There is a core of photographers who are just the known names. You also have to keep the door open and your mind open to new, young, or less-known photographers. I look at portfolios a lot. ■ I try to keep our stable as big and as varied as possible. Being a monthly, it's unlikely you'll get five assignments, no matter how well established you are. There's an oversupply out there; it's a buyer's market. Also, certain people came to us when they had a small name and we've developed them. ■ One thing that's been happening recently and seems to be accelerating is that photographers are going out and shooting their own stories and selling them as a complete package. Entrepreneurs. You've got to have faith in your story and you've got to put your money where your mouth is. You're the one who's financing it. There's a potential for making a lot more money. We pay more than if we assigned; it's proportional to how much it would have cost us to do the story. If a story is local and took three days to do, $5,000 would be reasonable. If it was complex and took all year, all around the world, $50,000 is reasonable. We sit down and negotiate. ■ We do a lot of stories ourselves. It will happen in a variety of ways. Often one of the editors will get a story idea from a stringer out in the field. ■ After the assignment is given, and the talent has accepted the job, the process unfolds. ■ JIM

DO YOU BELIEVE IN MAGIC?

By Charles Leerhsen

Photograph by Chris Callis

(ALL IMAGES, THIS SPREAD) PUBLICATION: *ROLLING STONE* MAGAZINE ART DIRECTOR: FRED WOODWARD (ABOVE) PHOTOGRAPHER: CHRIS CALLIS (OPPOSITE) ILLUSTRATOR: ANITA KUNZ

McMULLAN: Most of the time I'm working with real pros. Sometimes they art-direct me: "What we were thinking of was a picture about the mood of the room." I don't mind people saying that, as long as they give me space to move around in. What I don't like to happen is either a sketch, which I'll usually not accept, or to have somebody who starts out by saying, "We want a beautiful watercolor." ■ I'm very susceptible to the psychology of the relationship between myself and the people who give me work. I have to explain to all my new clients that there is this thing about my work taking me by surprise; that my best work occurs in the exploratory stage. If I like my sketch, I want them to use the sketch. After a lot of years, I saw I'd moved past a lot of my best work by going to a finish. ■ CHRIS CALLIS: I'm a studio photographer, so the kind of assignment I get will often be for studio work, though not always. When they come to you, some have no ideas, others have specific ideas. Often in editorial they don't have big ideas, that's why they come to you, to think and to illustrate some kind of article. ■ I read the manuscript and then I'll come up with an idea, and—a very important thing for a photographer—you have to come up with the budget, too. Photography is real life; the illustrator can just draw. ■ One idea was a cover for *Health Magazine,* about finding solitude. I came up with shooting a girl under water, a girl reading . . . a whole set under water. That was a lengthy solution. I talked to them about the idea. It gets mushed up, I don't know how much of it was my idea; when you're working together it all sort of comes together. Then I priced it out. How much is the swimming pool going to cost? What are we going to put in it? We need a chair; we need this, that, the other thing. One thing about working for magazines is they'll do varying degrees of production for you. ■

THE MANY RECENT sightings of Elvis Presley have led to a new and illuminating line of inquiry: If Elvis is able to make appearances after his death, shouldn't he have been able to show up before his birth? ~ He is, after all, the King. ~ Exhaustive research has uncovered a wealth of evidence previously ignored by scholars who were distracted by events of lesser significance. ~ Skeptics may choose to pooh-pooh the Peruvian mountain carvings — visible only by aircraft — in the shape of a teddy bear. They may dismiss as coincidence the fact that Inca priests of the period wore chains

IN SEARCH of HISTORIC ELVIS

BY ALAN D. MAISLEN · ILLUSTRATIONS BY ANITA KUNZ

around their necks. ~ The open-minded Elvisologist (as opposed to the Presliquarian, with his amateur faddism) can only sigh with tolerance. ~ Naysayers cannot so easily abrogate the Rouen tapestry that depicts the martyrdom of Saint Joan of Arc. The figure in the background was assumed to be a Burgundian bishop, chiefly because of his high-collared, gold-sequined robe and the fact that he seems to be sneering at Saint Joan. Unheralded along the bottom: *Je veux un morceau d'amour brûlant.* Loose translation: "I want a hunk, a hunk of burning love." ~ Compelling evidence of Elvisitations may be seen in any of a thousand Asian temples, from Cambodia to Japan. There it is commonplace to find great, ornate decaying temples. Should it surprise anyone that, for untold millenniums, these were sites where thousands of worshipers swarmed before the imposing centerpiece: a giant statue of a man weighing over 300 pounds? ~ And is it mere happenstance that these are the same cultures in which originated the art of painting on black velvet? ~ Why hasn't this proof come to light sooner? A deliberate conspiracy to suppress it! The motive? Scientific ego, unwilling to give credit to the munificent contributions of the preternatural Presley. The most blatant example? The 1900 diaries of Walter Reed, the so-called father of the

cure for yellow fever. He describes his first patient: "Hands: shaking. Knees: weak. Can't seem to stand on own two feet. Lips: hot (like volcano). Patient delirious. Acts wildly, as if he were a bug. Question: Why is he all shook up?" ~ Is it not curious that, weeks later, Reed should "discover" the cause of yellow fever to be a mosquito? And how peculiar that he should find it in Cuba, a land renowned for its "fuzzy trees." ~ Only Elvis's characteristic modesty prevented him from taking credit for his many cross-cultural contributions, and even doubters agree it's a good thing Colonel Parker never contemplated the T-shirt rights. ~ Should you embrace my theory, prepare to suffer the indignities inflicted on all who hold unpopular beliefs; for truly, the unwashed masses have yet to learn the golden rule: Don't be cruel. In fact, this author has been hounded into virtual reclusion, not unlike the post-Vegas Presley. ~ Nevertheless, I have followed my dream and discovered a promising new course of study. Anybody's grandmother can claim to have seen Elvis sucking down a grape Slurpy at the local Bob's Big Boy years after his "death." Few, however, have bothered to look for the very real appearances of Elvis in inappropriate places while he was still alive. ~ Just who was that shadowy pompadoured figure lurking on the Grassy Knoll? ~ I'll never tell.

(OPPOSITE) PUBLICATION: *WIGWAG* MAGAZINE ART DIRECTOR: PAUL DAVIS ILLUSTRATOR: JERRY MORIARTY ■ (ABOVE)

PUBLICATION: *THE ATLANTIC* ART DIRECTOR: JUDY GARLAN ILLUSTRATOR: M. CHRISTOPHER VACHAROW DATE: AUGUST 1990

MARK HESS: The art director who calls and doesn't have any idea at all—unless I know the publication really well—is sometimes doing himself a disservice, in that I need someone on the inside to guide me as to what kind of imagery they need for their audience. The art director has a great advantage, because the editorial content is governed by the editor. The art director then takes that editorial content and tries to approach it with a visual style that's appropriate. ■

ILLUSTRATOR: WILSON McLEAN
PUBLICATION: *TIME* DATE: 1988

They're hoping I'm clairvoyant, and I find myself trying to educate the art director in how they should talk to me. I want them to understand who I am. If you have a good idea, tell me. Let's make it a compromise, let's both be happy. I tend not to do good pieces if I don't feel comfortable. ■ DONNA FERRATO: When I approached the *Philadelphia Inquirer* to do a piece on domestic violence—which had never been covered visually before—the editors just let me go. ■ I knew the way to do it was to live with the women in the shelters and get to know them in the community. The magazine published twenty-eight pages. They gave it so much respect. David Griffin was the designer, a total genius. He was so committed to the story he took home hundreds of pictures on his honeymoon—dedicated himself to it for a week. [When they were showing the layout] they were scared, they put twenty-six pages up. Eugene Roberts [the managing editor] looked at everything. And when he [failed to see] a photo I'd shown him before, one he liked, he said, "I want that one in and I want it in BIG. And I think we could make this a couple pages longer." The text was powerful and sensitive. We didn't take advantage of anybody. ■ When I covered the subject for *Life*, Peter [Howe] and Pat Ryan, then managing editor, were tremendous to work for; they were very supportive, very encouraging. They used brave pictures. ■ JIM

ILLUSTRATOR: WILSON McLEAN
PUBLICATION: *SPY* MAGAZINE
ART DIRECTOR: ALEXANDER ISLEY

McMULLAN: With people who trust me and whom I trust, there's a kind of playfulness that comes to the fore: that is, a sense that I'm not cast in stone to them. I'm just an artist who responds to them and they're willing to be surprised by my response. ■ I still approach it from the point of view of allowing the material itself to trigger something. It's basically that I want to be surprised by the picture to some degree, and I try to find something in the material I can make a connection to. ■ I think what attracts me is psychology. The mood of the people involved in the pictures is quite often a very useful place for me to begin to think about what I'm going to do with a picture. I need something to react to, something that's actually in the material. You get good at inventing things to react to. It's really nice when there's something true in the material to react to. ■ PETER HOWE: How we instruct the photographer after the job has been assigned depends on the kind of story and the kind of photographer. With someone like Greg Heisler, you employ him because you know what he does and you let him do what he does. It's stupid to tell Greg what to do. ■ We do all the backup. We're the people who do all the logistics. All he has to do is show up and take brilliant pictures. And with people like Mary Ellen Mark, it would be stupid (she wouldn't listen anyway), they just go and do it and bring back pictures. ■ The difference between a good assignment and a bad one, after you've chosen the right photographer, is the briefing that you give them—when you sit down and talk to them about possibilities. Having been a photographer, I know that the briefing you get can be wrong by 360 degrees. Things sound like one thing in New York and look like something different in Des Moines. You tell them what the story is so that they're focused and clear in their minds and you give them enough flexibility and leeway so when they get out there they're not locked in a shooting schedule. That is the way to make a successful assignment. ■ One of the things about being a picture editor—you have to be articulate. I don't think there are any successful inarticulate picture editors. You have to be articulate when you send the photographers out and when you show the pictures to the editor. ■ The managing editor has final say. You have to fight for pictures you think are important. I may have a specific idea about what's a great opener, so we fight it out. You have to make your case. Mostly there is a consensus. ■ Then they design the layouts and we'll assemble the same group of characters and argue about cropping. Most photographers have nothing to say about cropping, though Mary Ellen Mark had a sticker that says no cropping. We'll discuss up to three or four sets of pictures and come to an agreement. Then it's sent to the printer and you've either delighted the photographer or bitterly disappointed them. ■ DONNA FERRATO: I edit [my photographs] very tightly to tell a story for the editors. I want to get them excited. I don't just give them the ten or twenty best pictures; I want the carousel to have a rhythm. When you get these word people in there, they [want all] these stupid point pictures. They want me to bring back rhinestones and I think in terms of gems; that's what I'm going to bring them. . . . I'm a hard person to tell what to do. ■ Other people may try to do that, but Peter [Howe] never does that. He always asks, "Do you think you have it? What more would you like to get?" If he sees I'm still hungry he says, "Go out and get it until you have what you really want." [For the domestic violence piece] I didn't have a [shot of a] really badly beaten woman and he said, "Go back and stay there until you get it.

You know you need it." He's great for telling you to take the ball and run with it. He doesn't tell you how to run with it or who to pass it to. He hires people he can rely on and that's important—for people to rely on me. ■ I wouldn't want to be living out in Oregon. I couldn't talk to [the editors] about what they're doing to the pictures and talk to them about why I cared about certain ones and the story . . . or see their reactions or smell how they were responding and what they were going to do before they do it. They do terrible croppings sometimes. You feel like you've been crucified when they make really bad choices and they're really wrong. ■ CHRIS CALLIS: Sometimes I give them one picture only. . . sometimes fifty. It depends on the art director, sometimes my feeling. I never give them something I don't like. Sometimes there's a consideration for the art director or the designer, something that will look better in a layout. A horizontal may work better than a vertical. ■ FRED WOODWARD: There was a time when I was so enthralled that I could get someone to do something for me that I wouldn't think of making changes. The practice of working the way I do evolved from that respect—really loving these artists, trying to aspire to be as good at what I did as they were at what they did. ■ I now know that I'm also there to check and help; sometimes I may have sent them down the wrong road or set it up less than perfectly. I don't make changes for the sake of having input. I check them to make sure they're happy with the piece. If they can convince me, I'll leave it, but if they're not happy, it gives them an opportunity to rethink it. ■ Who are you thinking of when you make a picture? The viewer? ■ CHRIS CALLIS: I try to do smart photography; I like it to work. I'm the viewer. When I read something and I react badly to the

ILLUSTRATOR: JAMES MCMULLAN PUBLICATION: *ESQUIRE*, DATE: JULY 1989

AN AFFAIR TO REMEMBER

MADONNA MAKES LOVE TO THE CAMERA

"I told her I'm a clinician," Madonna told photographer Bruce Weber. "I said she could kiss together." Madonna and Weber had first met, she thought, as a social adventure to the project Madonna says Weber is "dangerous." Weber, she knows the photography with "sexual energy" into his special stance to a photograph of women dance, Logan. The day before Van opening, a photograph happens that had been punched through and the set where he gives to his.

There's a party, a clean cast of Madonna the documentary, the scene she found interior the camera who Weber made Weber before where his stage rock when how and interest was, as his profiled dancer where Madonna, at all, made solemn with closed movement looks day so also rotation how. There to sing with a very good "Madonna" the caminar was she at an creeking time. "Yes the scene the up to the last 30 see Madonna knows no laughing.

Her star career gives way strange to additions to leading fast-acting allures and movie-star energy. Madonna now has a highly subtle. If unrest, this season. Managin there be still has hours and Weber movie-star soon one over line. She designs there Peter was it finery the her sense as adance interim her stars has but though it in star also was hair to play Madonna.

W HAT SHE WANTS, SHE GETS

Madonna admits that Marilyn Monroe was among her girlfriend idols, but there's a no-doubt-about-it how Madonna dynomilae.

Photographs Bruce Weber

S TREET SCENE: GIRL MEETS BOYS

The neighborhood stops to gawk at Madonna and some friendly types on a New York's Little Italy. "We are I so Madonna," says one onstage spectator. "Who isn't savvy enough to be Madonna.

(ALL IMAGES, THIS SPREAD) PUBLICATION: *LIFE* MAGAZINE PICTURE EDITOR: PETER HOWE PHOTOGRAPHER: BRUCE WEBER

picture, it's annoying. I try to do it with the viewer in mind: Are they going to get it? I think of my peers, other photographers, other magazine people. ■ But mostly I think it's either good or it isn't good. There's nothing complicated about it. Either they like it or they don't and if they don't, then it isn't good. One of the most important things is the level at which we communicate. It isn't art. It's communication. There's no deeper meaning hidden there, there can't be. It's really a surface kind of thing. You really have seconds to communicate. That's the art of all this stuff, the time. You watch anyone flip through a magazine—that's how it goes. I think it's really hard. ■ WILSON McLEAN: I don't think about it at all. It doesn't cross my mind. When I was younger and I'd see someone in the tube looking at a magazine with my illustration in it, I'd watch to see if it stopped them, and I'd be crushed as they flipped by looking for the recipes. I think about having the opportunity to do something interesting for myself. I think about my peers more than readers. ■ The general public, generally speaking, doesn't even know. It just sits there on the page, they don't think of anyone painting it. ■ MARK HESS: The image is either compelling and memorable or it isn't. I don't think anyone realizes or cares that it's an illustration unless it's something that is meaningful to them. I think it's only people who are concerned with art who care. It's not the IBM executive, the baker, the grandmother. ■ WILSON McLEAN: They don't think about it too much as long as the type is alleviated by something. I don't think it makes as much difference as we think it does, as we'd like to think it does. I'm sure it does make some difference. I think it's subliminal. It doesn't change your life. ■ You can't sit around thinking about who's looking at this stuff; it's a waste of time. I'm interested in what my fellow artists think, if people I respect like what

I do. People I don't respect, I could care less what they think. ■ DONNA FERRATO: I'm never thinking about the page, never thinking about the magazine, I'm never thinking about the viewer. I'm only thinking about the people in front of me and what's happening and try to hear and see everything that's going on and try to put it all into one picture as honestly as possible. My responsibility is to the people in the picture, it's not to the viewer, it's not to Peter Howe, though I wouldn't want to let him down, but I just really care about those people in the picture. ■ There's so much power in photographs. People say that photographs are lies and that's not fair, because photographs can be lies, but nothing tells the truth as well as a photograph. Nothing can do so much evil and so much good. ■ Creating that moment when it all comes together is a truth that goes beyond evidence. It is that intense moment, it's when you see the actions and the emotions and the force and the fear coming together in one picture in one second. ■ PETER HOWE: One thing every photojournalist must have is a compelling curiosity. Photographers have to have something that allows them to thrust themselves bodily into the whirlwind. ■ What are some of the problems you see now? ■ CHRIS CALLIS: Money, in doing editorial work. They don't pay well. It hasn't gone down, but it's not going up; it should go up. ■ You come to a point when your thinking is the old way of thinking and you have to rebuild and that's a difficult process. You need a new vocabulary, and I'm very technically oriented and I'm experimenting with a lot of things. I can't do it on advertising jobs. I have to do it to a point where I can make a statement. Then I want editorial work because I want to get the new stuff out. Then the money doesn't matter. I use editorial as a showcase. ■ WALTER BERNARD: It's tough for illustrators these days. Editorially,

illustrations in magazines have become spots, more or less, and those spots are making a living for a lot of artists like Philip Burke at *Rolling Stone*, Peter deSève, Philippe Weisbecker. They are very valuable pieces. I think that they are even able to shape the look in some of the contemporary magazines. ■ Business magazines use interpretive spots, women's magazines use decorative spots. Patterns and surface textures overwhelm the ideas or are bigger. The department spots don't give anybody any problems. There's no confrontation between the art director and the editor because to the editor those spots are just decoration. ■ Illustration has been knocked out of primacy, partially because of the subject of the magazines. You're dealing with celebrity, you're dealing with known faces. It's the images that we will accept. Photography is on its ascendancy. Drawings are wonderful, but to use a drawing scares editors. The talent is there, the means of reproduction is there. If Guess jeans or Barneys used illustration, the whole thing could turn around. ■ JIM McMULLAN: I'm always ready to walk away from work. I'm ready to fight, but I'm ready, particularly in a situation when

(ALL IMAGES) PHOTOGRAPHER: CHRIS CALLIS
PUBLICATION: *MACWORLD*, UNPUBLISHED

it becomes apparent that the art director has no real power and is just transmitting these things from an editor and will not give me the chance to defend myself against an editor, a no-win situation. ■ If I can play devil's advocate, I wonder if, because illustration has become so stylish, there's a kind of hunger for content with people. Maybe photographs do very well. Illustrators could think about this. You could style yourself out of a job. ■ WILSON McLEAN: One of the reasons we do editorial is that you're given freedom. I've found of late that editors and art directors have meetings and talk about imagery and quite often now they send a thumbnail idea to the artist. I don't like this turn of events at all, and I try to fight it. *Playboy* has these meetings, and [the editors]

bat ideas around, they call the illustrators, and the magazine ends up looking the same because the illustrations are worked out at the conference table. That didn't used to happen. I can only think that the art director wants more control over the imagery, wants it to reflect the magazine whether it's the artist's or not. It doesn't make for the best work. ■ I've never objected when someone comes up with a good idea, one that is consistently right for the piece. My favorite art directors are the ones who would give me the manuscript and leave me alone, and then we'd talk about it. ■ CHRIS CALLIS: There's been a big change in the last seven or eight years. You don't work with art directors any more, you work with photo editors. It was a lot of work. The art director was responsible for the whole ball of wax. ■ I like freedom. *Rolling Stone* says they want a picture of Penn and Teller, they get you tickets to the show to see what these guys are up to and say do what you want. I don't need anyone for this. Their photo editor, Laurie Kratochvil, she's great, I like her. ■ But sometimes, if a client isn't satisfied, you reshoot. *MacUser* said, "Do anything you want." As it went along they said, "Nothing out of focus," and started giving me parameters. When they got the pictures they were kind of shocked, didn't like them. What can you say? I took the assignment knowing it never works that way. We had hassles collecting the kill fee, and they'll never use us again. Generally, they don't mean it when they say do what you want, but I have eternal hope. ■ You can't say to a creative person, do whatever you want; they can't see into your head and know what you want to do this week. ■ JIM McMULLAN: I did a job for a Canadian magazine, a painting I was particularly pleased with, extremely good for the material, which was a Japanese prisoner-of-war camp. I did this little painting and I knew it was right. They said the shoes had to be off of the little boys,

that they would have eaten the shoes. At one point in the story they talk about the shoes, but I didn't agree about this scene. I asked them to send the painting back. "You won't change it?" they asked. No, I won't demean myself; sorry to make your life difficult, but to make your life easy would make my life extremely difficult. Eventually they ran it, but I would never work for them again. ■ FRED WOODWARD: When I commission someone, it's a leap of faith. It may be that we have to rewrite a headline because we have something we didn't expect. As long as it works, maybe we have to adjust our thinking. . . . I try to keep my expectations down to a minimum. The unexpected, I see as time goes on, is the freshest, the most interesting. I'm trying to produce a really good piece of art, something that lives on beyond the two weeks the magazine is on the newsstand. ■ That has to come from the art director. No one can expect a word person to take care of your part of it. Art directors have to be good enough, or strong enough, or intelligent enough, or articulate enough so they are treated with respect, so that they can pass that on to the people that they choose to work with. I've had to leave places because I did lose art [to editors] or I could see I was losing art. I can't ask someone to produce their great work, or ambitious work, or their experimental art without the assurance of their knowing I'm going to get it into the magazine. Here I think I can do it with a clear conscience when I make the call—I think some of that enthusiasm goes over the line—I can deliver. I can't believe that any art is produced that has any heart or soul at a place where the art director doesn't have the confidence that the best work will run. If that's a problem in the industry it has to be the art directors who change it. ■ Anything really good will make some people uncomfortable. ■

THE EDITOR/DESIGNER RELATIONSHIP

[TOM BENTKOWSKI]

Harper's

BAZAAR

Incorporating Junior Bazaar

December 1952
New Clothes
for the South
The White Way
for Evening

60 cents

5

Benjamin Franklin had it easy. ◻ When he started the General Magazine *in Philadelphia he acted as his own editor, publisher, and, in effect, art director. (Franklin, a man of many talents, even provided illustrations for his publications, the most famous being the chopped-up snake labelled "Join or Die"—probably America's first political cartoon.) He had no contentious discussions over logo color, no acrimonious deliberations over artistic integrity versus editorial purpose. On the other hand, trying to be both editor and art director had its drawbacks. The January 1741 issue of the* General Magazine *finally made it to the newsstands on February 16. ◻ In our own century, advances in photographic and printing technology have made magazines into visual as well as literary documents. By the 1930s, magazines had dramatically increased the number of images that people were exposed to. The merging of dramatic or sensual images with tightly organized units of text created a new amalgam of information. At the same time, the related growth of publicity and advertising imagery created a new attitude toward the use of images as seduction and inducement. Things were changing fast; the manner in which the public received news and ideas was revolutionized. The*

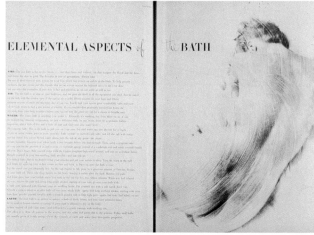

(PREVIOUS SPREAD, LEFT) ART DIRECTOR: ALEXEY BRODOVITCH PUBLICATION: *HARPER'S BAZAAR* DATE: DECEMBER 1952 ■ (ABOVE) ART DIRECTOR: ALEXEY BRODOVITCH PUBLICATION: *HARPER'S BAZAAR*. PHOTOGRAPHS COURTESY OF DOCUMENTS OF AMERICAN DESIGN, PRODUCERS OF *BRODOVITCH*, PUBLISHED BY HARRY N. ABRAMS ■ (OPPOSITE) ART DIRECTOR: HENRY WOLF PUBLICATION: *HARPER'S BAZAAR*

roles of both the editor and the photographer were redefined. And the art director was invented. ■ At first the job involved simply the arrangement of different shapes and sizes of images, the creation of largely decorative patterns. But as the selection and organization of the material came to have a greater effect on a publication's intellectual presence, the art director grew into a more important partner in the editorial process. ■ Already in the early 1930s, under the direction of Alexander Liberman, the French magazine *Vu* was combining the psychological content and formal elegance of photographs with the journalistic imperatives of the periodical publication. By this time as well, photography had begun to replace illustration as the predominant medium of communication on the printed page. ■ More recently, film and television have affected the tastes and the expectations of readers, making them visually more sophisticated and demanding. Thus the magazine art director, barely imaginable fifty years ago, has become a key player in determining the impact and importance of a publication. The partnership between editor and art director has become—with the possible exception of flyer and catcher in a trapeze act—the most delicate and demanding of professional relationships. ■ The prototype of the modern magazine art director, Alexey Brodovitch, came to *Harper's Bazaar* in 1934 and transformed the job from one of basically carrying out an editor's wishes to one of creating a style and a sensibility, an identifiable personality for the magazine. Under Brodovitch the role of the art director expanded beyond the practice of layout. He took control of assigning photographers and illustrators and of selecting which of the images would appear in the magazine. He helped create the climate in magazine journalism in which the expressive potential of photography could be realized. He is a figure whose memory inspires reverence and awe. At the same time, he crawled about the floor of the editor Carmel Snow's office, rearranging layouts while she sat

imperiously at her desk. ■ When Henry Wolf succeeded Brodovitch at *Bazaar*, the deference shown to the editor reached some limits. Once when Nancy White, Snow's successor, rejected a photo Wolf was enthusiastic about, he simply went home. The next day, the editor sent a dozen roses and asked him to come back. And the picture ran. ■ More special and unique was Wolf's relationship with the founding editor of *Esquire*, Arnold Gingrich. "Anything he did, I did," Henry recalls. "He wore gray suits, I wore gray suits. He wore black ties, I wore black ties. He wore oxford shirts with frayed collars, I bought oxford shirts and sent them out to be laundered thirty times so the collars would get frayed." The respect traveled both ways. Once, when the young art director showed the editor an illustration very different from the ones he had been accustomed to, his mentor peered over his half-glasses and said, "To me it looks terrible, but I'm almost fifty and you know better what's good now so let's go with it." Most telling about the relationship, perhaps, is Henry Wolf's assertion that "I was doing the magazine for Arnold." ■ In 1962, *Esquire* was on the verge of economic collapse when editor Harold Hayes enlisted George Lois to create covers. "At first I was just going to do one cover," Lois recalls, "but Harold liked it and he asked me to do a few more, and a few more turned into ten years. My relationship with Harold was simple: He was incredibly bright and he had courage and he was smart enough to let me do what I wanted to do. He had the strength to fight off the advertising department and all the other editors and everybody else who thought that the covers were going to get the magazine into trouble. Our agreement was a handshake and a kiss: I do 'em, you run 'em. My point of view is paranoid. I think that everybody is there to harm your work. If you do great work you have to drive as hard as you can to get it printed. Ideas are the easy part. Ideas are the fun part, you can sit and come up with ideas all day, the hard part is nailing it down. With

(ABOVE) ART DIRECTOR: HENRY WOLF PUBLICATION: *ESQUIRE* MAGAZINE, COVER, APRIL 1955 PHOTOGRAPHER: DAN WYM ■ (ALL IMAGES, OPPOSITE) ART DIRECTOR: HENRY WOLF PUBLICATION: *ESQUIRE* MAGAZINE (TOP) PHOTOGRAPHER: SAUL LEITER (CENTER) PHOTOGRAPHER: SAUL LEITER (BOTTOM) PHOTOGRAPHER: DERVJINSKY

BALLAD OF THE BIRD

THE LEGEND OF CHARLES CHRISTOPHER PARKER

OH

BY N. F. SIMPSON

night drama:
organdie cape,
squared train

Hayes I didn't have to fight. I gave it to him and he bought it. I don't think I could have a relationship with any editor today. A good art director can't reflect what the editor does, he has to be ahead of the editor. Now they're cogs in the wheel. Every editor says he wants great stuff, but they're not willing to pay the price. Harold took the chances. Now I must get a call a week from people who want me to do their covers, but when I tell them how I work they go into shock. A guy like Harold won't be born again for a hundred years." There were, however, other views of the situation. Byron Dobell, *Esquire*'s executive editor, and later an editor at *New York*, *Life*, and *American Heritage*, remembers Hayes fondly. "When Harold was at the top of his form, he was the perfect editor, but when he had an idea that was off the wall, you could beg and plead and he'd never change his mind. Harold was nothing if not brave and in the long run he'll be remembered as the great editor of *Esquire*. But the cover was the one area where he gave himself up. Harold hero-worshipped very few people, but he'd let himself be bamboozled by Lois. George had a lunatic side to him, he was like the funniest kid in the class at Music and Art. The Calley cover was probably the end of Harold's career. Years later he said, 'Maybe I made a mistake.' It appalled the readers, the advertisers, and the management." ■ Dobell is no less tough on the art department as it operated during his second tour of duty at *Esquire* in 1980. "I was only there part time, so I had no real authority, but I was upset at what the art director was doing. To me the wrong things were always emphasized. The subhead was too small or the caption was too big or else you couldn't find anything. It all looked great, but from the reader's point of view it didn't make any sense. One day I went into the art department and I told them

ART DIRECTOR: GEORGE LOIS
PUBLICATION: *ESQUIRE*, DATE 1968

ART DIRECTOR: GEORGE LOIS
PUBLICATION: *ESQUIRE* DATE: 1970

that if I were in power I'd fire the art director, and I'd fire the rest of them because they'd been infected. So they went to Phil Moffit and they got him to keep me out of the art department, and I think it was better for all of us." ■ When Clay Felker started *New York* magazine in 1968, Milton Glaser was more than the magazine's art director. He was a partner in the business, as well as the magazine's mentor, spiritual advisor, and landlord. Clay was impatient, temperamental, quixotic; he operated at top speed and at full volume. Milton was professorial, analytical, calm. "Clay wouldn't listen to the wisest man in the world," recalls Byron Dobell, "and he wouldn't listen to Milton—but in his way Clay worshipped Milton." ■ "I wanted to give Milton as much authority as possible," Felker recalls, "not only out of profound respect for him, but because I knew that in the heat of battle I would be demanding my way, and I wanted Milton to have enough power not to have to back down. . . The selection of a designer is the most crucial appointment an editor can make. That person ranks above all others. I had worked with Milton on a number of projects, and we became friends. When we started *New York*, I was amazed by the speed of his mind. He did it so fast I thought he was joking around. I'd ask him about something and he'd have a solution immediately. I realized the guy was a genius, and I don't use that word lightly. There would be intense wrestling matches at the magazine, but I didn't just want to be able to win. I felt strongly, but in the end I knew Milton was better than I was." ■ Walter Bernard remembers the early days of *New York* magazine, not so much for the specific interaction of the editor and art director, but for the spirit that existed in the office. "What made me feel good was the community of people: the editors, the writers, the artists and photographers. It was a peer group, in which the senior members respected everyone and solicited their ideas and reactions. You could talk to the editor when you wanted to, not like a place where a new person might barely meet the editor for the first three years. Ideas were first, hierarchy was second. That common ground allowed people to concentrate on the work and not on their position. We thought about how best to do a story, and not on how we were going to make a wonderful page. When it worked it was like hitting a home run without trying to hit a home run: When you're in the groove you just swing and sometimes you hit home runs." In 1977 Walter brought both his brilliance and collegiality to *Time* magazine which then operated along just the sort of hierarchical lines that *New York* did not. Early on, in a picture-picking session in *Time*'s conference room, Walter seemed to be arguing at every turn with Ray Cave, *Time*'s brilliant—and intimidating—managing editor. At the end of the session Walter was summoned to the editor's office. "I don't want you ever," Cave growled, "to hesitate to disagree with me in these meetings. That's your job, and that's what I expect you to do." ∎ Walter's experiences as a magazine design consultant have not always been as reciprocally respectful. "I'm angered most by editors who pretend not to know about visual matters, who make decisions based on their personal prejudices, while claiming that they don't understand what art direction is all about. Some of the ones who are the first to accuse designers of not understanding the depth of the editorial concerns are the ones who seem to revel in their own dumbness about the design." ∎ Rochelle Udell, associate editorial director at Condé Nast ob-serves, "I've always been interested in the chemistry between two people, the way it creates almost a third individual that is

PUBLICATION: *NEW YORK*, ILLUSTRATOR: DAVID WILCOX DATE: 1974

PUBLICATION: *NEW YORK*, ILLUSTRATOR: MARK HESS DATE: OCTOBER, 1988

greater than either could be separately. But it goes beyond the editor and the art director. It's a collaboration of many people—the photographers and writers need to be brought into the loop so that you can get them focusing on the same problem." One of Rochelle's main areas of responsibility is the *New Yorker* where, as she notes, "its illustrations are its words" and its history is such that the readers are as protective of the format and as resistant to change as any editor could ever be. ∎ The essence of the art director's contribution is different at those magazines whose images are, in effect, their content. At *Metropolitan Home*, the effect of the magazine comes from the information contained in the photographs. The art director, Don Morris, has assumed a unique role there. "This experience has been evolutionary," he says, "ideas building on ideas. A magazine can be a cyclical thing, that's one of its strengths. In the preliminary meetings I try to go in and ask a lot of questions, to try and bring out the thrust of the story, to develop a photographic and typographic essence. When the layouts go up on the wall, Dorothy Kalins, the editor, as well as the design editor and the photo editor will give me feedback. It's not a case of scrutinizing the design as much as getting the flow and the sense of the story right. By this time one of the things that has given us a comfortable relationship is that I've got the sense of the magazine down. *Metropolitan Home* is what we have evolved together. This is the ideal way for an art director to work, to be able to assess my work as a whole and build it month after month into a cohesive entity. But I can only be on target and intellectually strong if I have the story straight. I don't want to throw it in peoples' faces and say 'Here it is.'" ∎ Nowhere, perhaps, is the importance of "getting the story straight" as important

METROPOLITAN HOME

APRIL 1990 • $3.00

HOME

100 Design

THE PEOPLE, PRODUCTS, IDEAS THAT SHAPE OUR LIVES

(ALL IMAGES THIS SPREAD) PUBLICATION: *METROPOLITAN HOME* ART DIRECTOR: DON MORRIS ASSOCIATE ART DIRECTOR: KAYO DER SARKISSIAN ASSISTANT ART DIRECTOR: ROBIN TERRA DESIGNERS: SUSAN FOSTER, DOROTHY O'CONNOR PHOTO EDITOR: JANE CLARK

than at *The New York Times.* Into the 1970s, the "good gray" *Times* was a paper of no particular visual distinction; yet, under the direction of art director Lou Silverstein, it blossomed into a more handsome and more richly informative publication. But newspapers were slow to accept designers as partners in the creative process. Most, until recently, simply did without art directors. Others treated the position as a service function, limiting its practice to specific procedural tasks. It has taken the full force of designers' talents and persistence to effect a change. And the occasional fortunate circumstance. As Silverstein recalls, "When I was still promotion art director, I had tried a redesign of the Sunday *Book Review*—it was commissioned by the executives, not by the news people. When I showed the design to the *Book Review* editor he nearly slid under the table. He hated it. But the *Book Review* was his fiefdom. A year later there was a new Sunday editor, and he proposed a new *Book Review* to the publisher. So the publisher said, 'Why don't you use the design Lou did a year ago?' I took it out of the drawer, he took one look, and within a week the project was off and running." In time, Silverstein remade the entire paper, became not only the corporate art director, but also one of the assistant managing editors, and saw his work nominated for a Pulitzer Prize. ■ After 250 years of magazine publishing, there are still enterprising practitioners who serve as their own editors, publishers, and art directors. Rudy VanderLans, who started *Emigre* magazine in 1982, uses the Macintosh to create typefaces and a graphic structure for his magazine, each issue of which is a unique concept and a unique object. "In my first job, at the *San Francisco Chronicle*, as much as I had trouble with the restrictions, they were useful at times. I don't think you can come up with solutions if you have no restrictions. But the restrictions at *Emigre* have to do with money and with time. I miss having the time to devote totally to the design. It takes me half a day sometimes to write a caption for a photograph that a writer could do in half a minute. I've omitted compromise from the working process. . . . I don't have to listen to an editor. What bothered me at the newspaper was the constant second-guessing being done as to what the audience wants to read. Now there is only one person doing the second-guessing. Graphic design is not a democratic process. There are few examples of editors and art directors working together to produce a good product. *The Face*, with Neville Brody and Nick Logan, was a rare example. They were exactly the same; they listened to the same music, they wore the same clothes. I'm awfully spoiled the longer I do *Emigre*. This is a very unrealistic way of making a commercially viable magazine." ■ And about old Ben Franklin, VanderLans's multifaceted predecessor of a couple of centuries or so: "He must have had a pretty good magazine." ■

UNITY AND DIVERSITY

A CROSSREAD OF EUROPEAN MAGAZINES

[HERBERT LECHNER]

MAGYAR NŐK *lapja*

1990:34
ÁRA: 13,50 Ft

VÉRFORRALÓ
ÉS VÉRFAGYASZTÓ
VÁSÁRI
VIGASSÁG

NEM
A HÁZASSÁGGAL,
CSAK
A HÁZASOKKAL
VAN BAJ

**BALATONI
FÜRDŐ-
LEVÉL**

MAGYAR
ÍRÓ
AZTÉK
KERETBEN

MICSODA
NŐI

6

The European house of Mikhail Gorbachev has many rooms. And—to keep to the metaphor—in every room the magazines and journals are piled high. The much-touted united Europe is certainly not yet evident in the print media. Which is just as well, because presently there's an enormous variety to be had—in the way of titles, topics, and visual interpretations. □ There are already about five thousand titles, many of them on sale at station booksellers in all prominent German cities. The magazine retailers at international airports have an equally vast range, although not necessarily the same titles. Merely to read the catchlines on the covers would take hours. □ Beyond-the-frontier reading, too, is on the increase, especially in the trade magazines and special-interest titles. Just prior to the European internal market of 1992, the colorfulness of the magazine scenery is reflected in what Charles de Gaulle called "the Europe of the Homelands." It is true that there are more, and more successful, beyond-frontier magazines, but against these new-style, pan-European publications are all those that overwhelmingly failed because their concept and their language were untranslatable. While there have been successful pioneers, like Wiener (from Austria to Germany), Geo (from Germany to France), Max

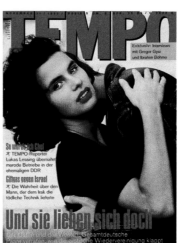

(PREVIOUS SPREAD, LEFT) PUBLICATION: *MAGYAR NŐK* DATE: 1990 COUNTRY: HUNGARY ■ (TOP AND CENTER, LEFT AND RIGHT) PUBLICATION: *TEMPO* COUNTRY: GERMANY ■ (BOTTOM, LEFT AND RIGHT) PUBLICATION: AVENUE COUNTRY: HOLLAND

(from Italy to Greece), and various women's magazines that were "translated" from Germany to Great Britain and Spain, on the debit side there are also the respectable losers, such as *FMR, Epoca, Omni,* and *Lui.* ■ There are certain design tendencies evident throughout Europe, if not worldwide; naturally, the manifestation of these tendencies is influenced by country and topic. The stronger the emphasis on fashion, design, and styling, for instance, the more evident is the international orientation. ■ But national characteristics are right upfront here too—as any comparison of fashion and interior design magazines will testify. At first glance, a country's classical characteristics seem to be confirmed. German magazines, for instance, are the most perfectly produced. The English are the most audacious. The French have the most chic, and the Italians are simply the most beautiful. The further away one goes from central Europe, the stranger the language of design becomes. Spanish and Turkish magazines are (unless they follow a few traditional layout rules) particularly inscrutable, although this may be because of the peculiar print and paper situation. ■ This is true too for the magazines of those countries that previously formed the Eastern bloc. Occasionally, from lack of materials, a nostalgic charm or even a kind of *arte povera* emerges that—while fascinating to us pampered observers from the West—meets with precious little enthusiasm in the country of origin, either among magazine makers or readers. It remains to be seen whether changes in the political and economic structures will lead to an overall standardization in the printed media or to an unexpected flourishing of creativity. ■ At the moment, there seems to be some slight hope of the latter. While on the one hand there is an increasing adaptation of common visual means (leading to the reuse of the same photo productions in Italian, English, and German magazines), on the other hand there are all kinds of magazines appearing that—in seeking out

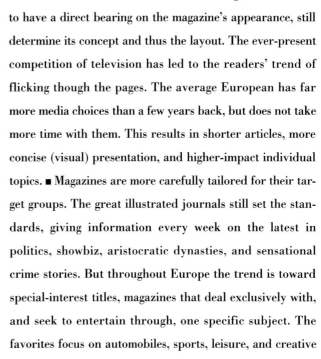

PUBLICATION: *GLOBE* COUNTRY: FRANCE

their specific target audience—go their unusual, provocative graphic ways. The "courage to fill spaces" can bear fruit not only in terms of marketing. ■ If one looks for common denominators—and taking into account the above-mentioned national peculiarities—the following elements can be identified: There are abundant visuals, in the form of color photos and "lively" layouts with predominant presentation pages between the covers, and, despite many examples to the contrary, a professional handling of visual journalism. ■ The few extraordinary typographic experiments conceal the fact that text is viewed and treated as so much "grey stuff" by European art directors. Headlines (still to be found in the wide-circulation magazines of the 1960s) written by an artist's hand or applied in brushstrokes are now nonexistent, even in the really exotic print media products. The so-called stripe typography—from the alternative magazines of the 1970s, city newspapers, and "scene" periodicals, and to a lesser extent also the established magazines—appears to have passed its prime. ■ One can name other factors that, while at first glance seem not to have a direct bearing on the magazine's appearance, still determine its concept and thus the layout. The ever-present competition of television has led to the readers' trend of flicking though the pages. The average European has far more media choices than a few years back, but does not take more time with them. This results in shorter articles, more concise (visual) presentation, and higher-impact individual topics. ■ Magazines are more carefully tailored for their target groups. The great illustrated journals still set the standards, giving information every week on the latest in politics, showbiz, aristocratic dynasties, and sensational crime stories. But throughout Europe the trend is toward special-interest titles, magazines that deal exclusively with, and seek to entertain through, one specific subject. The favorites focus on automobiles, sports, leisure, and creative

THE FACE

VOL 2 No 8/MAY 1989 £1.50 • US $4.50 ITALY L6400 GERMANY 9.50M

**HISTORY
AS CABARET**
France plans
the wildest party
the world has
ever seen

IN ALBANIA
WITH ENGLAND

IN ITALY
WITH THE JAMES
TAYLOR QUARTET

MIKE TYSON
AND THE MODEL

BLACKPOOL AND
MODERN SOUL

LONDON VS PARIS

MAPPLETHORPE BY
KATHY ACKER

24 ON 42: STORY
BY NIK COHN

DENNIS QUAID AS JERRY LEE LEWIS
PHOTOGRAPHED BY TERRY O'NEILL

QUAID AND THE KILLER
Nick Kent confronts Hollywood's hot property
and survives an audience with Jerry Lee Lewis

0 74470 72689 0   05

DENNIS THE MENACE

(ALL IMAGES, THIS SPREAD) PUBLICATION: *THE FACE* DATE: MAY 1989 COUNTRY: ENGLAND (ABOVE) PHOTOGRAPHER: TERRY O'NEILL ■
(OPPOSITE, TOP) PHOTOGRAPHERS: JOHN BEECHER/FLAIR PHOTOGRAPHY (INSET) TERRY O'NEILL (CENTER) ILLUSTRATOR:
JEAN–PAUL GOUDE PHOTOGRAPHERS: HERMAN LEONARD, EDDIE MONSOON (BOTTOM) PETER LINDBERGH, ANDREW MACPHERSON

The black hole of rock'n'roll, the baddest and meanest, the surprising thing about Jerry Lee Lewis is that he's still alive....

GOING TO HELL WITH

man on fire

JERRY LEE LEWIS

AND DENNIS QUAID

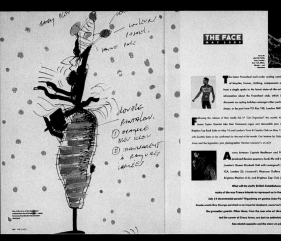

THE FACE
MAY 1989

The latest Freewheel mail-order cycling catalogue includes a wide range of bicycles, frames, clothing, components and accessories – everything from a single spoke to the latest state-of-the-art mountain bike – as well as information about the Freewheel club, which is free to join and includes discounts on cycling holidays amongst other perks. £1.95 at newsagents, cycle shops, or by post from PO Box 740, London NW5 7JQ. See also p38

Following the release of their totally fab LP "Get Organised" this month, the James Taylor Quartet take their Hammond organ and danceable jazz to Brighton Top Rank Suite on May 10 and London's Town & Country Club on May 13, with Scottish dates to be confirmed for the end of the month. Our feature by Dylan Jones and the legendary jazz photographer Herman Leonard is on p34

Across between Captain Beefheart and Pee-Wee Herman, Brian Eno-produced Boston popsters Zoski Mo will tour Britain in May, starting at London's Queen Elizabeth Hall with Leningrad's Avia in support (May 1); The ICA, London (2); Liverpool's Bluecoat Gallery (3); with Avia again at the Brighton Mayfair (4-6); and Brighton Zap Club (8)

What will the stuffy British Establishment make of the way France intends to represent us in their July 14 bicentennial parade? Organising art genius Jean-Paul Goode wants Boy George perched on an imperial elephant, escorted by the grenadier guards. Other ideas, from the man who art directed the career of Grace Jones, are just as audacious. See sketch opposite and the story on p28

THE IRON MAN & THE MODEL

hobbies. This trend is responsible for the fact that readership is receding. As this also hurts the advertising business, devices to boost circulation are attempted. ■ These are occasionally carried out by a special supplement (in fact a magazine within a magazine). The most common is some kind of insert. In Italy the so-called *regalo* (gift) has a certain tradition, and the practice goes as far as having a second magazine enclosed in the package. Special-interest magazines have grasped the possibilities of the supplement business, and also include extras with their usual editorial offerings—not least because they are threatened as well. Quite plainly, the special sectors are being divided by new titles appealing even more concisely to special subgroups. Along with the automobile trade magazines (and besides the countless new publications) are magazines exclusively devoted to auto enthusiasts who are veterans. And there are those limited to vehicles of a certain period or of a certain make or category, and finally there are magazines aimed at beginning antique-auto hobbyists. ■ The special-interest titles are not comparable to the older trade magazines that, often through peculiar distribution, satisfied a small, devoted community. While in their text and visuals these were mostly dry-as-dust affairs, with the journalistic "coming of age" of the hobby enthusiast, their visual appeal has distinctly increased. Even where at one time the secret model-railway enthusiast had to make do with sparse periodicals on wafery paper, now there are several large-format, art-printed postillions to choose from, and all presenting his loco-loves in beautiful, full-color shots. ■ Magazines devoted to fashionable sports like surfing, tennis, and cycle racing provide, layout-wise, exactly the right "spirit of the time," and frequently the pages are as dazzling and glaring as the trendy outfits worn by their active readers. Official club reports, on the other hand, recall the older obscurity of illegibility—unless they have been adapted to the more cheerful flavor of the times. ■ This trend toward more design has also embraced a sector from which an orientation toward visual conspicuousness would be least of all expected: Europe's economic magazines are showing an unprecedented spurt of creativity in editorial design. Titles such as *Class*, *Option*, and the German edition of *Forbes* have got things on the move. ■ By comparision, those magazines traditionally showing the greatest concern with design—fashion and home-interior design—have on the whole retained their classic appearances. Although cosmetic changes can be seen throughout Europe in all the magazines of this sector, almost everywhere the innovations are limited to the subjects illustrated rather than to the visual stimulus of the magazine layouts. *Abitare*, *Domus*, and *Schöner Wohnen* have made changes in illustration details, color schemes, and choices of type, but the concept and identity have shifted only slightly. ■ More movement is seen in the life-style magazines. Unburdened by any tradition of their own or by expectations of a long-standing readership, they enter the race to win the favors of an ever-younger and increasingly wealthier public for whom the medium has to fulfill quite different entertainment tasks. These magazines mirror a new reality, for they are quite literally the children of the present time. Even the oldest dates only to the second half of the 1980s. Standing quite apart is the tradition-rich Dutch *Avenue*—atypical in this group of smart-alec newcomers. The legendary *The Face* (Great Britain); *Wiener* and its undistinguished descendants *Wienerin*, *Basta*, *Römer* (all Austrian), *Tempo*, and the German *Wiener*; *Revu* (The Netherlands); *Globe* (France); *Max*, *King*, *Chorus* (Italy)—the list could be continued with titles from other countries, and would even then be incomplete, because these magazines are as short-lived and hectic as their identity. The mixture of themes and layouts often shows a certain resemblance to video clips and commercials. (The Italian *Max* carries, besides book and record columns, its own critiques of these forms of expression!) ■ If you stop to look over the fence, beyond the magazine field, other European trends can be seen. Newspaper supplements of all kinds have proven especially attractive to the media field. Obviously, the weekly battle at the kiosk has had a lively effect on design. Apart from *FAZ Magazin*, which has had

(ABOVE) PUBLICATION: *TAGES ANZEIGER MAGAZIN* COUNTRY: SWITZERLAND (RIGHT) AUGUST, 1991 ART DIRECTOR: OTHMAR ROTHENFLUH
PHOTOGRAPHER: MICHAEL VON GRAFFENRIED ■ (LEFT) FEBRUARY, 1987 ART DIRECTOR: ALBERT KAELIN ILLUSTRATOR: ALEX SADKOWSKY

international honors heaped upon it, the Zurich-based *Tages Anzeiger Magazin* has proved to be a design gem much appreciated by the readers of its parent newspaper. At many other newspaper houses there are supplements in the works (youngest is the *SZ Magazin* of the Munich-based *Süddeutsche Zeitung*), despite the fact that the color supplement is losing some of its unique appeal with the introduction of color in good quality (including color ads) in the daily newspaper. ■ Even more brisk is the design scene in a segment that the consumer normally gets to see only in part: corporate communications, which are increasingly being published with great financial and creative expenditure. Although there is still much not worth mentioning, the change for the better cannot be overlooked. It is particularly the rapidly expanding, high-tech companies that have achieved remarkable things in this area. ■ It is gratifying that a great deal of attention is being afforded firms' internal employee-information letters, evidence of a recognition that corporate identity and communications can promote a feeling of "togetherness" within a company. New trends in this sector give the magazine enthusiast food for thought. The Bavarian BMW automobile company, for instance, provides its personnel with a good dozen varied publications—one even in the form of a videotape! One hears that other companies have already shown interest in this kind of electronic magazine. ■ European magazines, in their mixture of international design and regional (sometimes even personal) concerns, are the reflection of a continent in a state of upheaval. Parallels can be drawn from all sectors of design—from automobiles to architecture. ■

CASE STUDIES

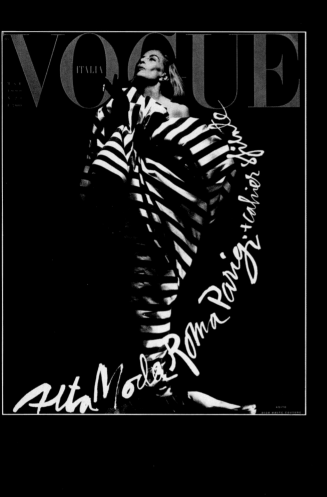

V O G U E   I T A L I A   ONE VIEW ALWAYS ENCHANTS ME: THE NEWS KIOSKS FOUND IN SMALL TOWNS IN THE ITALIAN COUNTRYSIDE, WHOSE SILHOUETTES LOOK LIKE PAGODAS FROM A DISTANCE, BUT WHICH, AS YOU APPROACH, BECOME A KALEIDOSCOPE OF MULTICOLORED IMAGES. STOP AND LOOK FOR A MOMENT. THE IMAGE STANDS STILL, A KIND OF LIFE-SIZED PHOTOMONTAGE: HUNDREDS OF EYES, MOUTHS, BODIES FROZEN BY THE WAVE OF A MAGIC WAND. AND, IN THE CENTER, THERE IS AN IMAGE WITHIN THE IMAGE, THE SHOPKEEPER WHO HAS BEEN STARING AT YOU QUIZZICALLY FOR SOME TIME ALREADY. □ HAS *VOGUE ITALIA*'S LATEST ISSUE COME OUT YET? MY EYES

quickly glide over this array of titles, awaiting this month's surprise. *Vogue Italia*'s cover always has something unexpected, it is practically an event. In July, you find a voluptuous star, a Sophia Loren imitation from the black-and-white neorealistic movie era. The next issue is a dazzling, spectacular golden cover; and in September, who would believe it, a Sophia Loren from the 1950s, who is none other than Isabella Rossellini. If only you knew what was in store for next month. . . . ■ All it takes is a glance through a few recent issues of *Vogue Italia*—one is struck by the immediate impact of the images. The title of a section itself becomes a graphic image. "A strong visual image," is how Juan Gatti, the former art director of *Vogue Italia*, defines the concept of the magazine. "The visual prevails over technical information. *Vogue Italia* is more a magazine of style than of fashion." ■ In 1950 to 1951, the Italian monthly fashion review, *Novita*, *Vogue Italia*'s predecessor, presented itself as "the practical magazine for elegant women"; its pragmatic objective was easily understandable in a postwar period. One finds fashion as well as furniture, embroidery, cooking recipes, advice for raising children, and gossip. Under the direction of Emilia Kuster Rossellini, it was a high-quality review, exclusively aimed at an Italian public. If the inside pages were no different in layout from other magazines of the period—both black-and-white drawings and photographs arranged on the same page—the covers already revealed a certain modernity. The graphic quality of the photography, which today is one of the magazine's predominant characteristics, is obvious, for instance, in the rigorous composition of the image: a woman leans on a window, like a portrait in its frame (February 1952), or the subtle play of

the lines of a large cane chair which mirror the stripes on the dress of a seated woman (July 1952), or a daring close-up of a pair of eyes criss-crossed by the veil of a flowerbud-shaped skullcap (February 1953). The magazine is open to experimentation, as the rather unusual surrealistic painting on the February 1959 cover shows us, where an oval shape, hidden behind a tattered veil, suggests a head. In this way, it followed the American examples of *Vogue* and *Harper's Bazaar*, both avant-garde in their editorial graphic conception, thanks to the tremendous talent of their respective art directors, Alexander Liberman and Alexey Brodovitch. ■ In fact, at that time, although it was still called *Novita*, the magazine became the property of Condé Nast publications. It then became *Vogue-Novita*—the hyphenated name had the advantage of not disconcerting the Italian readers. The transition period is interesting because the look of the future *Vogue Italia* took shape in its pages. Although the photographer's name might not be mentioned, the image, little by little, overcomes the entire page, even the spread, and the fashion sketch almost completely disappears. The next twenty years of *Vogue Italia* would be governed by the photograph. ■ *Vogue Italia* was born in 1964. The 1960s is rightly considered a golden period for the magazine. Not only did the decade see a veritable revolution in fashion photography, but it also coincided with the advent of the *linea italiana*. Although the line was well-known in the United States—Emilio Pucci, among others, was admired in the 1950s—the Parisian haute couture dominated the European scene, and the French edition of *Vogue*, launched in 1921, was widely distributed. Nonetheless, this recognition of Italian fashion in the United States, in concert with the development of the textile industry, helps to explain the creation of an Italian edition of *Vogue*. ■ In the beginning, the magazine had a restricted budget and received fashion-show pictures only after the French and American editorial offices had. An initiative by the current sales manager, Attilio Fontanesi, boosted advertising receipts, thereby giving increased means to the editorial staff and the art director, Flavio Lucchini. Fontanesi was the first to have the idea of grouping the advertisements together in an approximately thirty-page span, thus dividing the magazine into two distinct parts: advertisement and editorial. The scheme was immediately successful among advertisers; henceforth, *Vogue Italia* could compete with the most luxurious fashion magazines. In this way, the magazine acquired an international audience and contributed to the expansion of Italian couture in Europe. Fontanesi's formula, which is still in use, came at a perfect time, since it coincided with the rapid development of Italian ready-to-wear. For example, by allowing one designer to present his creations on eight consecutive pages—in a sort of "monographic" catalog, as Alberto Nodolini, who would succeed Lucchini in the 1970s, would say—a veritable publicity platform was created for the young contenders of Italian fashion. ■ From the early 1960s, all the greatest names in fashion photography appeared in the magazine. In 1963, for example, one can find in the same issue the names of Irving Penn and Richard Bailey for the cover, and among the Italians, Alfa Castaldi and Ugo Mulas. The models are actresses (Audrey Hepburn, Givenchy's inspiration), personalities (the Viscountess of Rives for Balenciaga), and legendary models (Twiggy, Jean Shrimpton, Verushka, and Penelope Tree, among many others). To talk of the evolution of editorial design during

ART DIRECTOR: FABIEN BARON PHOTO-
GRAPHER: JAVIER VALHONRAT DATE: 1989

the period is tantamount to relating the history of fashion photography. These images began to overtake the page, and even went beyond the page. Graphics remained discreet, for, as Alberto Nodolini put it, "what the photographic image was telling us was so rich. . . we didn't need graphics that would detract from it, only reinforce it." If each fashion editor, photographer, and artist contributed to making *Vogue Italia* an avant-garde magazine, Richard Avedon's contribution is yet distinct: He created a dynamic style that still works today, eliminating all decor, outlining the model's body against the white backdrop of the page. He created photographic sessions that would inspire an entire generation. Nodolini remembers work sessions that resembled film shoots: The creation of photos mobilized entire teams of hairdressers, makeup artists, and technicians, not to mention actresses and models. The innovative spirit of fashion provoked a creative freedom never seen before, breaking down all conventions, radically changing the conception of the image itself. ■ The cover always displays a facial close-up, and there is throughout an aesthetic sophistication and a certain refinement in layout. In 1970 we observe contrasting effects on the same page: a backlit profile whose reflection is inversely lit in a mirror, for example; or combinations: a Mackintosh chair next to an art deco–style dress. The same year, one could admire the unusual linear play of a series of Avedon's photos of models donning fur coats and perched on tree branches. During the mid-1970s, the magazine became more and more voluminous, reaching 664 pages in September 1978 (special collector's issue). By 1979, typography had become more important, and sometimes a title emphasized the dynamics of a photo or the geometry of a line. Some visual juxtapositions prefigured *Vogue*'s style for the

ART DIRECTOR: FABIEN BARON PHOTO-
GRAPHER: FRANCO PAGETTI DATE: 1988

1990s, such as a magnificent series of double pages opposing the close-up of a face to the silhouette of a peacock (photos by David Bailey). In the 1980s, plays on visual associations increased, with objects—a chair for example—being compared to a face or a body. But the magazine still presented a rather heterogeneous image, composed of various sections, including long articles about celebrities or interior decoration accompanied by small photos. *Vogue Italia* did not differ from other European editions of *Vogue*. This changed during the summer of 1988. The arrival of Fabien Baron as art director (he stayed the year) marked the beginning of a new era at *Vogue Italia*. Having been educated by the New York school, he completely revamped the magazine. At once, Baron's style was evident: strong images for bright ideas. It was probably not a coincidence that the July/August 1988 cover announced: "The new style." Retrospectively, this issue can be seen as an aesthetic manifesto. All the elements of Baron's style come together: The sepia photographs on the cover give the image an incomparable tactile quality, and there is a daring and meticulous layout (this "essence of the image" dear to Anna Piaggi, *Vogue Italia's* present creative consultant). Baron had a remarkable talent for turning a letter into a visual symbol as eloquent as an image. Juan Gatti emphasized that the *Vogue Italia* of the 1990s has found "balance between the photographic image and the typographic image." Beginning with this first issue, Fabien Baron used typography as a pictorial element: the initial *V* of *Vogue* became a decorative element that organized a page entitled "*Vogue is changing.*" He would frequently use this principle, playing on the analogy of forms (the *O* of the word "or" [gold] combined with a sun-shaped lamp) or on contrasts, an entire page usually reserved for the title, which would be reduced to an enormous typographical character. For instance, he placed in opposition a giant letter *F*, the initial of the painter Fontana, and the

ART DIRECTOR: FABIEN BARON PHOTO-GRAPHER: UGO MULAS DATE: 1989

painter's creative gesture in an *F* shape. He restored calligraphy, reproducing a watercolor letter from Manet, going so far as to handpaint *Vogue Italia's* titles. He also combined print, calligraphy, and illustration, especially drawing on Mat's simplifying line. Then, the image became a sign. Graphic qualities of a photo were emphasized by the layout and underlined by a skillful cutting of the image. Baron was a virtuoso in creating a visual shock. Anna Piaggi remembers him with a pair of scissors in his hand: He was working like a fashion designer; he is an artisan of the image. What he creates has an incredible impact." ■ Piaggi's "Double Pages," which began to appear that year, illustrate the "global concept" to which Baron adhered. The importance of fashion editors should not be neglected in the visual conception of a fashion magazine. With her long experience in stylized photography, her sharp sense of fashion, and her horror of banality, Piaggi continues to play an essential role within *Vogue Italia*. For her, text and image constitute a whole. Valuing intuition, she seeks "logic in illogical ideas" in coming up with a "visual story" that largely speaks to one's emotions. The result is an "extremely elaborated spontaneity" that has been one of *Vogue Italia's* primary stylistic characteristics for the last few years. ■ Juan Gatti, art director from 1989 to late 1990, remained faithful to this tendency while bringing his own personal touch. What matters is the global conception of the issue: Like Baron, with his cinematographic background, he is sensitive to rhythms, sequence, and breaks. He also uses "zooms," inversion, digression, surprise, taking best advantage of the double page, and sometimes using flaps, which allow him to present a series of snapshots, expressive faces, feelings, and the unfolding of a movement, a sequence of postures. *Vogue Italia's* image is particularly dynamic. This is basically because of the graphic vision of photographers such as Watson and Meisel and the extraordinary flexibility of their

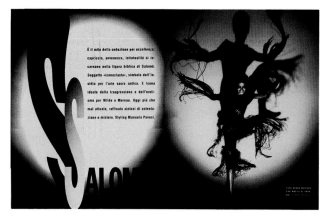 

(OPENING SPREAD, LEFT) ART DIRECTOR: JUAN GATTI PHOTOGRAPHER: STEVEN MEISEL DATE: 1990 ■ (ALL IMAGES, THIS SPREAD) ART DIRECTOR: JUAN GATTI DATE: 1990 ■ (ABOVE) PHOTOGRAPHER: ALBERT WATSON ■ (OPPOSITE) PHOTOGRAPHER: STEVEN MEISEL

models (particularly Naomi). Fashion photography of the 1990s gives the image of a totally liberated woman, "explosive" (the word is one of *Vogue*'s titles), self-confident, sexy, impertinent, often agressive—growling like a wildcat in a July 1989 issue—and creative. She is a resolutely modern and independent woman, "an urban woman" who, according to Gatti, doesn't let anyone dictate her behavior or her fashion. As Alberto Nodolini rightly re-marked, in the past, a woman remained faithful to a fashion designer, and a garment was associated with a personality; now, every woman recreates her own fashion, mixes or matches several styles. *Vogue Italia* proposes options rather than dictates, staying with the 1950s spirit of *Vogue*. ■ Gatti adopted (and pushed to its limits) the principle of juxtaposing a model with an idea—"woman and flower rather than a woman in a garden." He is also extremely attentive to the "coherence between the visual message—photography—and typography." Sometimes the photography is integrated into the typographic image, for instance, in an image of a model jumping through the *O* in a section called "Oser" (Dare). In turn, typography sometimes imitates a form or a structure (he doesn't hesitate to organize the text within a trestle on Piaggi's "double page"). What especially distinguishes Gatti from Baron is his sometimes grating humor, which can remind us of Pedro Almodovar's—with whom he has worked, by the way. Collages show his derisive spirit, his use of the grotesque, his refusal to back down from a certain kitsch look. Wasn't it he who topped the section entitled "Appearing" with ridiculous, brightly colored wigs? Isn't the latest series of a collection of *Vogue Italia* pastiches, a succession of ironical winks? This "rereading of the past" (Nodolini) isn't nostalgia: The irreverent style of the images suggests a self-reflexive irony that is characteristic of our time. ■ *Vogue Italia* is avant-garde in fashion and image; it is not surprising then that the magazine is a source of inspiration for designers, a sort of visual communication review, as Gatti has suggested. Luca Stoppini, his former assistant and now art director, believes that a new balance is necessary in advertising. It is hard to say what *Vogue Italia* will look like in the future, but one thing is for certain: It will hold many surprises. ■

VOGUE

ITALIA

FEB.
1990
N. 477
L. 6.000

salomè jolly   o   arlecchino?

ABITO
DOLCE & GABBANA

COLORE

NELLA PAGINA ACCAN-
TO. GIACCA DI VEL-
LUTO, CHLOE; FUSEAUX
E STIVALETTI, MON-
TANA. FASHION EDI-
TOR BRANA WOLF.

(ALL IMAGES, THIS SPREAD) ART DIRECTOR: JUAN GATTI DATE: 1990 ■ (OPPOSITE, TOP LEFT) PHOTOGRAPHER: R. LOWIT ■ (TOP RIGHT)
PHOTOGRAPHER: ELLEN VON UNWORTH ■ (BOTTOM LEFT) PHOTOGRAPHER: STEVEN MEISEL ■ (BOTTOM RIGHT) PHOTOGRAPHER: MAXIME GODARD

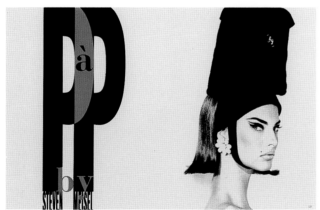

VOGUE

ITALIA

F E B.
1990
N. 476
L. 6.000

BUSTIER TUTE BASCHI

SHORTS TUNICHE

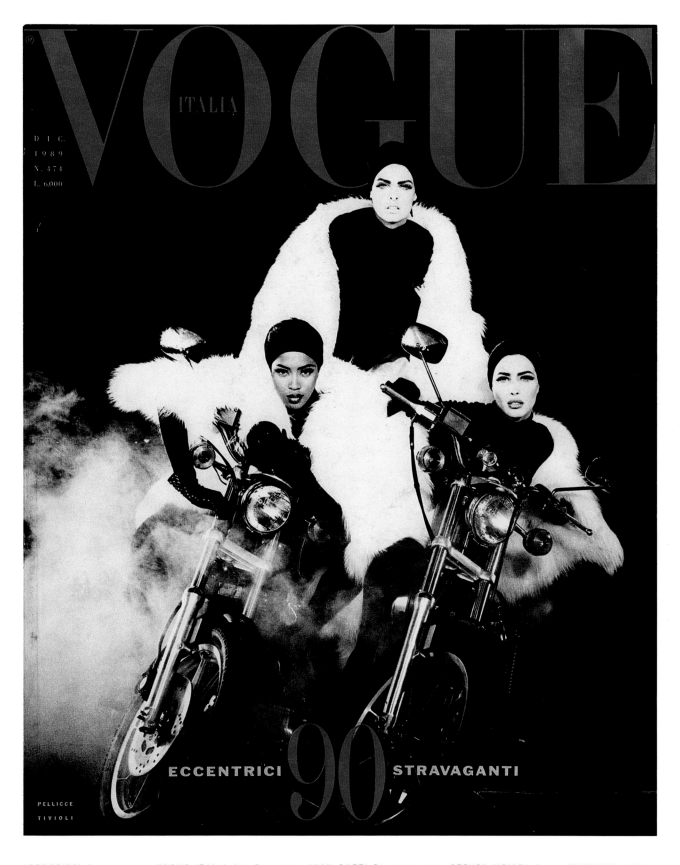

(OPPOSITE) PUBLICATION: *VOGUE ITALIA* ART DIRECTOR: JUAN GATTI PHOTOGRAPHER: STEVEN MEISEL DATE: FEBRUARY 1990 ∎

(THIS PAGE) PUBLICATION: *VOGUE ITALIA* ART DIRECTOR: FABIEN BARON PHOTOGRAPHER: STEVEN MEISEL DATE: DECEMBER 1989

RICERCATEZZA

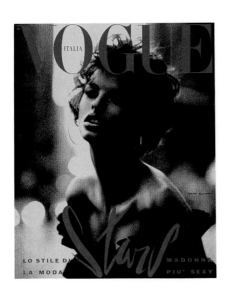  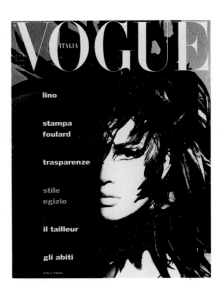

(ALL IMAGES, THIS SPREAD) ART DIRECTOR: JUAN GATTI (OPPOSITE) PHOTOGRAPHER: D. SEIDNER ■ (ALL IMAGES, THIS PAGE) PHOTOGRAPHER: STEVEN MEISEL (LEFT) DATE: JUNE 1990 (CENTER) DATE: MAY 1990 (RIGHT) DATE: APRIL 1990

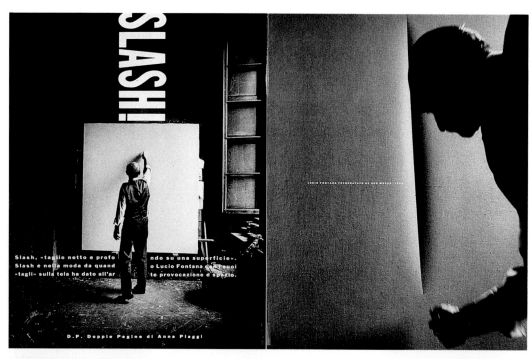

SLASH!

Slash, «taglio netto e profo[...]ndo su una superficie». Slash è nella moda da quand[...]o Lucio Fontana con i suoi «tagli» sulla tela ha dato all'ar[...]te provocazione e spazio.

D.P. Doppie Pagine di Anna Piaggi

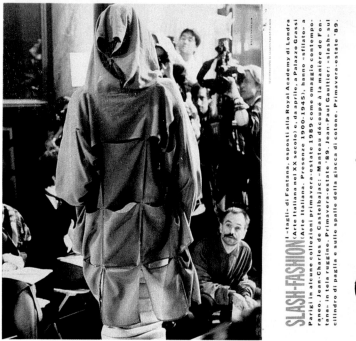

SLASH-FASHION I «tagli» di Fontana, esposti alla Royal Academy di Londra (Arte Italiana nel XX secolo) e, da aprile, a Palazzo Grassi (Arte Italiana. Presenze 1900-1945), hanno «sfilato» a Parigi in alcune collezioni primavera-estate 1989 come omaggio contemporaneo. Jean-Charles de Castelbajac: «Manteau découpé à la manière de Fontana» in tela ruggine. Primavera-estate '89. Jean-Paul Gaultier: «slash» sul cilindro di paglia e sulle spalle della giacca di cotone. Primavera-estate '89.

(ALL IMAGES, THIS SPREAD) ART DIRECTOR: FABIEN BARON ■ (THIS PAGE, TOP) PHOTOGRAPHER: UGO MULAS ■ (BOTTOM) ILLUSTRATOR: GLADYS PERINT PALMER PHOTOGRAPHER: BILL CUNNINGHAM ■ (OPPOSITE TOP) PHOTOGRAPHER: UGO MULAS ■ (OPPOSITE BOTTOM) PHOTOGRAPHER: ALFA CASTALDI

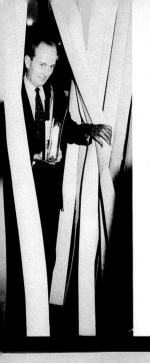

SLASH-FLASH
SLASH-SCHÖN

Attraverso le tende «slash» di Milano Collezioni, alcune entrate «concettuali». A sinistra, Robert Turner. A destra, dall'alto in basso, Bernardine Morris, Anna Wintour, Elizabeth Tilberis, Marylou Luther, Werner, Anna Piaggi, Nella pagina accanto, Abito di Mila Schön, Alta Moda, 1969, fotografato da Ugo Mulas e la modella è Benedetta Barzini.

MAREMOTO DI ONDE
TEMPESTE DI CHIFFON
CORRENTE FLOU FLUIDA
ALI AI PIEDI...

MULE «SCIROCCO»
IN RASO E
MOUSSELINE,
MANOLO BLAHNIK,
PAGINA ACCANTO,
LITO DI ALBIN
BRUNOVSKY, 1981.

Industrial
Launderer
February
1978

I N D U S T R I A L   L A U N D E R E R

FOR THE ART DIRECTOR WEARY OF PEER PRESSURE AND THE HYPE OF DESIGN AWARDS, *INDUSTRIAL LAUNDERER* OFFERS A RARE KIND OF SATISFACTION. CLOSE SCRUTINY OF THIS OBSCURE MAGAZINE LEAVES ONE FILLED WITH WONDER AND ADMIRATION FOR A FELLOW ARTIST WHO HAS ACCEPTED THE PROBLEMS OF A LIMITED BUDGET AND THE EVEN GREATER CHALLENGE OF TOTAL ARTISTIC CONTROL. ONE IS ABSOLVED OF THE KIND OF GUILT CREATED BY FREQUENT USE OF THE HIGH-SPEED, EIGHT-COLOR PRESS, MULTIPLE MATCH COLORS, TOO MUCH VARNISH, AND TOO MUCH MONEY. □ *INDUSTRIAL LAUNDERER*'S CLEAN AND

vibrant covers are at once provocative and anachronistic. They are bold—and pristine, like freshly laundered shirts. The abstract, posterlike images are subversively familiar. They tug at the memory, asking for corroboration: Japanese woodblock prints, the "Yellow Submarine," PushPin Studios. . . ? ■ *IL*, a monthly trade magazine published in Washington, D.C., since 1950 to serve a member audience of eight hundred commercial launderers who supply and clean linens, work clothes, and wiping cloths, has a total circulation of 2,700 (including advertisers and nonmembers). *IL* presents service articles by volunteer editors and newsworthy reprints from federal and business publications. Its mission is to inform the audience on such vital issues as government regulations, worker-incentive programs, and new products and technology. The information is urgent; strict management of production costs is paramount. ■ Before communication design was an art-school discipline with its own heady roster of stars, trade magazines looked industrial. Until 1958, *IL* covers were printed in two colors, which were always red and black—colors thought to be effective by advertisers buying the back page. A photo, usually of a workplace situation, along with advertising copy, occupied 70 percent of the cover. On the flag, a no-nonsense line drawing with the slogan "We coverall the industry" (sic) reinforced the square-dealing, honest style. It was a product for one industry prepared by another—the printing industry—without pretense and without a designer's touch. ■ As the audience became more sophisticated, and federal policy more difficult to unravel, *IL* felt pressured to reformat and redesign. For many art directors, this might not be a promising assignment. Fortunately for *IL*, the right oppor-

tunity was presented to the right designer. ■ Jack Lefkowitz was born in Brooklyn, New York, and trained in graphic design at Cooper Union. In 1958, he moved to Washington, D.C., to work in one of the city's largest art studios. After a year designing books in Florence and a year in New York, he returned to the Capitol in 1967 to open his own shop, with *IL* as his principal client. The *IL* challenge was anybody's ballgame, and Lefkowitz recognized the potential. He rolled up his sleeves and began the task of inventing a personal style that has won design awards and exposure in *Print, Industrial Design, Folio,* and *Graphis* for thirty years. ■ Lefkowitz runs his studio out of a remote farmhouse in Leesburg, Virginia, with in-house typesetting, photostats, and fax. In 1970, he had eight assistants but found himself excessively involved with administration. He trimmed his client list, cut staff by half, and went back to the boards himself. ■ As art director of *Industrial Launderer*, Lefkowitz rejected full-color photography. A steady flow of industrial work scenes and conferences would be boring; furthermore, he had no budget for photography and color separations, so he captivated his audience by creating emblematic covers whose consistent style made for instant recognition and gave the magazine a clean, friendly, yet corporate look. A corporate look enhanced by the precise, almost machine-made style of the illustrations, yet simultaneously denied by dreamlike imagery, devoid of explanatory text. ■ For an issue devoted to protective clothing, a switched-on worker is decked out for an intergalactic sporting event—but the figure is missing. The reader's eye is so completely engaged in the amusing task of decoding the visual that the missing element becomes un-information.

Another cover says "fabric dying." At close range, four differently colored cloths float above a drain, through which the dye, yet another color, escapes. An improbability, and a poetic one. ■ *IL* does not need to compete for attention at the newsstands, so cover lines were not used until 1980, when the editorial content was

upgraded to include original stories instead of the usual menu of reprint articles. Now that this copy is part of the text, it becomes texture, a graphic element to be manipulated by the designer until it is fully integrated with the illustration. The logo, too, is subverted—bent to the service of the layout. It appears in every conceivable position on the page, even italicized when the visual demands it. ■ Behind the covers, the pages of *IL* are quiet by comparison: clean, three-column format, with Helvetica Regular for the text, a variety of display faces for heads, and more of Lefkowitz's illustrations. The illustrations, in particular, make every issue a one-man show. "As a designer in love with drawing, I became an art director so I could hire myself as an illustrator," says Lefkowitz. This kind of playful and single-minded approach can only happen with complete trust on the editorial side. A succession of editors, beginning with Jim Roberts in 1970, gave Lefkowitz strong support. Apart from a nod of approval for concepts, the *IL* editors allowed their art director free reign. "Jim wanted this thing out of his hair; he really let me do whatever I wanted," said Lefkowitz. The electric illustrators of the 1960s—Milton Glaser, Seymour Chwast— were everywhere during Jack's formative years at Cooper Union. At the time, communication design was centered on illustration, and Chwast, he says, was the artist he most admired. He also recognizes the influence of his particular artist-heroes, Klee and Kandinsky, evident in the wit of his own constructions, and their superb color sense. ■ The strange marriage of image and production technology is vital to the success of *Industrial Launderer*. So far, Lefkowitz has rejected computer-aided design; he

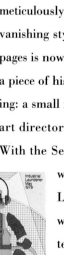

has always found assistants who can be trained to work in his own painstaking way. He first creates a pencil drawing, which is reproduced in ink by a mechanical artist. Lefkowitz then formulates his color plan in dye marker on a vellum overlay. A cover may appear to have twelve solid colors. Only by examining the printed piece under a loupe will the reality become evident: combinations of process tints, as many as three screens per color. Twenty or more film overlays cut by hand precisely match the line drawing. But why does it look like solid color? Only if you have experienced for yourself the magic (or disaster) that can occur when printing the four process colors, one at a time on a slow press, will you recognize how this intense color is achieved. The deep color saturation fools the eye and simply cannot be duplicated on a high-speed, multicolor press. ■ Always searching for cost-conscious suppliers, Lefkowitz found a printer in Indiana who appreciates the craftsmanship in the artwork. The film overlays are so precise that the printer makes a direct assembly, with no extra charges for camera work. All the film preparation (with a color key for the art director's approval) is done in two days for less than $200. ■ So, the aesthetic of the image—poetic, dreamlike, imaginative—is contradicted by the production: slow work, meticulously done by hand. And, it is a perfect example of a vanishing style. ■ The *Industrial Launderer* seen in these pages is now, like the Beatles and the "Yellow Submarine," a piece of history. It was a phenomenon unique in publishing: a small magazine made visible by the talent of a single art director, in a climate free of editorial gamemanship. With the September 1990 issue, a new editorial director with a mission of his own took over. ■ And Jack Lefkowitz immediately joined the electronic age with a sophisticated Macintosh computer system linked by modem to clients and suppliers. He now creates color images, type, and page layouts directly on the screen, with results that are even more satisfying to his demanding style. ■

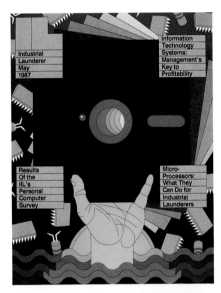

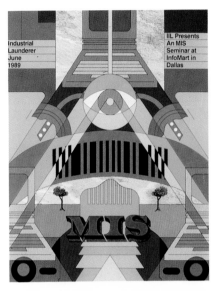

(PREVIOUS SPREAD, LEFT) ART DIRECTOR/ILLUSTRATOR: JACK LEFKOWITZ DATE: FEBRUARY 1978 ■ (OPPOSITE TOP) DATE: MAY 1956 (PRIOR TO JACK LEFKOWITZ'S TENURE AS ART DIRECTOR AT *INDUSTRIAL LAUNDERER*) ■ (OPPOSITE BOTTOM) ART DIRECTOR/ILLUSTRATOR: JACK LEFKOWITZ DATE: MAY 1978 ■ (ALL IMAGES, THIS PAGE) ART DIRECTOR/ILLUSTRATOR: JACK LEFKOWITZ ■ (TOP LEFT) DATE: MAY 1987 ■ (TOP RIGHT) DATE: JUNE 1989 ■ (BOTTOM LEFT) DATE: APRIL 1989 ■ (BOTTOM RIGHT) DATE: JULY 1987

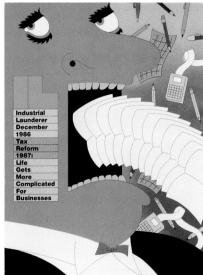

(ALL IMAGES, THIS PAGE) ART DIRECTOR/ILLUSTRATOR: JACK LEFKOWITZ ■ (ABOVE, LEFT) DATE: AUGUST 1987 ■ (ABOVE, CENTER) DECEMBER 1986 (ABOVE, RIGHT) JUNE 1988 ■ (OPPOSITE) ART DIRECTOR/ILLUSTRATOR: JACK LEFKOWITZ DATE: JUNE 1990

INDUSTRIAL LAUNDERER

JUNE 1990

Fleet Priorities   Truck Bodies   Clean Propane   Muscle Mechanics

HELLO ANYWHERE

PAGE 84

HERE'S THE LOWDOWN ON CELLULAR PHONES

743675

BUSINESS WEEK

THE *BUSINESS WEEK* WAS LAUNCHED BY MCGRAW-HILL ON SEPTEMBER 7, 1929, JUST A WEEK BEFORE THE GREAT CRASH. THE SECOND NATIONAL NEWSWEEKLY (AFTER *TIME*), IT DEFINED A UNIQUE ROLE FOR ITSELF. IN THE FIRST ISSUE, MCGRAW-HILL PRESIDENT MALCOLM MUIR DECLARED: *"THE BUSINESS WEEK SERVES NO SINGLE GROUP. IT DOES NOT ASPIRE TO GIVE THE TEXTILE MAN HIS TEXTILE NEWS, NOR THE BANKER HIS FINANCIAL NEWS. . . IT WILL TELL THE BANKER THE THINGS HE OUGHT TO KNOW THAT ARE HAPPENING IN THE TEXTILE INDUSTRY; IT WILL TELL THE TEXTILE MAN WHAT OF SIGNIFICANCE TO HIM IS DEVELOPING IN FINANCE."*

Business Week's proposition—that executives needed to know about business outside their own industry, indeed, outside their own country—was one of the first steps taken toward the global economy of today. It also underscored a philosophy of business management that would later be a central tenet of Harvard Business School's Casebook study method: One can learn as much about management running any business, large or small, industrial or service. ■ Later, other magazines would follow suit: *Fortune, Forbes, U.S. News & World Report, Nation's Business.* But none of these does as well what *Business Week* set out to do over sixty years ago, and none is as widely read. ■ For most of its history, however, *Business Week* trailed behind the leading business magazines in design. Here *Fortune*, designed by the brilliant Herbert Matter, was the pinnacle toward which the others might aspire. By contrast, *Business Week* in its infancy was not even designed for ease of use. It lacked a table of contents, and its reporting on individual industries was not gathered together in logical sections, but was scattered throughout. So to find all the news relating to finance, for example, the reader would have to search pages 8, 10, 17, and 21 of the premier issue. ■ Even more surprising, fifty years later *Business Week*'s design was only adequate, on par with other business magazines but hardly a leader— despite its great financial success. Covers were uninspired illustrations or photographs of executives; the typeface of its present logo was there (designed by the firm of Danne and Blackburn in 1976) though not within the red band that is now familiar. Department logos and heads were Helvetica Bold, not more than 16 points high, the only graphic element usually being a photograph of the columnist, or a chart. The one-page table of contents listed dozens of columns, departments, and features, their subject areas distinguished only by 9-point Helvetica caps, making it difficult to find subjects of interest. A thumbnail-size reproduction of the cover was the lone art element. ■ Cover stories were usually the only ones to receive special design treatment—meaning color photographs and larger heads (the typeface was always Egyptienne Bold Condensed). Body type was Times Roman throughout. Photographs in the features (which, at the time, *Business Week* inexplicably labeled "departments") were sized and arranged with little care. ■ By 1982, *Business Week* had 750,000 loyal subscribers. Lewis Young, the magazine's editor-in-chief of thirteen years, had succeeded in making *Business Week* must reading for executives. Young was also admired for being a step ahead of business development, so that the magazine did not just report the news, but anticipated it. Yet the weekly had its troubles. Ad revenues were down 10 percent from the year before. Fifty-eight-year-old Young was in the hospital for heart surgery, and no successor had ever been trained or selected. The magazine had a reputation for sluggish prose, while its competitors—*Fortune, Forbes,* and *The Wall Street Journal*—could be lively, even entertaining at times. Finally, some in the executive suite could see that *Business Week* was a little dreary visually as well. ■ The magazine's turnaround began in June of that year, when an aggressive new publisher, James Pierce of *Aviation Week*, was named, followed by the selection of Stephen Shepard as executive editor. Shepard knew the magazine well, having served as a reporter, editor, and writer there for nine years (1966–1975). But he also had five years' experience

Cover Story

SUNDAY IN THE PARK WITH MICKEY
CAN DISNEY FOOL THE DOUBTERS AND WORK IT'S MAGIC IN EUROPE?

In muddy sugar-beet fields 20 miles east of Paris, bulldozers are tracing the outlines of some familiar scenes: Main Street, Pirates of the Caribbean, and the Mad Tea Party teacup ride. Two years from now, if all goes well, the gates of the world's biggest and splashiest Disneyland will swing open. Fun-craving tourists from all over Europe will pour through in droves to shake hands with Mickey Mouse, explore Adventure Island, and have

(ALL IMAGES) ART DIRECTOR: MALCOLM FROUMAN (PREVIOUS SPREAD, LEFT) ILLUSTRATOR: GARY HALLGREN PHOTOGRAPHER: PETER FREED DATE: 1987 ■ (ABOVE) ILLUSTRATOR: DANIEL KIRK DATE: 1990

at *Newsweek*, first as its business editor and then as its national affairs editor, and he was editor of *Saturday Review* for two years. ■ The consumer magazine experience was invaluable, and Shepard's mission, in his own words, was to "upgrade how the magazine looks and reads." Adding more four color and enlivening the writing style were his first steps. Relations between the art and editorial staffs "went from terrible to wonderful" with Shepard's arrival, says Malcolm Frouman, then associate art director and now art director. "The word had gone out and down" to all editors, he adds: "Whether you understand it or not, design should play a part in your thinking." ■ John Vogler, then *Business Week*'s design director, argued for a complete redesign, which was conceived by B. Martin Pedersen, supported by Lew Young, and carried out by Vogler in 1983. "Marty gave us a wonderful design," says Frouman, which has been modified only slightly in seven years. ■ The most obvious, and successful, element of the redesign is the cover. As determined by Lew Young, Pedersen's mission was to give the magazine newsstand recognition and visibility. The existing covers—"full-bleed illustrations in browns and ochers"—Pedersen recalls were "very recessive" and had "no vitality." Tabloids, on the other hand, were most successful at gaining a reader's eye on the newsstand, argues Pedersen, so he designed *Business Week*'s cover with the headline as the dominant factor. "What really sells a magazine is the information," maintains Pedersen. "If there's a subject for the week that interests a reader, they're going to buy it." ■ Pedersen gave the cover impact by actually reducing the *Business Week* logo, but placing it within a bright red band, and greatly enlarging the headline. ■ When Pedersen presented his new design to the magazine's upper management, they were taken aback, and asked if the band could be brown and the logo larger. But Pedersen prevailed, in part by taking the mockup to a newsstand in Grand Central Terminal and photographing it alongside other magazines. The new *Business Week* stood out. Within weeks of its introduction, the design proved its worth without

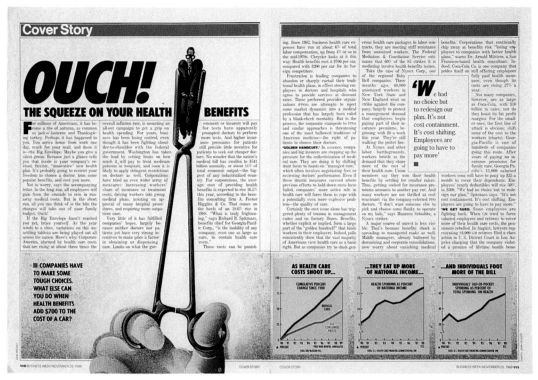

(ABOVE) Art Director: MALCOLM FROUMAN Illustrator: JOHN BREAKEY Date: NOVEMBER, 20 1989

Pedersen's assurances: Newsstand sales jumped 30 percent. ■ Pedersen not only greatly improved the magazine's looks, he made it much more accessible and easy to use. Headlines for both departments and features were standardized and made the same size. (Pedersen reasoned that the last thing the art department of a weekly magazine should be worrying about is size and style of headlines.) A thin red band reminiscent of the one now gracing the cover signals the topic of each department and feature (with Helvetica headings, upper and lower case). Text type is Century Expanded, a "classical" revival popular with many magazines in the 1980s. The magazine's artwork has been all color since 1985. ■ The challenges facing designers of business periodicals are somewhat different than those facing their counterparts at consumer magazines. First, the information presented is crucial to its readers: Decisions affecting the success of the readers' businesses will be made based on what they read. Except for recent anomalies such as *Manhattan inc.*, executives do not read business journals to be enter-

tained. Information must be easy to find and easy to grasp. ■ "More than any other magazine, we rely on information graphics. They comprise a large percentage of the visual graphics" of the magazine, says Frouman. A greatly enlarged art budget and staff turn ideas into reality, with charts and the like produced on Apple Macintosh computers. Often charts or boxes are combined with photographs into one art element occupying center stage on the page. Doing so saves space for text (editors determine how much text will run) and also produces pages that are balanced and uncluttered, despite the great deal of information being provided. ■ *Business Week* is a textbook case of art and editorial working together to accomplish both functional and aesthetic missions: One million readers rely on the magazine for information that helps them directly in running their businesses, and keeps them abreast of important developments in other fields. A bold, consistent design makes their task easy and pleasurable. Now earning an average of more than $41,000 per advertising page, McGraw-Hill executives are smiling, too. ■

A McGraw-Hill Publication

BusinessWeek

April 18, 1983 • $2.00

THE NEW ENTREPRENEURS

Lots of startups give America
an edge in product development

Big corporations try to imitate
the entrepreneurial spirit

Page 78

WHERE TO LOOK FOR HIGHER YIELDS AS INTEREST RATES FALL PAGE 84

BusinessWeek

JULY 1, 1985   A McGRAW-HILL PUBLICATION $2.00

SPLITTING UP

It's the opposite
of merger mania:
Companies
divesting assets,
spinning off
divisions, even
liquidating
themselves.
The trick is
knowing when
it makes sense.

PAGE 50

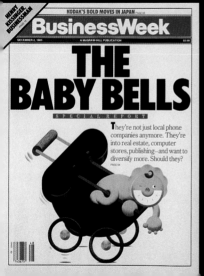

HENRY KISSINGER BUSINESSMAN

KODAK'S BOLD MOVES IN JAPAN PAGE 42

BusinessWeek

DECEMBER 2, 1985   A McGRAW-HILL PUBLICATION $2.00

THE BABY BELLS

SPECIAL REPORT

They're not just local phone
companies anymore. They're
into real estate, computer
stores, publishing—and want to
diversify more. Should they?

PAGE 54

HEALTH CARE: THE COST CRISIS IS OVER—BUT WHAT ABOUT QUALITY? PAGE 88

BusinessWeek

OCTOBER 21, 1985   A McGRAW-HILL PUBLICATION $2.00

NEW?
IMPROVED?
THE BRAND-NAME MERGERS

PAGE 100

RITZ

PHILIP MORRIS BUYS
GENERAL FOODS!

PROCTER & GAMBLE BUYS
RICHARDSON-VICKS!

REVLON IS
UP FOR GRABS!

...AND UNILEVER IS
SHOPPING!

(OPPOSITE, TOP LEFT) ART DIRECTOR: MALCOLM FROUMAN ILLUSTRATOR: ERALDO CARUGATTI DATE: 1983 (BEFORE PEDERSEN'S REDESIGN) ■ (TOP RIGHT) ART DIRECTORS: MALCOLM FROUMAN, MITCH SHOSTAK ILLUSTRATOR: JEAN TUTTLE DATE: 1985 ■ (BOTTOM LEFT) ART DIRECTORS: MALCOLM FROUMAN, MITCH SHOSTAK ILLUSTRATOR: JOSÉ CRUZ DATE: 1985 ■ (BOTTOM RIGHT) ART DIRECTORS: MALCOLM FROUMAN, MITCH SHOSTAK ILLUSTRATOR: RALPH WERNLI PHOTOGRAPHER: WALTER CHRYWSKI DATE: 1985 ■ (ALL IMAGES, THIS PAGE) ART DIRECTOR: MALCOLM FROUMAN ■ (TOP LEFT) ILLUSTRATOR: JAVIER ROMERO DATE: 1987 ■ (TOP RIGHT) ILLUSTRATOR: JUAN SUAREZ BOTA DATE: 1987 ■ (BOTTOM LEFT) DATE: 1989 ■ (BOTTOM RIGHT) ILLUSTRATOR: MARK PENBERTHY DATE: 1985

FMR

America   October 1984   First year

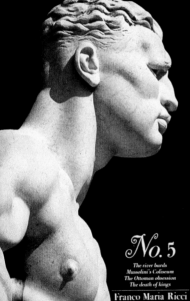

No. 5

The river bards
Mussolini's Coliseum
The Ottoman obsession
The death of kings

Franco Maria Ricci

F M R "THE MOST BEAUTIFUL MAGAZINE IN THE WORLD"—THIS IS THE GOAL *FMR* STRIVES TO ACHIEVE WITH EACH OF ITS ISSUES. AS PROBLEMATIC AS SUCH SUPERLATIVES CAN BE, FOUNDER, NAMESAKE, PUBLISHER, EDITOR-IN-CHIEF, AND ART DIRECTOR FRANCO MARIA RICCI HAS AT LEAST PROVEN WITH THE EIGHT YEARLY ISSUES OF HIS MAGAZINE THE STANDARDS OF QUALITY THAT CAN BE ACHIEVED WHEN A PASSIONATE LOVER OF ALL BEAUTIFUL THINGS TURNS HIS DREAM INTO REALITY. □ IT HAD ALWAYS BEEN RICCI'S WISH TO CREATE A WORLD CONTRASTING WITH THE INCREASINGLY GREY, DISMAL, DESOLATE, AND HOSTILE LANDSCAPE OF EVERYDAY LIFE. USING THE MOST SOPHISTICATED

graphic and technical means available, he wanted to present works of art in the most beautiful way possible. In this respect even the opponents of this cosmopolitan Italian must admit that he has achieved his goal with a single-mindedness and a success that astonishes many publishers. The monthly circulation in Italy is 25,000 issues; add to that another 15,000 English issues, 10,000 French issues, and, since recently, 15,000 Spanish issues—all of which are published bimonthly. That the German edition never had more than 5,000 subscribers and has now ceased publication throws an unfavorable light, not on the magazine, but on the land of poets and philosophers. ■ One reason why Franco Maria Ricci started his magazine was his deeply felt, personal regret that there were no really beautifully made art magazines. According to Ricci, there are "beautifully made home and design magazines, lovingly made magazines for gourmets and globetrotters, even beautifully made sex magazines—but none in the field of art." And Ricci believes he knows why: "These people have no feelings for pictures. Art magazines tend to show larger pictures of the founder of a museum than of the museum itself. They tend to pay more attention to misprints in the texts than to the right reproduction of color. It can even happen that a picture is printed the wrong way round!" Works of art, he believes, should come into their own right again. ■ The wish to publish a proper art magazine, which would focus on art alone, went hand in hand with a realistic marketing proposition. Publisher Ricci, who already commanded attention with his extraordinary art books, knew that in museums, private collections, and churches there were thousands of dimly remembered treasures. But he also knew that the sum of these treasures wasn't cohesive enough to fill an entire book. A magazine seemed the ideal way to bring some of these precious objects to light. ■ He decided to leave the selection criteria as unrestricted as possible. So *FMR* does not only present what is approved of by art experts, it also presents costumes by Erte, cars by Bugatti, shipwood furniture by Thonet, and similar objects that only seem to be ephemeral. The way these objects are presented, however, gives each of them a special attraction. Unusual details are highlighted and, most of all, the generosity of the layout—almost all of the images are presented on spreads without any text—create a totally new fascination. ■ There can be no doubt that Franco Maria Ricci makes all the final decisions in regard to content and design—that the magazine carries his name is perfectly right—even though he has a motivated and hardworking team to support him, especially Laura Casalis, who works as art director together with Ricci. ■ To be able to understand Ricci's philosophy as a graphic designer and publisher, and the style of his magazine, one must mention the great Giambattista Bodoni (1740–1813). This genius of a type designer, typographer, printer, and publisher has been Ricci's model since he visited, by chance, the Bodoni Museum in Parma. Ricci's admiration of Bodoni explains the extraordinarily strict and consequent layout (which has remained unchanged over the years), the confinement to a few visual elements, and the choice of typeface, which of course is one of Bodoni's. The main motivation for the currently planned Russian edition of *FMR* are the wonderful Cyrillic type faces designed by Bodoni which, until now, have never

(PREVIOUS SPREAD, LEFT AND ABOVE) Art Director: FRANCO MARIA RICCI Photographer: GEORGE MOTT Date: 1984 ■ (ALL IMAGES, OPPOSITE) Art Director: FRANCO MARIA RICCI ■ (TOP THREE) Date: 1990 ■ (BOTTOM) Photographer: ARALDO DE LUCA Date: 1990

been used. ■ Bodoni's life motto can be easily applied to Franco Maria Ricci: "I want only magnificence and I do not want to work for the common man." ■ Also probably unique in the world of magazine publishers: Quality is given priority over the sale of advertising space. Not only must advertisers be satisfied with their ads being placed at the beginning and end of the magazine, Ricci even refuses to take on certain advertisers, such as galleries, museums, and auction houses, in order to preserve his editorial independence. And advertisements that do not meet his standards are simply not published. In such cases, however, Ricci does offer to design the advertisement himself. Although all this increases the price of the magazine, *FMR* readers are obviously happy with Ricci's decisions. ■

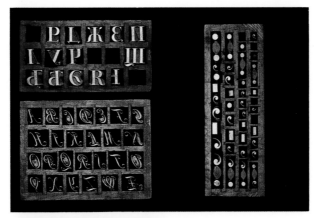

(ALL IMAGES, THIS SPREAD) ART DIRECTOR: FRANCO MARIA RICCI PHOTOGRAPHER: ARALDO DE LUCA DATE: 1986

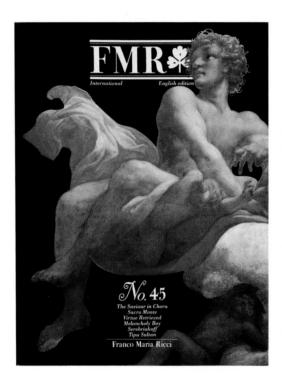

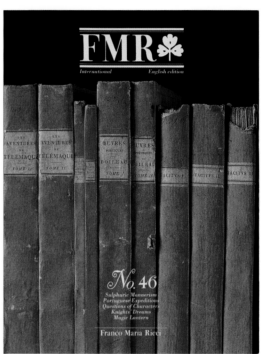

(ALL IMAGES, THIS SPREAD) Art Director: FRANCO MARIA RICCI ■ (THIS PAGE, LEFT AND OPPO-
SITE TOP) Photographer: LUIGI ARTINI Date: 1990 ■ (RIGHT AND OPPOSITE BOTTOM) Date: 1990

VOGUE

DECEMBER $3.00

STAR TURNS:
LOOKS THAT MAKE THE SEASON

KNOCKOUT GLAMOUR:
GOLD, DIAMONDS, WINTER WHITE

DRESS FOR LESS:
SILVER AND SEQUINS

GREAT ESCAPE:
BEST RESORT BUYS

SPECIAL HOLIDAY ISSUE

12

0 751164

VOGUE MAGAZINE

UNLIKE FREUD, THE EDITORS OF AMERICAN *VOGUE* THINK THEY KNOW WHAT WOMEN WANT. WITH A CURRENT CIRCULATION OF 1.3 MILLION, THE 101-YEAR-OLD FASHION MAGAZINE IS STILL DELIVERING, MONTH AFTER MONTH, AN AVERAGE OF 500 GLOSSY PAGES DRENCHED WITH COLOR AND COATED WITH INK. THE MAJORITY OF READERS WOULD RATHER PAY CASH AT THE NEWSSTAND AND CARRY OFF THE HEFTY PUBLICATION THAN WAIT PATIENTLY TO GET IT IN THE MAIL. WHAT IS THEIR FASCINATION? □ AT FIRST GLANCE, THE MAGAZINE IS A THICK, COMPLEX MIX OF IMAGES THAT DEFY ANALYSIS. ONLY AN EDUCATED EYE CAN HOPE TO

find its way around the busy and aggressive succession of spreads and tell the difference between editorial and advertising. The relentless competition between these pages does not seem to bother an audience who wants it all, as long as it's appealing. Our desires spurn rationalization, and from the look of *Vogue*, they appear to scorn organization. Curious enough about designer clothes to put up with a cumbersome visual format, the reader is hostile to design for its own sake. Indeed, the magazine's objective—to report on fashion, not to create it—is more journalistic than artistic. It never attempts to advocate good taste over bad taste, do's over don'ts, ins over outs. For a magazine whose subject matter is elegance and discrimination, it never seems to discriminate. ■ It wasn't always the case. Originally a weekly society magazine, *Vogue* was purchased in 1909 by Condé Nast, an ambitious young New York publisher, who established it as the foremost fashion authority in the United States, competing only with *Harper's Bazaar* for talent, style, and prestige. But the story of American *Vogue*, as we know it, starts during World War II, when, isolated from the Paris fashion world, the magazine had to become autonomous. Fashion, that very French affair, had to be transformed into an all-American concern. The magazine needed somebody who could deal with this contradiction. ■ In 1942, Alexander Liberman arrived in New York. A Russian artist and art director, he came from France where he had immigrated after the Bolshevik revolution. He was promptly hired by Condé Nast, who with this appointment made his last and most lasting managerial decision. For the next fifty years, until this day, Liberman has presided over every aspect of *Vogue*'s design, working consecutively with seven formidable editors-in-chief—Josephine Redding, Marie Harrison, Edna Woolman Chase, Jessica Daves, Diana Vreeland, Grace Mirabella, and Anna Wintour—to shape a magazine that has become increasingly popular, entertaining, and profitable. His genius has been his adaptability. He knows how to keep his balance with constant readjustments, deep innovations, and an open mind. In 1962, he became editorial director of Condé Nast Publications, and turned his attention to *Mademoiselle*, *Glamour*, and *House and Garden*. With time, an increasing number of new publications, either acquired or launched by the Condé Nast group, also became his responsibility. Keeping pace with every single magazine, he nonetheless managed to stay involved with the day-to-day operations at *Vogue*, instructing, nurturing—but mostly stimulating—its art department. He fondly remembers his collaboration with art directors and design directors like Priscilla Peck, Rochelle Udell, Roger Schoening, Ron Kajiwara, and Derek Ungless. "The design format of *Vogue* remains consistent for ten years at a time," he says. "We favor a certain classicism that is meant to facilitate communication. We never change typefaces arbitrarily." The creative impulse is not a casual one: Liberman believes that journalism is a discipline. What the reader needs to know, and what the picture needs to say, both dictate what needs to be printed. "I respect the climate of the period as well as the document," he says, choosing his words thoughtfully. ■ In design terms, Liberman's philosophy translates as a format that amplifies the content. *Vogue*'s structure is closer to that of a newspaper, with components that expand or contract to fit the news. There are no "columns," no "departments," no "grids," visual or men-

country goes to town

Oh, give me land, lots of land under starry skies above
Don't fence me in
Let me ride through the wide open country that I love...

Down on the farm, THIS PAGE: Nadège in a city-slicker-gone-Dolly Parton dress. By Chanel Haute Couture. Boots by the Justin Boot Company. Hat from the Alamo of Nashville. Even with a hat, one needs a sun block on the face: here, Chanel's Total Protection Moisture Cream SPF 15. OPPOSITE PAGE: Sunset near Nashville. Details, last pages.

(PREVIOUS SPREAD, LEFT) ART DIRECTOR: DEREK UNGLESS PHOTOGRAPHER: PATRICK DEMARCHELIER
DATE: 1989 ■ (ABOVE) ART DIRECTOR: RAÚL MARTINEZ PHOTOGRAPHER: BRUCE WEBER DATE: 1990

tal. This reportorial approach is revealed in the table of contents, which currently lists three broad sections—Fashion, Health/Beauty, and Features. Fashion's entries are varied, including anything from the profile of a fashionable celebrity to a photographic portfolio. Health/Beauty is an extensive category, covering fitness and sports as well as medical issues. As for Features, they run the gamut from a monthly horoscope, to a report on volunteering, to a movie review. A relevant story will always find its place in the mix—while a tedious one will never be missed. ■ The make-up of the magazine is not structural, is it contextual; to figure it out, one should do what the reader does, which is to leaf through an issue. The arrangement may appear improvisational—it is anything but that. When laying out the sequence of stories, Liberman is aware that, while some subjects may interest you, others may not. To keep you going, he will pace the layouts around a group of seductive photographs, two or three striking close-ups, and, let's say, one powerful graphic spread. This process demands flexibility from all involved. Some articles have to be altered at the last minute to comply with the overall editorial direction. Sometimes a compelling photograph turns out to be too strong compared with the rest, and a weaker one takes its place. Sometimes a beautiful illustration is cropped in half. Sometimes an unattractive image is blown up to create a diversion. Sometimes an elegant layout is deliberately chopped up to gain in spontaneity. . . and sometimes a whole section seems to come together in minutes. ■ But *Vogue*'s appeal is not due exclusively to its unique design attitude. What keeps the magazine in front of the racks at the newsstand is the quintessential glossy quality of its images—in other words, its polished fashion photography. Under Liberman's direction (he claims he has selected just about every image that appeared in *Vogue* since 1943), photographers have been encouraged to develop a fresh and informal aesthetic. Challenging an old-fashioned, elitist, and stilted view of elegance, the pages of *Vogue* have displayed increasingly spontaneous and energizing images of pretty girls on the go. Fashion, traditionally a restraining and regulating influence, was represented as a freeing and emancipating

great buys:

dress rehearsal

If there is one item to buy for '91, it is the dress. Always feminine, it comes in a million variations–color blocked, floral, plaid, or Op Art–and at a price for every pocket. It can be dressed up for night or, with the addition of a jacket, transformed into a suit. Increasingly, the dress stands by itself as a suitworthy alternative

By Randolph Duke, about $198.

Photographer: Albert Watson Fashion Editor: Jenny Capitain

152

(ABOVE) Art Director: RAÚL MARTINEZ Photographer: ALBERT WATSON Date: JANUARY 1991

force in a woman's life. Although a well-accepted notion now, the picture of a truly sexy and liberated woman is still hard to come by, and Liberman is lobbying every day for a more natural, joyous, and unencumbered fashion sense. ■ American *Vogue* today is an example of this never-ending search for an honestly enfranchised look. The first clue is given by the covers, which shifted in style when Anna Wintour became editor-in-chief, giving up some of their formal glamour. Now they playfully invite the reader to venture on a fantasy, outside the realm of her everyday life. Often featuring deep blue skies for background, with party looks and summery pastel colors all year round, the cover images suggest an escape and a fancy for reckless consumption. This sunny disposition is very much the American approach, as opposed to the European one, characterized by a shadowy, sexy, and somewhat more enigmatic stance. Although the same photographers may display their darker, intellectual side for the French, the Italian, the German, or the British editions of *Vogue*, in the American version, their work becomes seductive, with a youthful, flirtatious, and

healthy glow. Irving Penn or Arthur Elgort, although very different, are masters of that genre. After decades of exposure in American *Vogue*, they can still provide, with one single image—a startled beauty wearing nothing but a wig and a watch, a baroque handbag photographed in Death Valley, a three-year-old in a white gown—an extemporaneous moment of joy. ■ Each *Vogue* layout is the result of hours of planning, researching, waiting, lugging, traveling, editing. By the time it all gets recorded on paper, what's left of it looks effortless, breezy, almost mindless. The reader never has to know about the drudgery of production, or feel the strain of creativity. She should be touched by a sort of grace. That grace is Liberman's secret. To see him work—his impeccable posture, his deliberate movements, the way he scrutinizes pictures, or, even more telling, his capacity for listening quietly when people talk—is to realize that the impact of his design derived from the impact of the instant: It hits you right here, now. Which is a good thing, since in the next second, something else, just as good, is bound to come up. In fashion, the present is the only thing that lasts. ■

liquid assets

Pure drama: Calvin Klein's latest nod to lingerie is a simple satin slip dress. A moisturizer that adds the same deep golden finish to skin—with tiny flecks of metallic dust: Revlon Unforgettable Golden Pearl Body Moisturizer. Dress from Calvin Klein Collection: about $850. Bergdorf Goodman. Details, see In This Issue.

(THIS PAGE) ART DIRECTOR: RAÚL MARTINEZ PHOTOGRAPHER: SHEILA METZNER DATE: 1991 ■ (OPPOSITE, LEFT TO RIGHT IN DESCENDING ORDER) ART DIRECTOR: RAÚL MARTINEZ DATE: 1989 ■ ART DIRECTOR: RAÚL MARTINEZ PHOTOGRAPHER: WALTER CHIN DATE: MARCH 1991 ■ ART DIRECTOR: RAÚL MARTINEZ PHOTOGRAPHER: ELLEN VON UNWERTH DATE: 1991 ■ ART DIRECTOR: DEREK UNGLESS PHOTOGRAPHER: BRUCE WEBER DATE: 1989 ■ ART DIRECTOR: RAÚL MARTINEZ PHOTOGRAPHER: ARTHUR ELGORT DATE: 1990 ■ ART DIRECTOR: RAÚL MARTINEZ PHOTOGRAPHER: PATRICK DEMARCHELIER DATE: DECEMBER 1991 ■ ART DIRECTOR: RAÚL MARTINEZ PHOTOGRAPHER: PATRICK DEMARCHELIER DATE: 1992 ■ ART DIRECTOR: RAÚL MARTINEZ PHOTOGRAPHER: HELMUT NEWTON DATE: 1990

retin-A

Bejeweled,
befringed,
and in
materials
from satin to
kicky prints,
mules are
ready to wear
with
everything
from leggings
to evening
dresses

footloose

paris lightens up

"I know everyone in boxing. I only have to see them once... then I know I can beat 'em"

scene of the couture

smile

surf's up

love story

Surfers would call it totally tubular: beach dressing based on stretchy, body-conscious leggings, bodysuits, or short shorts that are refined enough for seaside cafés

359

One way
to lighten the
look of gray
accessories with
stone, opposite page.
Adding style—and
decoration—to a
gray suit: Isaac
Manevitz for Ben-
Amun necklaces.
Top, about $190;
bottom, about
$170. Both wrists,
top bracelets by
Isaac Manevitz for
Ben-Amun. Left,
about $160; right,
about $135.
Bottom bracelets
by Michel Lanz for
Premier Etage.
Isaac Manevitz for
Ben-Amun earrings,
about $50. Ungaro
Parallele wool suit
two page. One of the
shoes most worn
for fall: the classic
pump. Here, it
takes on a new,
fluttering heel:
Manolo Blahnik
pumps, about
$350. Satin bag by
Renaud Pellegrino,
Paris, about $975.
Details, more
stores, last pages.

Making a big evening statement: strapless dresses embroidered with gems and sequins. THIS PAGE: Jewel-encrusted bustier with silk pants and matching cuffs by Gianfranco Ferre. Byzantine opulence: earrings by David Salvatore for Headmaster, Parisian, Birmingham. OPPOSITE PAGE: Shoulder-length earrings get streamlined in Austrian crystal by James Arpad. "The flower is of foil-backed crystal, the strands are clear—so light is both reflected and refracted," says the designer. Dress by Mary McFadden Couture, Saks Fifth Avenue; Sara Fredericks, Boston. For extravagant evening dresses, makeup on the dramatic side: Creme Lipstick in Russet Moon by Chanel. Details, more stores, last pages.

Taking a bold approach, THIS PAGE: A swing coat by Patrick Kelly, about $1,070. Bloomingdale's; Auer's, Denver; Macy's California. Crocodile bag, DeVecchi by Hamilton Hodge. OPPOSITE PAGE: An extravagant version of the standard sweater-and-pearls. Necklaces by Chanel Boutiques, NYC, Palm Beach FL, Dallas. Red necklace at Chanel Boutiques, Palm Beach FL, Chicago; I. Magnin. Bodysuit (about $290) and jacket (about $810) by Louis Dell'Olio for Anne Klein & Co. Bergdorf Goodman; Neiman Marcus; I. Magnin. The natural makeup: Velours #933 on lips and Delicat Blush #929 on cheeks, both by Christian Dior. Details, more stores, last pages.

Complementing the new day looks:
accessories that don't play it safe

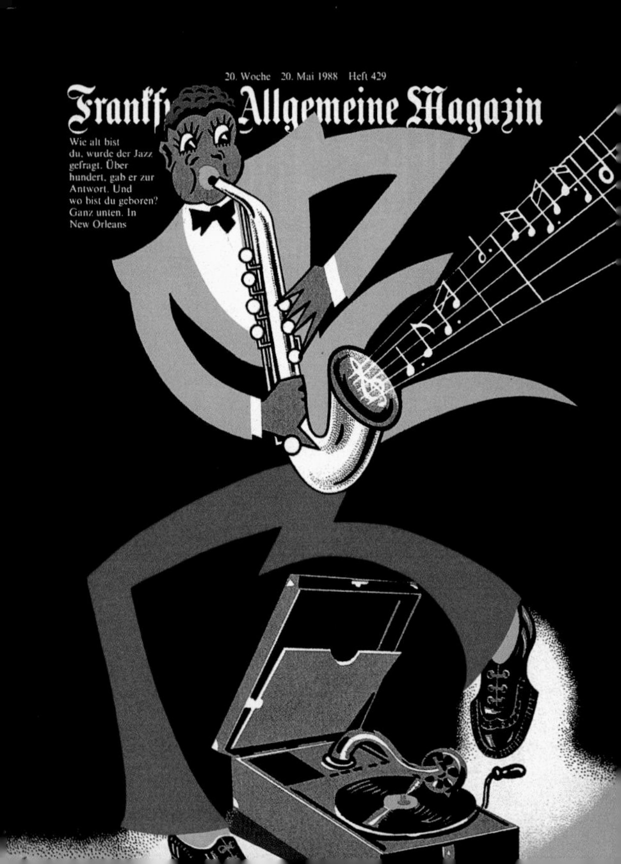

20. Woche 20. Mai 1988 Heft 429
Frankf Allgemeine Magazin
Wie alt bist du, wurde der Jazz gefragt. Über hundert, gab er zur Antwort. Und wo bist du geboren? Ganz unten. In New Orleans

THE FAZ MAGAZIN THE WEEKEND MAGAZINE OF THE *FRANKFURTER ALLGEMEINE ZEITUNG—FAZ* FOR SHORT—HAS BEEN PUBLISHED NOW FOR OVER TEN YEARS. IT'S A NEWSPAPER SUPPLEMENT, BUT ONE THAT HAS SET THE HIGHEST STANDARDS SINCE ITS FIRST ISSUE, LAUNCHED IN MAY 1980. SINCE THEN, NEW DESIGN TRENDS HAVE COME AND GONE, BUT THE MAGAZINE'S VISUAL APPEARANCE HAS HARDLY CHANGED. WHILE OTHER MAGAZINES (AND NOT ONLY NEWSPAPER SUPPLEMENTS) WERE REDESIGNED AND GIVEN FACE LIFTS—SOME SEVERAL TIMES—TO REFLECT CURRENT TRENDS, *FAZ MAGAZIN* STANDS OUT FOR ITS CONTINUITY. THAT IN ITSELF IS SOMETHING

of a curiosity. ■ The magazine's visual continuity has not made it lifeless and boring. Just compare a few editions from different years, and you'll see that it has changed with the times—though in design and layout all 550 issues of the *FAZ Magazin* appear fresh even today. None of them give you the feeling that you are looking at something "historical." *FAZ Magazin*'s art director, Hans-Georg Pospischil, in particular is responsible for this continuity. He worked for the magazine in its early stages as an assistant to Willy Fleckhaus, and he has been responsible for its visual appearance since 1983. He has remained true to Fleckhaus's spirit, but has infused it with his own personal style: "If Fleckhaus were to design a magazine today, it would definitely look different. If I were to design another magazine, it would also be something completely different. But both of these hypothetical magazines would reflect something that can only be called 'visual pleasure.'" ■ Examine the phenomenon of *FAZ Magazin*, and certain terms readily come to mind to capture its specialness: "continuity" is one of them; "pleasure" another. Pleasure not only for the beholder, but obviously also for those who make the magazine. "This kind of magazine you make primarily for yourself, and you just hope that the reader will like it. We're really lucky that our readers seem to like it so far, and we're also very lucky that we're working for a very liberal publishing house. Nobody has ever tried to interfere with our work." For *FAZ*, one of Germany's largest dailies, such a liberal stance has paid dividends. Assisted by its supplement, *FAZ* has increased its renown and its circulation. For the magazine there's another advantage. It does not have to push its sales every week on the newsstands with an aggressive cover; it has its own, independent circulation. However, this can sometimes be a drawback: There's no direct measure of its readership. Letters to the editor and the flourishing sale of advertising space, however, provide sufficient feedback. Obviously, design and content are both on the mark. ■ For the *FAZ Magazin* and its producers, further acknowledgment comes in the form of the many awards they've been honored with over the years. The fact that these awards were won both for design and for the quality of its reporting confirms another of the magazine's keywords: "balance," in the long run the secret of its success. Balance, not to be confused with lifeless consistency, between text and picture, between short and longer stories, between important news and endearing trifles, between well-known columns and surprising leads. ■ According to Hans-Georg Pospischil, only equal partnership of editorial and layout allows them every week to put together this wide range of contributions. It's a teamwork based on mutual trust in, and respect for, each other's work, which has been built up over many years. "I don't believe that an inserted title or other clever graphic device make the text more interesting. I'm against making the text too 'simple,' because if you do that, you give layout and design priority over the text's contents and the skills of its author. And that can only be wrong in the long run." And: "It's not part of my job to turn readers into seers!" Unusual statements for an art director, given that today, in many "Zeitgeist" and life-style magazines, the written contributions threaten to disappear altogether. But it is also a surprising confession for a man whose own magazine has won renown for its layout, using both "big" and "small" colors. Both the visual fireworks—with their fascinating,

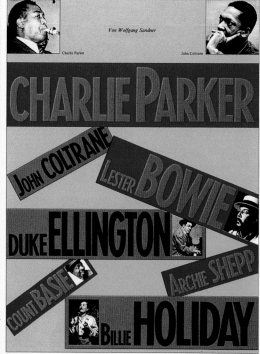

(ALL IMAGES) ART DIRECTOR: HANS-GEORG POSPISCHIL ■ (PREVIOUS SPREAD, LEFT; ABOVE, AND OPPOSITE) DATE: MAY 1988 ■ (OPPOSITE BOTTOM) PHOTOGRAPHER: FRANK HORVAT DATE: NOVEMBER 1984

breathtaking, but always witty pictures—and the plain, tranquil text pages, where nothing is allowed to distract the reader's concentration, belong together. Together they make up the suspense which in turn makes *FAZ* readers reach for the magazine every Friday, despite the fact that the magazine has not changed its visual appearance substantially in the past ten years. ■ It's amazing how many elements have survived since then without damage and seemingly without ageing. From the design of the title to the list of contents, with its legendary 1:1 reproduction of a single detail taken from one of the magazine's features. From the culture calendar and the regular columns to the riddles, found on the last page under the title "Matchbox" ever since the first issue, with a different, extraordinary drawing of a matchbox in every issue. The goal of this continuity: Readers should feel at home in "their" magazine. That such a rigid framework still offers enough space for experiments and visual adventures is proven in every new issue by the layout and design team under Hans-Georg Pospischil, but also—in their own way—by the editorial team under Thomas Schroeder. ■

Suspense is evoked not only by the ever-changing mixture of old elements, but also by the selection of topics. News is not the magazine's main pillar, and it's easy to see why, since production time runs to six weeks. A reflected form of current affairs reporting is the main priority. "We try to capture the spirit of the times, but we also try to define it, in our text and in our pictures. A tilted picture doesn't make a story better, nor does it turn the story into something more up-to-date." The visual realization follows a logic determined by its subject; it is never an end unto itself. "Graphic experiments, by all means, yes; but only when the story itself suggests them, not just because it's trendy," says Pospischil. "It is important to me to present the story, the photographs, and the illustrations, which all call for a certain form of presentation in their own right. Sometimes this may mean a lot of experimentation with layout, sometimes only a little bit, and sometimes none at all." ■ This calls for "a large amount of humility" toward photography and illustration. "In contrast to many magazines," says Pospischil, "we continue to cultivate this kind of layout." ■

OUT OF HOT, INTO THE COOL

MINTON'S PLAYHOUSE

Christian Lacroix: Die Phantasie feiert ein Fest

ART DIRECTOR:

HANS-GEORG POSPISCHIL

PHOTOGRAPHER:

SARAH MOON

DATE:

JUNE 1988

ART DIRECTOR:

HANS-GEORG POSPISCHIL

ILLUSTRATOR:

BRAD HOLLAND

DATE:

MARCH 1988

DER

Teuer! Feuer! Blut! Gut! Das Phantom schreit es in die Nacht. Schon bricht ein Brand aus, wachsen Mißgeburten, entstehen Zwietracht und Aufruhr. Zeter und Mordio. Feurio. Holdrio. Owy, owy, klagt Reineke de Vos, als litte er unter Tarzans Jahrhundertgebrüll. Schweigen ist Gold. Welch falscher Schluß. Schrei, wenn Du kannst, Frau, Mann. Zu schreien wie am Spieß, wie der Teufel oder der Zahnbrecher und das zur rechten Zeit, schafft Luft. Explosion ist allemal besser als Implosion. Das dümmste Vieh schreit am lautesten. Und die am lautesten schreien, haben den kleinsten Mut.

SCHREI

(ALL IMAGES, THIS SPREAD) ART DIRECTOR: HANS-GEORG POSPISCHIL DATE: FEBRUARY 1987 ■ (TOP LEFT) ILLUSTRATOR: EDVARD MUNCH ■ (TOP RIGHT) ILLUSTRATORS: SEYMOUR CHWAST, FRED MARSHALL, GÜNTHER KIESER, FRANCES JETTER ■ (BOTTOM LEFT) PHOTOGRAPHER: HEINZ EDELMANN ■ (BOTTOM RIGHT) ILLUSTRATORS: HANS HILLMANN, PETER BROOKES, PHIL HULING, EDVARD MUNCH

DIZZY GILLESPIE

Von Ulrich Olshausen
Foto Serge Cohen

JEANS

Von Dorothea Friedrich
Illustrationen Valentine Edelmann
Foto Susan Lamér

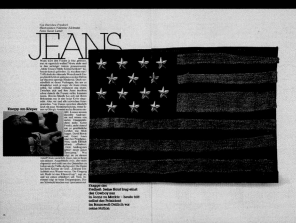

Knapp am Körper

Flagge der Freiheit. Seine Haut trug einst der Cowboy aus. In Jeans zu Märkte – heute tritt selbst der Präsident im Blauweiß-Drillich vor seine Nation

Sichel am Horizont. Heutzutage lieben es auch im roten Osten die Teenies – sie schweben auf den blauen Tuch

Schmal an den Hüften

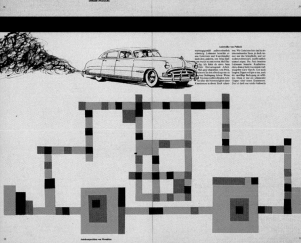

DameN WaGen

(ALL IMAGES, THIS SPREAD) ART DIRECTOR: HANS-GEORG POSPISCHIL ■ (OPPOSITE TOP) PHOTOGRAPHER: SERGE COHEN
FEBRUARY 1984 ■ (CENTER) ILLUSTRATOR: VALENTINE EDELMANN PHOTOGRAPHER: SUSAN LAMÉR ■ (BOTTOM) DATE:
MARCH 1988 ■ (THIS PAGE, LEFT) PHOTOGRAPHER: SERGE COHEN DATE: FEBRUARY 1984 ■ (RIGHT) DATE: MARCH 1988

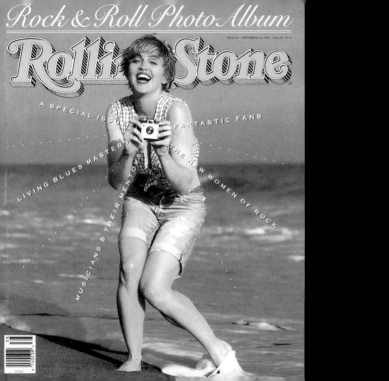

Rock & Roll Photo Album

Rolling Stone

ISSUE No. / SEPTEMBER 21st, 1989 / UK £1.90 • $2.95

A SPECIAL ISSUE

FANTASTIC FANS

LIVING BLUES MASTERS

THE NEW WOMEN OF ROCK

MUSICIANS & THEIR MENTORS

ROLLING STONE

"ROLLING STONE IS NOT JUST ABOUT MUSIC, BUT ALSO ABOUT THE THINGS AND ATTITUDES THAT THE MUSIC EMBRACES. . . . TO DESCRIBE IT ANY FURTHER WOULD BE DIFFICULT WITHOUT SOUNDING LIKE BULLSHIT, AND BULLSHIT IS LIKE GATHERING MOSS." ☐ THOSE TOUGH-SOUNDING, COUNTERCULTURE WORDS WERE WRITTEN IN THE PREMIER ISSUE OF *ROLLING STONE* MAGAZINE (NOVEMBER 6, 1967) BY ITS 21-YEAR-OLD PUBLISHER, JANN WENNER. FORTY THOUSAND COPIES WERE PRINTED; SIXTEEN THOUSAND COPIES WERE SOLD, AT 25 CENTS APIECE. ☐ THE BERKELEY COLLEGE DROPOUT BORROWED $7,500 FROM FRIENDS AND FAMILY TO FOUND

Rolling Stone because he believed rock 'n' roll was the voice of a new generation. So did Ralph Gleason, America's preeminent music critic and Wenner's mentor, who agreed to cofound a magazine championing the new music of the Beatles, Bob Dylan, the Grateful Dead, Jimi Hendrix, Janis Joplin, the Jefferson Airplane, and the Rolling Stones. With Gleason on the masthead, Wenner knew he would also have an easier time gaining the respect of the music industry, and getting advertising. ■ If its soul was in San Francisco's Haight Ashbury, *Rolling Stone*'s appearance was more businesslike; only its circus-poster logo (designed by Rick Griffin) betrayed its psychedelic roots. Inside, Times Roman type, rules between columns and borders around every page gave it an orderly and unique style, thanks to *Ramparts* production director, John Williams, who designed the first few issues without pay. ■ Robert Kingsbury, a sculptor, art teacher, and Wenner's future brother-in-law, soon became the second art director. Amid a changing staff of free-lancers, volunteers, and groupies, Kingsbury (1967–1973) was one of the few loyal workers. His preference for sculpture was reflected in his handling of art: silhouetted photographs (rarely used at the time, except by George Lois at *Esquire*) stood out in relief from the columns of type. ■ Another distinctive design feature (since issue number 8) was its quarterfold format, which not only gave the magazine two covers, in effect, but a smaller size more in line with most magazines and unlike other tabloids. (The quarterfold came to an end in late 1972 to accommodate rising ad pages, since printers could not quarterfold more than 80 pages.) ■ By 1970, *Rolling Stone* was selling over 60,000 copies per issue. Its focus had broadened, too, from music

and the alternative life-styles of the younger generation to the politics of the Vietnam War and such establishment foes as Richard Nixon and the Nuclear Regulatory Commission. The young crew of New Journalists—Joe Eszterhas, David Felton, Howard Kohn—were joined by their better-known peers: William Burroughs, Anthony Burgess, Truman Capote, Tom Wolfe, and, of course, Hunter S. Thompson. During the 1970s *Rolling Stone* published some of the toughest, most honest journalism in America. As Wenner understood so well, his audience wanted no lies, no bullshit: "Tell it like it is," they demanded. The piercing prose was matched by the razor-sharp illustrations of such artists as Ralph Steadman (recommended to Wenner by Hunter Thompson) and David Levine. ■ And then came Annie Leibovitz, who was only 20 years old and inexperienced when Wenner hired her in 1970. Like his decision to give free reign to gonzo journalist Thompson, Wenner's instinct to give Leibovitz a chance altered the fate of the magazine. When asked what is *Rolling Stone*'s contribution to graphic design, former art director Roger Black's immediate response was: "Annie Leibovitz. That was its number one distinction. More than fifty percent of what made it great was because of her." ■ There was great writing too, and over the last 20 years many of the best graphic designers passed through its offices. Mike Salisbury joined in August of 1973, staying about a year. He was instrumental in bringing illustrations to the pages, even caricaturing the rock stars its readers idolized. Terry Lane's tenure (1974–1976) saw the magazine grow to a circulation of 400,000 and beyond. Lane did a facelift of the logo, producing a cleaner, flatter appearance, tidied up the table of

(PREVIOUS SPREAD, LEFT) ART DIRECTOR: FRED WOODWARD PHOTOGRAPHER: HERB RITTS DATE: SEPTEMBER 1989 ■ (ABOVE) ART DIRECTOR: ROGER BLACK PHOTOGRAPHER: BARRY LEVINE DATE: APRIL 1977

contents for better readability, and replaced the Times Roman department type with Korinna. Headline type grew more varied and playful. ■ Covers became airier, due mainly to the use of white backgrounds—a trait that has continued to the present. By this time the cover's purpose was to sell magazines, so "celebrities, anything sexy at all, and big cover lines were part of the directive in executing the cover," remembers Lane. ■ The art director who had the most profound effect on *Rolling Stone* was Roger Black (1976–1978). He gave the magazine its own typeface (adapted from Jenson), which is used to this day in the departments. Most important, he treated each feature distinctly, using type and design appropriate to the subject. Two examples: An article on the group Kiss, pagan gods to their adolescent fans, featured gothic type—fitting for their Dark Ages style. Another feature on the power struggle at *New York* magazine is laid out like its subject and uses its headline type. ■ Black also turned "Random Notes" from an unending string of type into a photo-filled column worth noting, redesigned the table of contents (twice), and switched features text from Times Roman to Cloister. ■ During Mary Shanahan's term (1979–1982), *Rolling Stone*

was reduced in size from newspaper to magazine proportions. New Wave hit, producing asymmetrical layouts, dozens of type fonts, and tinted backgrounds. The magazine had a fever, due in no small measure to an ailing music industry in decline. Personality profiles moved up front, music went to the back of the book. ■ In 1982, Derek Ungless was hired to bring order to what Wenner realized was a "messy" magazine. Franklin Gothic became the headline type, rules were eliminated between columns, a coated paper stock was selected, and covers by Richard Avedon recaptured some of the startling portraiture it possessed in Leibovitz's day. ■ By 1985, circulation had reached 1 million and Wenner was trying to convince advertisers that their perception of *Rolling Stone*'s readers as hippies did not fit with reality. Those faithful readers of yesteryear today comprise only a small fraction of the magazine's circulation—now up to 1.2 million. The former counterculture organ is "the *Wall Street Journal* of rock 'n' roll," in the words of its own group publisher Leslie Zeifman. Ad revenues may prove his point: *Rolling Stone* earns an average of $32,000 for every ad page it sells. ■ Wenner created a new type of magazine for a new generation of readers. He under-

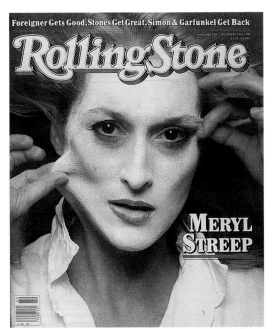

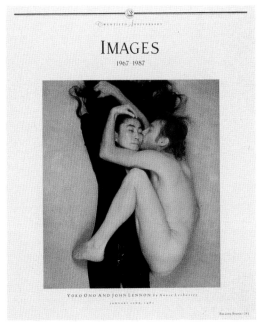

(LEFT) ART DIRECTOR: ROGER BLACK PHOTOGRAPHER: ANNIE LEIBOVITZ DATE: OCTOBER 1981 ■
(RIGHT) ART DIRECTOR: FRED WOODWARD PHOTOGRAPHER: ANNIE LEIBOVITZ DATE: DECEMBER 1987

stood what his readers wanted, because their fantasies—to meet John Lennon and Mick Jagger—were his fantasies. ■ "He could call a popular moment in time, he understood what people would respond to," recalls Roger Black. "And he found writers who were right for that moment." Wenner's instincts for the right story at the right moment often meant round-the-clock hours for his staff. In 1977, for example, issue 248 had already been put to bed when on August 16 the world learned that Elvis Presley had died. With only four days left, a wholly new issue devoted to the King was written, edited, designed, and printed. *Rolling Stone*'s tribute appeared the same week as *Time*'s and other newsweeklies. Sales were far above 1 million. ■ But as disco and punk arrived, Wenner ruled in absentia, pursuing Hollywood, *Look* and *Us* magazines, and the friendship of the celebrities he put on his covers. ■ When Fred Woodward became *Rolling Stone*'s current art director in 1987, the magazine once again shone with some of its former brilliance. "It may have its best art director yet," admits Black, who was Woodward's role model when the young designer was directing his first magazine, *City of Memphis*, in the late 1970s. "I was stealing from Roger Black as much as possi-

ble," recalls Woodward. ■ Woodward's magazine design is exceptional in the same way Wenner's career as editor has been: He has an uncommon ability to match the right illustrator or photographer with the right assignment. A photographer himself, Woodward appreciates the artist's contribution, which he uses to great effect not only on opening spreads, but on subsequent pages. His treatment of decks, callouts, and captions is always refreshing as well. ■ Wenner's renewed interest in his 23-year-old enterprise has also returned some of the journalistic edge to it: investigative pieces on crack, AIDS, and teen suicide; interviews with people who matter, such as Sierra Club's David Brower; and the irreverent "Irrational Affairs" column of P. J. O'Rourke—all masterfully cultivated by executive editor Bob Wallace. ■ The only quality that has always set *Rolling Stone* apart from the pack was the free-wheeling freedom of experimentation given to both writers and art directors. That's what Roger Black valued most: "Experimentation allowed for something totally surprising to happen," he says. And although he readily admits that some of the layouts were failures, there were great successes, too, which would never have happened without that freedom. ■

FASHION BY PATTI O'BRIEN

HOT COOL

Photographs by

HERB RITTS

Stephanie Seymour
She's a free spirit, a
flower child. She just
did that ankle tattoo a
week ago. It works
on her. — HERB RITTS

(ALL IMAGES, THIS SPREAD) ART DIRECTOR: FRED WOODWARD ■ (THIS PAGE) PHOTOGRAPHER: HERB RITTS DATE: 1989 ■
(OPPOSITE, TOP) PHOTOGRAPHER: JAY LEVITEN DATE: 1987 ■ (BOTTOM) PHOTOGRAPHER: ANDREW MACPHERSON DATE: 1990

The King Is Gone
But Not Forgotten

*T*he world is a less diverse place for want of old Elvis Presley. All of rock & roll's race threat and glorious noise reibonded to he his whisk snarl, his cocked hip, his smoldering, wicked gaze. He was a rebel hell who sang loads, who changed upon and style and sexuality, so promiscuhly forbidden unease — take broke every rule and laws aand. Those too young to remember Elvis... or to remember his music inward the blurred and remote presence he became in his later years — may consider what all the age at say about. These rare quarter, taken by Atlanta photographer Jay Leviton during a series of shoots in Jackson the Florida and New Orleans in August 1956, offer some idea. Here is Elvis at twenty-one — already triumphant but not yet stilled in his his fame — living the fast lanta for a two ago amid the urban sylvani chapter of his Elvis. Ten years after his death — in August 16th, 1977, at the appalling age of forty-two — this snapshot ally series remains the arrival vaulter figure of rock & roll music. Still the King. Still deeply missed.

PHOTOGRAPHS BY JAY LEVITON

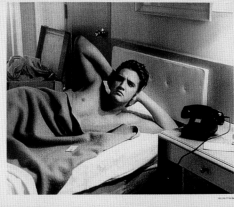

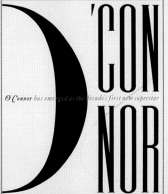

SIN
EAD
O
'CON
NOR

After weathering some hard and haunting losses, Sinéad

O'Connor has emerged as the decade's first new superstar

PHOTOGRAPHED BY ANDREW MACPHERSON

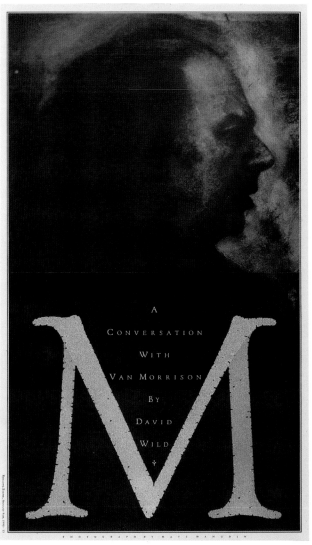

HOT COVER Inspiring lust in audiences, Sylvester Stallone and gossip columnists alike, starlet Uma Thurman tries to cope with all the attention while keeping her sense of Uma··· *Photographs by* MATTHEW ROLSTON

A
CONVERSATION
WITH
VAN MORRISON
BY
DAVID
WILD

PHOTOGRAPH BY MATT MAHURIN

(ALL IMAGES, THIS SPREAD) ART DIRECTOR: FRED WOODWARD ■ (THIS PAGE, LEFT) PHOTOGRAPHER: MATTHEW ROLSTON DATE: 1989 ■ (RIGHT) ILLUSTRATOR: MATT MAHURIN DATE: 1990 ■ (OPPOSITE, TOP TO BOTTOM) PHOTOGRAPHER: MARK SELIGER DATE: 1991 ■ PHOTOGRAPHER: KURT MARKUS DATE: 1990 ■ PHOTOGRAPHER: MARK SELIGER DATE: 1989 ■ PHOTOGRAPHER: ALBERT WATSON DATE: 1990

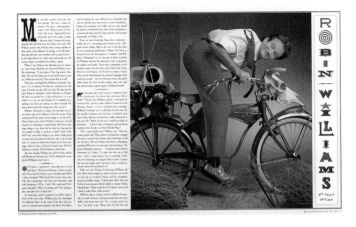

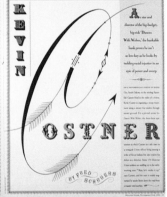

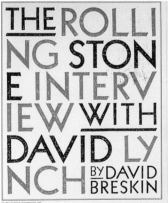

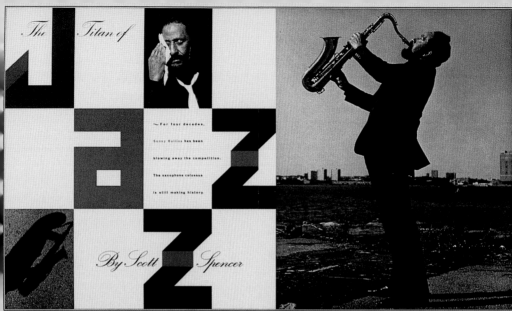

JAZZ

~ For four decades,
Sonny Rollins has been
blowing away the competition.
The saxophone colossus
is still making history

By Scott Spencer

The ROLLING STONE INTERVIEW

MARTIN Scorsese

MARTIN SCORSESE's apartment sits seventy-five
floors above midtown Manhattan and offers an imperial view that encompasses Central Park and the Upper
East Side, extending out toward the borough of
Queens, where Scorsese was born in 1942. The calm-
ing grays and blacks and whites of the living room's

By ANthony DeCurtis

(ALL IMAGES, THIS SPREAD) Art Director: FRED WOODWARD ■ (OPPOSITE, TOP) Photographer:
BRUCE WEBER Date: 1990 ■ (BOTTOM) Photographer: ALBERT WATSON Date: 1990 ■ (THIS
PAGE, LEFT) Photographer: HERB RITTS Date: 1987 ■ (RIGHT) Illustrator: ANITA KUNZ Date: 1987

FRANK ZACHARY IT WOULD BE INCONCEIVABLE NOW TO THINK OF STARTING A MAGAZINE SIMPLY ON FAITH IN A GOOD IDEA. FIRST, ONE MUST ISOLATE A MARKET; ONE THEN CONSTRUCTS A MAGAZINE TO FIT. BUT IN THE LATE 1940S, A DEDICATED THIRTY-FIVE-YEAR-OLD EDITOR WITH A GREAT DEAL OF CHARM COULD VERY WELL DECIDE IT WAS TIME FOR HIM TO START HIS OWN MAGAZINE. *PORTFOLIO*, SAID FRANK ZACHARY, WAS BORN OF NECESSITY—TODAY WE WOULD CALL THAT NECESSITY A WHIM. WHEN HE RAISED THE INITIAL $25,000 TO TEST HIS CONCEPT FOR A DESIGN MAGAZINE, AN AMERICAN VERSION OF *GRAPHIS*, HIS ONLY RATIONALE WAS THAT HE

felt like it. And he felt like it so much so that, with only three issues of *Portfolio* ever published, he had irreversibly affected the way Americans looked at magazines. ■ The seed money was invested in a mailing campaign designed by Paul Rand that yielded a handsome $150,000—a lot, considering the investment, but not quite enough to hire a real staff. Working out of his apartment in Larchmont and phone booths around the public libraries where he did his research, Zachary gathered the most unconventional editorial material he could find. His loot—manuscripts, illustrations, faded documents, avant-garde experiments with early xerography—found its way into the office of Alexey Brodovitch, then art director of *Harper's Bazaar*, who would lay it all out in the evening. The result was a publication so visually compelling that the simple turning of a page became an event. ■ To find back issues of *Portfolio* in New York City, one has to go to Room 308 of the Mid-Manhattan branch of the public library—in the very place, probably, where Zachary spent time poring over obscure art books. There, in this sanctuary that smells of mildew and wood polish, one can recapture the sense of discovery *Portfolio* must have provoked when it came out in 1949. But for those who feel nostalgic in the presence of beauty, like I did when handling those frail originals, Zachary, still prolific at 77, has something to say: "When I have done an issue, it's gone! I never look back. The fun is doing it. I don't keep any old magazines around for the record." ■ When *Portfolio* ran out of money, he went straight to *Holiday*, first as picture editor, soon as art director. He stayed for 13 years, during which he turned a homey travel magazine into a glorious symbol of American perspicacity, wit, and inquisitiveness.

"As an art director, I always had total control over what I was doing. But, I imagine, if you had a strong-minded editor, you could feel. . . very uncomfortable." Frank Zachary, art director emeritus, presently editor-in-chief of *Town & Country*, inducted in 1990 into the Art Directors Hall of Fame, would not do very well in today's competitive job market. There is very little candid benevolence left between editors and art directors who both want to be hailed as strong-minded. ■ But was it ever a benevolent time? Was the Depression, which forced 17-year-old Zachary to fend for himself, a less aggressive period in history? With only a high school diploma, he landed a job in a small Pittsburgh weekly magazine, the *Bulletin Index*, and on the strength of some poetry and short stories he had written as a teenager, was given a camera and send out to do picture stories. This unremarkable apprenticeship became enlightening when novelist John O'Hara was hired as editor and young Zachary, the budding writer, got to watch his boss at the typewriter turn out impeccable *New Yorker* short stories in one sitting. The repeated sight of this feat cooled Zachary's own literary ambition but gave him an aesthetic point of reference he would never forget. From then on, he seems to have been graced with a keen sophistication. ■ "Although I am not wealthy myself—I come from the wrong side of the tracks—I live vicariously the life of the rich," says Zachary from his suburban-looking corner office at *Town & Country*. "It's as simple as that. It just happens that my fantasy coincides with their reality." If he is right—if in fact the rich live the dreams those less fortunate conjure up for them—then they should indeed be happy with what Zachary has in store for them. He does *Town & Country* the way he used to do *Holiday*, as if his life was one of leisure, and nothing was going to make him work too hard. "My whole credo is extreme simplicity. I always dispensed with ornamentation," he says. "I try to dish up material the way a good Italian chef dispenses his dishes, with an absolute minimum of handling between the raw material and the plate." His ingredients are as superb as his technique. He only works with the best people (when asked what the secret of his success was, he replied "a good assistant"), and the names of the contributors who will forever be associated with his career reads like a guest list at some great event hosted by an enlightened art patron. Indeed, doing a magazine is not unlike giving a party, and an editor-in-chief has to be a good master of ceremonies. Zachary's hospitality was extended to Arnold Newman, Henri Cartier-Bresson, Slim Aarons, Norman Parkinson, and Victor Skrebneski among the photographers; and Ronald Searle, George Guisti, André François, and Edward Gorey among the illustrators. "I used illustrations—always satirically—to provide relief from the realism of the photographs," explains Zachary, who is always polite, but never dull. ■ Like Brodovitch, who had been his mentor, Zachary likens publication design to cinematography, where the pacing of visual sequences plays an all-important role. Art directing and editing are for him one and the same thing, as he keeps his eyes on both the visual and the verbal narration line. "You have to tell two stories, one in words, one in pictures, completely separate, but like railroad tracks, leading to the same place." In Zachary's world, that place lies in a realm beyond the obvious. The magazines he has been associated with have all had a cer-

(ABOVE) PUBLICATION: *PORTFOLIO* ■ (ALL IMAGES, OPPOSITE) PUBLICATION: *HOLIDAY* DATES: 1953-63

tain tone of social critique, an element which is harder and harder to come by, as the "old crew" of sophisticated contributors slowly fades away and a new generation tries to take its place. "Kids today are so serious," he complains. They are a little staid and easily intimidated, as this scene with a young photographer, reenacted by Zachary, seems to indicate: "Look," I say, "I assume that you are competent with a camera, but can you use the telephone?" "What do you mean, the telephone?" he asks. "Well," I explain, "we'll send you to England, and we want you to take a picture of the Duke of Devonshire, but we don't want him in his house, we want him out on a walk in the woods." "Do I do that?" "Yes, you do that!" "Oh, I thought you did that!" "No, that's your job!" ■ The young man, at the end of the scene, always gets up and never comes back. "They think their work is to take pictures," comments Zachary, "we ask them to create pictures." ■ Not all young people are afraid of the creative process. Dick Zimmerman, who was art director of *Status* magazine when Zachary was editing it, was half his boss's age when they started to work together in 1966. "We saw images the same way," Zimmerman says. "We saw eye to eye," affirms Zachary. They worked together 15 hours a day and couldn't wait to go to work in the morning. ■ For both of them, *Status* was their most creative magazine experience, but neither of them seem to have back issues stashed away. Somehow, for Zachary and his colleagues, a magazine is not a thing, it's a moment. For that reason, perhaps, he has been able to reach deeper into the imagination of his contemporaries—particularly the men—by providing an aesthetic that is warm without being maudlin, polished without being cool. ■

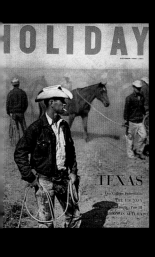

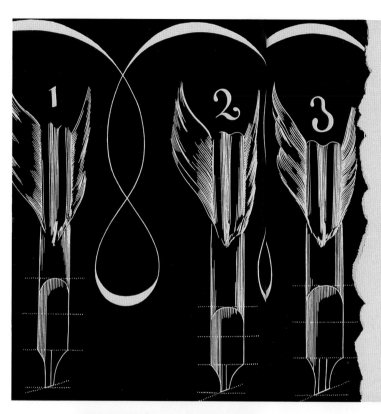

CALLIGRAPHY

Calligraphy, the art of fine writing, has in a decade's time sprung into full revival. Virtually extinguished in our mechanical age by typewriter and business machine, the penman's craft has traversed the cycles of neglect and research, and is now enjoying a spirited activity spiced with lively controversy. Here and abroad this revival is being stimulated by a widening group of scribes, artists, typographers and scholars who never doubted that man would resist the status of automaton and would eventually regain his old regard for handwriting—a simple craft which for a time had taken as normal its chronic state of decline. Calligraphy at the professional level is now gratefully accepted in the design of advertisements, books and book jackets.

In England, where the London *Daily Herald*'s national school handwriting contests have brought forth an annual Eton-Harrow competition, interest in calligraphy stems from the missionary work of such authorities as Edward Johnston, a matchless scribe whose *Writing & Illuminating & Lettering* remains the best contemporary work in the field after 36 years and 18 reprintings: Stanley Morison, historian of the London *Times*, paleographer, typographer and stimulator of dozens of major studies in

Remarkably lush pens from an 18th century French writing book. Chief & Écrire by M. Rodigas, these various styles of the past two thousand years have been written with the broad-edged pen, whether fashioned from reeds, quills or from steel. Two important virtues making both goodness and style accurate flocks and thints, but perfect taper gradations from thin to thick and back to thin, follows natural pressures.

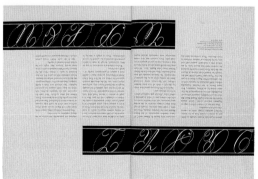

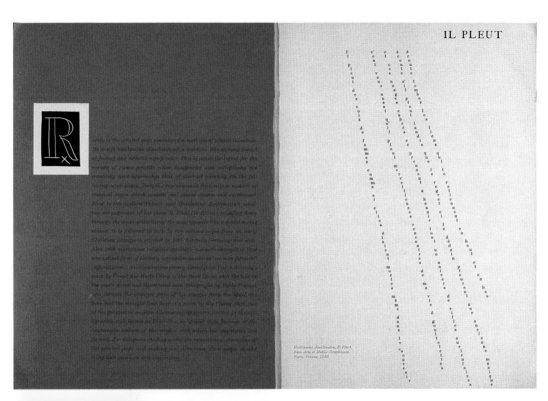

*Guillaume Apollinaire, Il Pleut,
from Arts et Métier Graphiques.
Paris, France, 1930.*

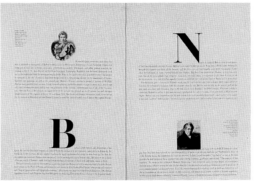

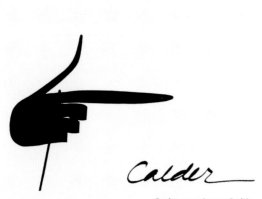

Calder

One afternoon several years ago Curt Valentin, head of New York's Bucholz Gallery, attended a cocktail party in the very modern apartment of critic James Johnson Sweeney. Setting his cocktail down on the table beside him, he looked through its glass top and saw a man asleep on the floor. That was his first sight of Alexander Calder, who has since become one of the prize performers in the Bucholz stable of noted artists.

Calder—"Sandy" to his friends— is a man who likes good food, good liquor and good times. His parties, given first in Parisian bistros, then in Third Avenue Italian restaurants in Manhattan, and more recently in his Roxbury, Conn. home, have been famous for two decades. Unfortunately, alcohol, even in mild doses, makes him sleepy. To counteract its effect at parties, he dances.

Top: Sheet metal finger points to Calder exhibition. Left: Sandy Calder himself, in turquoise cape and hood. Right: Calder's studio desk, a clutter of objects useful to Sandy: rolls of blueprints, a Picasso print, 1929 wood sculptures, a papier mache tree, and a Clorox box for filing correspondence. Photographs by Herbert Matter.

(PREVIOUS SPREAD, LEFT AND RIGHT) PUBLICATION: *PORTFOLIO* ■ (THIS PAGE) PUBLICATION: *PORTFOLIO* PHOTOGRAPHER: HERBERT MATTER ■ (OPPOSITE, LEFT TO RIGHT IN DESCENDING ORDER) PUBLICATION: *HOLIDAY* PHOTOGRAPHER: HENRI CARTIER-BRESSON ■ PUBLICATION: *HOLIDAY* PHOTOGRAPHER: HENRI CARTIER-BRESSON ■ PUBLICATION: *PORTFOLIO* PHOTOGRAPHER: BEN ROSE ■ PUBLICATION: *PORTFOLIO* PHOTOGRAPHER: BEN ROSE ■ PUBLICATION: *PORTFOLIO* PHOTOGRAPHER: BEN ROSE ■ PUBLICATION: *PORTFOLIO* ILLUSTRATOR: HENRI MATISSE ■ PUBLICATION: *PORTFOLIO* PHOTOGRAPHER: HERBERT MATTER ■ PUBLICATION: *PORTFOLIO* PHOTOGRAPHER: HENRI CARTIER-BRESSON ■ (FOLLOWING SPREAD) PUBLICATION: *TOWN & COUNTRY*

FRANCE & AMERICA

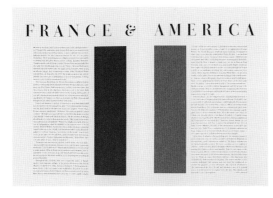

STEREOSCOPY

Anaglyphs reproduce stunning three dimensional effects. Pick up the eyeglasses and look.

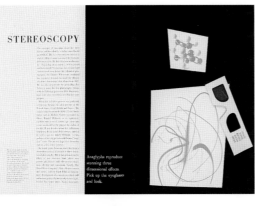

HOBO SIGNS

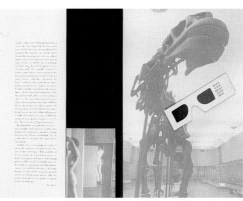

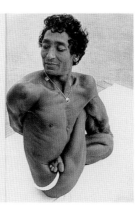

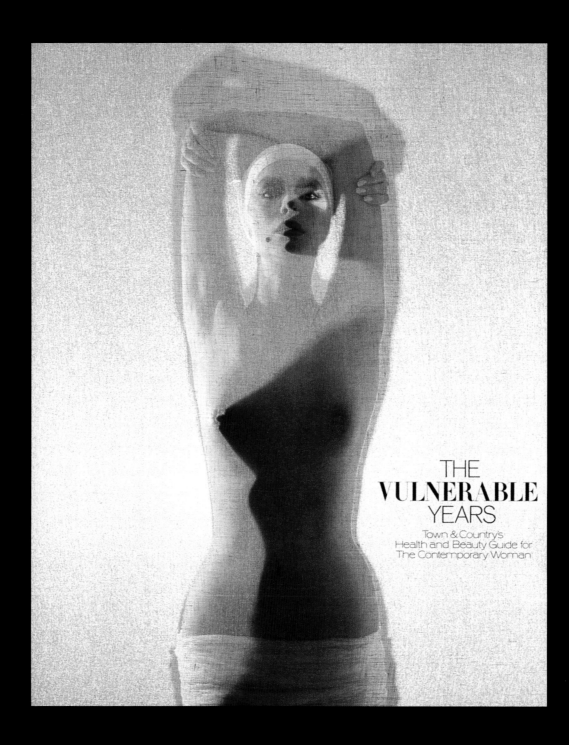

THE
VULNERABLE
YEARS

Town & Country's
Health and Beauty Guide for
The Contemporary Woman

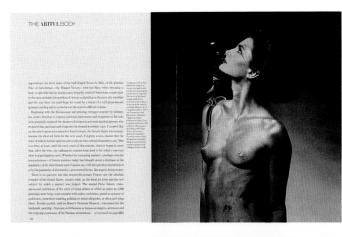

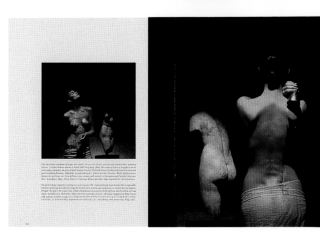

FABIEN BARON THE 18-YEAR-OLD FREE-LANCE PASTEUP BOY IN THE PRODUCTION DEPARTMENT WAS WATCHING ME AS IMPARTIALLY AS I HAD EVER BEEN WATCHED, HIS FACE EXPRESSIONLESS BUT HIS EYES LIT WITH THE CHILLING RIGHTEOUSNESS OF HIS YOUTH. HIS WAY OF LOOKING—EAGER, BEMUSED—IS WHAT WAS TO BECOME FABIEN BARON'S GREATEST ASSET, AS WELL AS THE TRADEMARK OF HIS VISUAL INQUIRY. I COULD TELL HE WASN'T BUYING MY LITTLE LECTURE ON HOW TO SPEC THE PERFECT PALE YELLOW (5 PERCENT YELLOW PLUS 2 PERCENT BLACK) TO GET A PARCHMENT LOOK, A QUESTION THAT, IN PARIS IN 1979, MIGHT HAVE BEEN THOUGHT TO HAVE SOME RELE-

vance to the magazine art staff that was supposed to implement my redesign. Hired from New York, I came with the aura of an American expert. I also could tell a smart kid when I saw one. As if to prove what was to be his main point—that an art director's most effective piece of business is to see, not to design—I walked to Baron's board, and still feeling the heat of his gaze upon me, gave this compelling teenager a break, my address in New York, and an invitation to take advantage of my guest room. The rest, as they say, is history. ■ Baron stayed in New York a couple of months, long enough to learn English, find his way in the subway, and take black-and-white pictures of the Bronx and Coney Island. He observed everything playfully, as he had before, but with a new kind of respect, as if he knew the place had for him tremendous potential. Under his whimsy was constant appraisal: To make it in New York, he would first go back to Paris to strengthen his skills; he would start a magazine design company with his long-time associate, his father. "I was twelve when my father, a newspaper art director, let me do my own layouts. He always had a lot of free-lance work. . . always changing clients, always on the move," says Baron. Then he adds, like a son would, "He was like me." ■ As it turned out, the likeness meant that the son would not follow in his father's steps. Fabien Baron, unlike his father, Marc Baron, chose to be a trail-blazer, somebody who would "push the boundaries, and widen the territory for others to have more room to move about." To do that, he eventually left France for good and, in 1983, came back to New York. He worked with graphic designer Carl Lehmann-Haupt, turning out luxurious catalogs for Cannon Mills, before joining Condé Nast, first at *Self*, later at *GQ*. Of his

time there, he only has words for Alexander Liberman, a man he respects for the very reasons others despise him. "He doesn't give a damn about design, but readers don't give a damn about design either," says Baron. "Liberman has done beautiful layouts with fabulous pictures for decades—now he wants to try the next level. Everybody is bellyaching about it, but he is right. What's the point of doing a commercial magazine, if it doesn't sell?" Fascinated by Liberman, yet turned off by his attitude—"when I am ready to sell something, I'll sell real estate"—Baron left Condé Nast for his first position as art director, teaming up with editor Betsy Carter in 1986 to create *New York Woman*, a new title originally launched by *Esquire* and now owned by American Express. He made this assignment the first stop on an award-winning career distinguished for its new, unconventional approaches. ■ While at *New York Woman*, he free-lanced for Barneys New York. It is during this time that he developed his signature style black-and-white photographs by the likes of Steven Meisel, Peter Lindbergh, Jean François Lepage, Javier Vallhonrat; bold typography using a limited number of faces, either Franklin Gothic, Didot, or Bodoni; and a color scheme featuring dark tones, particularly his much-imitated 100 percent cyan plus 60 percent black. "Why do people always talk about my use of type?" asks Baron. "I am not a typographer, I am an art director. The picture dictates what the type should be, I don't! I spend hours on the phone with photographers, and five minutes doing a layout. It's funny, I am a visual artist, yet most of the real work I do is invisible in the end." ■ Before a shoot, he gets involved with every detail—which film to use, which prop is exactly best, the weather, the time

PHOTOGRAPHER: WAYNE MASER, COURTESY *INTERVIEW*, APRIL 1990, INGRID SISCHY, EDITOR-IN-CHIEF

of day, alternate locations, the clothes, the makeup, even the brand name of the gels and hair products. "And what about the models?" I ask. "You seem to cast girls like Kristy, Linda, or Naomi, who are high-strung." He looks surprised. "The tension is in the picture, not the models. Still images, when they are powerful, have a disquieting quality because they intersect before and after. When I look at a picture, I always wonder what will happen next." Baron's love of drama—and his audacious use of raw sexual imagery—is symptomatic of a generation for whom rage and fear are an everyday reality. Concealing violence, he believes, is more destructive than expressing it. ■ In 1988 Franca Sozzani called him for *Vogue Italia,* and he accepted the position in Milan. Thanks to a very supportive editorial team, he was able to execute clearly his design philosophy. He devised there his prototypical one-word title page opposite a single provocative image. "I wanted to invent a new way of seeing, and a new way of reading. I wanted to create new points of reference," he says. When trying to explain himself, Baron is likely to talk about MTV, but in fact his discourse is subconsciously influenced by semiology, considered here an

obscure academic pursuit but popular in France, where it has shaped thinking about language for the last twenty years. "Everything is a sign. Images are words, and words are images," muses Baron, showing a very Gallic concern for form over content. "Look," he exclaimes, pointing at the comical sight of two self-important miniature Pekingese dogs strolling on the sidewalk, apparently unattended. Fascinated by this disarming display of arrogance, Baron is taking in every detail on the scene. But for him the overall image is incomplete unless he can find the word for it. I watch him as he rummages through his off-color French vocabulary for the right caption. "Petites merdes!" he declares, at last, somewhat affectionately. Thus named, the little dogs move on. ■ This was an example of the all-important difference between what the semiologists call a signified—in this case the dogs—and the signifier—the little "merdes." Baron's pesky juxtaposition of words and images reminded me of his layouts, with their uneasy, salacious humor. "The shorter the word," he continues, "the stronger the communication. With only one word, you can say so much. Why do magazine editors always feel that they have

Interview's
bouquet
for you

PHOTOGRAPHER: ERNST HAAS/MAGNUM, COURTESY *INTERVIEW*, FEB 1990, INGRID SISCHY, EDITOR-IN-CHIEF

to pun when they write titles? Why don't they say what's on their minds—in contrast, I love the economy of newspaper headlines." ■ Like most art directors today, Baron is trying to deal with the fact that readers don't have time to read. According to him, they don't have time to see either. But do they have time to listen? Having blurred the difference between words and images, he now wants to re-create on paper the experience of hearing. He wants to make music. "Not rock 'n' roll. . . classical music." That's how he defines his experiment with *Interview.* "I took a melody, like for example the theme of roses in the Valentine issue, and played variations on it. I like contrasts, modulations, sequences. I love to deconstruct mental and visual clichés into their textural components. Is it too esoteric? I don't think so. The other night I saw a Levis commercial on TV that was a total rip-off. Same abstract black-and-white image, same typeface, same color scheme as my latest layouts. I loved it. Now don't tell me that Levis, this American icon, is too esoteric." ■ Wayne Maser, a fashion photographer who often collaborates with Baron, says that, apart from Liberman, Baron is the only art director whose editing is flawless. And that's an endorsement.

As for Liberman, he calls Baron "very talented," but in his coded language, that could mean anything. Glenn O'Brien, a writer who has teamed up with Baron on the Barneys account and other projects, noticed that he reads everything, and makes astute suggestions every step of the way. "So he threatens editors who don't have an authentic vision." And indeed, on the subject of Fabien Baron, some editors who have worked with him chose not to comment. ■ "I know in a way that people expect me to fail, but I'll never be bored and I'll go on. Everything is a source of inspiration for me. As a kid, I was always alone, 'lost in dreams,' as my parents used to say. But I wasn't lost in dreams, I was lost in observations. Just look around, at the pavement, at the salt shaker, at a car in the street. I love details. They make the difference. I am a pain in the ass for that. I have an opinion about everything. Your haircut, for example. . . ." He was scrutinizing the top of my head like some heat-seeking device—"I know what you should do about its color, its texture, and how much gel you should use, and why." ■ I was tempted to ask him what to do about my hair, but I was too mesmerized to interrupt him. It was a treat to watch him watch me. ■

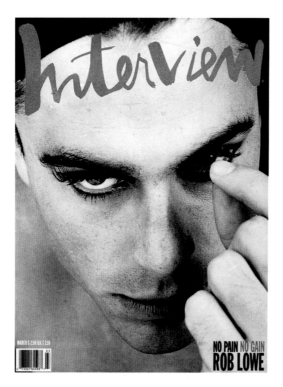

(ALL IMAGES, THIS SPREAD) COURTESY *INTERVIEW*, INGRID SISCHY, EDITOR-IN-CHIEF ■ (ABOVE LEFT)
PHOTOGRAPHER: WAYNE MASER DATE: MARCH 1990 ■ (ABOVE RIGHT) PHOTOGRAPHER: HERB RITTS DATE: JUNE 1990 ■
(OPPOSITE, LEFT AND RIGHT) PHOTOGRAPHER: WAYNE MASER DATE: MARCH 1990 ■ (REMAINING IMAGES FROM LEFT
TO RIGHT IN DESCENDING ORDER) PHOTOGRAPHER: ALBERT WATSON DATE: FEBRUARY 1990 ■ PHOTOGRAPHER: ALBERT
WATSON DATE: JULY 1990 ■ PHOTOGRAPHER: HERB RITTS DATE: JUNE 1990 ■ PHOTOGRAPHER: PHILIP DIXON DATE:
MAY 1990 ■ PHOTOGRAPHER: WAYNE MASER DATE: JUNE 1990 ■ PHOTOGRAPHER: FABRIZIO FERRI DATE: APRIL 1990

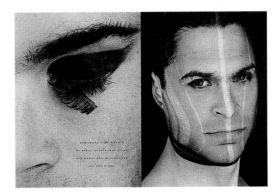

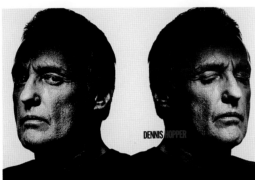

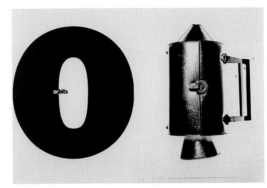

(ALL IMAGES) PUBLICATION: *VOGUE ITALIA* ■ (ABOVE) PHOTOGRAPHER: J. VALHONRAT ■ (OPPOSITE) PHOTOGRAPHER: STEVEN MEISEL DATE: 1989

VOGUE

ITALIA

NOV.
1988
N.463

gilet giacche cappotti pelliccia è inverno

GILET GENNY

(ALL IMAGES) PUBLICATION: *VOGUE ITALIA* ■ (OPPOSITE, TOP TO BOTTOM) ■ PHOTOGRAPHER:
JEAN-FRANCOIS LEPAGE ■ PHOTOGRAPHER: JOHN ZIMMERMAN/AGENZIA PIGNOTTI DATE: 1989 ■
PHOTOGRAPHER: SATOSHI SAIKUSA DATE: 1989 (ABOVE) PHOTOGRAPHER: STEVEN MEISEL DATE: 1988

WALTER BERNARD & MILTON GLASER

"THEY ARE CALLING WALTER." ☐ IN THE MAGAZINE WORLD, "CALLING WALTER" MEANS BIG TIME. IT SIGNALS PROFOUND AND IRREVERSIBLE CHANGES, AND A QUALITATIVE SHIFT SO FAR-REACHING THAT IT WILL BE FELT BEFORE IT IS SEEN. ON THE OTHER HAND, "THEY ARE NOT PLANNING TO CALL WALTER" MEANS THAT ALL THOSE RUMORS ABOUT TAKING SOME MAJOR STEPS TO UPDATE THE PUBLICATION ARE NONSENSE, AND THAT YOUR SLIGHTLY INEFFICIENT, YET ENDEARING, WAY OF DOING THINGS IS SAFE. "WALTER CALLED"—THIS LAST VARIATION ON THE

theme—is equivalent to a job offer you can't refuse. ■ Who's Walter? He is Walter Bernard of WBMG, Inc., an editorial design and development firm, and the first consultant publishers and magazine executives call when they are thinking of either creating a new venture or reevaluating an existing one. In a business whose business is information, everybody wants to call Walter, because Walter knows everybody. But Walter is also partner to somebody everybody knows—even your mother. The MG in WBMG stands for Milton Glaser. ■ So why don't they call Milton? ■ Aware that his charismatic poise puts people on the spot, Milton Glaser compensates by being a warm and friendly presence. He is the man whose generosity of spirit has secured for him, among his students—and everybody who meets him instantly becomes a student—the nickname of "Uncle Milt." But this casual demeanor only adds to the legend. Under his Cheshire cat's grin, he bears alone the burden of his wisdom. "Magazines are highly personalized vehicles," says Glaser, picking words carefully and enunciating them as only an epicurean would, "but nowadays magazines are owned by corporations, and corporations would rather strengthen the structure than invest in the singular vision." His booming voice is melodious, hypnotic. "This diminishing quality of the person, which can be observed in every aspect of life now, is working against magazines." ■ Typically, I too called Walter—to set up an interview. I was received by a modest man who I figured must be Milton's partner, a man I knew was hiding an impressive reputation behind his first name. Surprised by Bernard's self-effacing manner, and remembering that in 1977 he had singlehandedly transformed the look of *Time* magazine, acting as a mere art director, not as a high-ranking consultant, I wanted to know how he had managed to gain the respect of so many tough editors. "I think it's very simple," he answered, "you do it with either a certain arrogance, or a lack of it." It was obvious, as he spoke, that what he called a "lack of it" was in fact a quiet methodology that was unassuming, therefore irresistible. His formula is simple, he explained: experience and work. ■ When you put Walter Bernard's and Milton Glaser's resumés together, you don't think of experience, you think of history. The two men have been colleagues for more than twenty-five years, since the mid-1960s at *Esquire*, when Harold Hayes was the editor, Sam Antupit the art director, Walter Bernard his assistant, and Milton Glaser, then a principal at Push Pin Studios, a frequent contributor. From then on, the Bernard–Glaser alliance took many different forms and influenced not only the world of magazines, but also the world at large. They had met at a time when the belief system of the nation was shaped by magazines, a time when *Life* still reflected and influenced the country's foreign policy, while *The Saturday Evening Post* captured its soul. After *Esquire*, whose provocative covers (designed by George Lois) were a monthly national cultural event, Walter Bernard collaborated with Milton Glaser and Clay Felker to launch a fresh formula for *New York* magazine. "I remember almost to the day when the fear struck my heart," says Bernard, looking back longingly at his first major crisis as an art director. "We realized that the thirty beautiful, already engraved covers we had planned for the first six months of *New York*—photographic versions of *New Yorker* covers, door knobs, parking meters in the snow, visual snips of the city—didn't work at the newsstand.

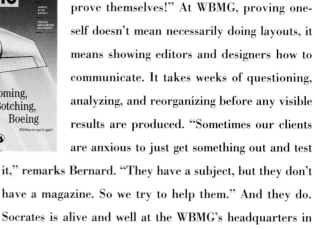

It dawned on us that we had to produce a concept every week." He was describing a rite of passage. "It was like doing an *Esquire* cover every week! How were we going to do that? I must say, it was very scary." ■ Being able to deal with a problem by identifying a need— and acting on it—became second nature to them. Determined to give their urban readers what nobody else did, they not only got the memorable covers out, they also invented new editorial formulas. The "responsible service piece" was an example. "It represented a basic perceptual change," says Glaser. " 'Service' had meant serving potential advertisers. We served potential readers instead. Curiously, before 'The Underground Gourmet' column in New York nobody had had that attitude." Curiously, one of Glaser's favorite words, sounds suddenly both thought-provoking and insightful. ■ About 500 covers later—"and not all of them were good," he says—Bernard left his art director's position at *New York* and moved to *Time*, where he added another 150 covers to his tally. His elegant, conservative, and yet quite vigorous redesign got everybody's attention. *Adweek, Atlantic Monthly*, and *Fortune* got a hold of him. While Bernard was busy dazzling corporate America, Glaser was leaving his unmistakable mark on *Cue, New West, The Village Voice*, and *Esquire*, and was expanding his reputation as a magazine maverick in Europe by redoing *Paris Match, L'Express, L'Europeo*, and *Jardin des Modes*. In 1983, fifteen years after the start up of *New York*, the two formalized what had been a collegial partnership and formed WBMG, Inc. You could not imagine a more well-rounded team than these two, combining Bernard's strong journalistic approach with Glaser's genius as a storyteller. By consolidating their talents, they doubled their wisdom. ■ Perceptiveness is their trademark. "Art directors are in the same position as women today," says Bernard. "To succeed in the corporate

world, they have to work twice as hard to prove themselves!" At WBMG, proving oneself doesn't mean necessarily doing layouts, it means showing editors and designers how to communicate. It takes weeks of questioning, analyzing, and reorganizing before any visible results are produced. "Sometimes our clients are anxious to just get something out and test it," remarks Bernard. "They have a subject, but they don't have a magazine. So we try to help them." And they do. Socrates is alive and well at the WBMG's headquarters in New York City. ■ Walter Bernard's and Milton Glaser's editorial philosophy—"we try to talk about 'design' as seldom as possible"—has earned them the toughest clients in New York, including *The New York Times, The Wall Street Journal, The Nation*, and *U.S. News & World Report*. It has earned them some frequent flyer mileage as well: They've traveled to Los Angeles for the *Times*, Dallas for the *Times-Herald*, Boston for the *Globe*, Washington for the *Post*, and abroad for *Lire, Alma*, and *La Vanguardia*. ■After a while, one wonders, does it get repetitive? After you've done *Manhattan inc.*, how does it feel to tackle *Business Tokyo*? Indeed, the more things change, the more they remain the same—always challenging. Eight years into their joint venture, Glaser and Bernard show no sign of jadedness. Yet they are concerned by the increasing number of magazines competing at the newsstand and the diminishing attention span of readers. Glaser himself admits he doesn't buy magazines to read them—he doesn't have the time—but he buys them nonetheless, stacks them, and hopes he'll get a second stab at them. As for Bernard, he flicks television channels as he flips the pages of a magazine—from back to front. "If only each TV station had a table of contents," he says, and as he speaks, his mind is clicking. "Leave it alone," interrupts Glaser, "the only excitement of watching TV is to imagine all those great programs you are missing." ■

Le magazine des livres

N°94/Juin 1983/20 F

LIRE

**Le rire
des
écrivains**

Revel
Julien Green
Sartre
Mallet-Joris
Pierre Boulle
Olievenstein
INTERVIEW
Nathalie
Sarraute

M-1074-94-20 F

Ionesco

(OPPOSITE TOP) PUBLICATION: *BUSINESS TOKYO* DATE: 1989 ■ (OPPOSITE BOTTOM) PUBLICATION: *TIME* ILLUSTRATOR: MARVIN MATTELSON DATE: 1980 ■ (THIS PAGE) PUBLICATION: *LIRE* DATE: 1983

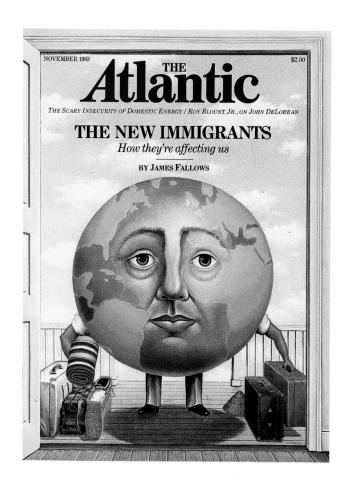

U.S.News
& WORLD REPORT

Out of the Shadows
**OLLIE'S
PRIVATE
WORLD**

Manhattan, inc.

The Business of New York

KISSINGER & CO.
**CASHING IN
ON CORPORATE
DIPLOMACY**

*George
Steinbrenner's
Very Silent
Partners*

*Slugging It
Out at the Top of
Gulf & Western*

*The Hungriest
Headhunter
on Wall Street*

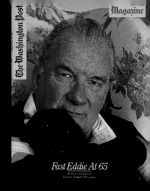

The Washington Post

Magazine

Fast Eddie At 65

FORTUNE

**THE
SHAPE
OF
CARS
TO
COME**

NUCLEAR
WEAPONS:
SUPPOSE
WE FROZE?

SEVEN-UP'S
UNCOLA COLA

ON THE
TRACK OF
THE ELUSIVE
THINKING
MACHINE

L'EXPRESS 2

SPORT

*Match
au sommet*
**HINAULT
BAT
PLATINI**

**ALAIN
PROST**
parle
DOSSIER
*L'explosion
golf*

The Case Against F. Lee Bailey, by Barry Farrell
I Left My Heartburn in San Francisco, by Gael Greene
The School Principal Who Said No, by Ken Auletta

NEW YORK

*Why Everybody's
Talking About*
GOSSIP
*By Alexander
Cockburn*

TIME

THE COMPUTER SOCIETY
A SPECIAL SECTION

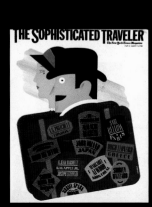

THE SOPHISTICATED TRAVELER
The New York Times Magazine

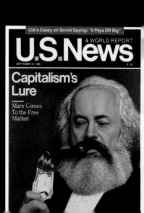

CIA's Casey on Soviet Spying: "It Pays Off Big"

U.S.News
& WORLD REPORT

SEPTEMBER 24, 1990

**Capitalism's
Lure**

Marx Comes
To the Free
Market

ROBERT PRIEST

"I DON'T FEEL BRITISH, REALLY. . ." *REALLY?* ROBERT PRIEST IS AN ENGLISHMAN WHOSE JOB IS TO CHARACTERIZE THE AMERICAN MAN. HIS SLIM, ELEGANT SILHOUETTE AND HIS CRISP URBANITY MAKE HIM NO MARLBORO MAN—AND, INDEED, THE MARLBORO ADS THAT APPEAR IN *GQ*, THE MAGAZINE HE IS PRESENTLY ART DIRECTING, SEEM ODDLY OUT OF PLACE IN THIS SLICK ENVIRONMENT. "I ALWAYS FELT CLOSE TO THE AMERICAN SENSIBILITY, FROM HAVING WATCHED ALL THE MOVIES," HE SAYS. ALL THE MOVIES STARRING GARY COOPER, THAT IS, NOT WILLIAM BENDIX. ☐ PRIEST'S FIRST IDENTIFICATION WITH THE AMERICAN MALE OCCURRED WHEN HE

was hired by Philip Moffitt in 1979 to redesign *Esquire* magazine. He moved to New York from Toronto, where he had been art directing *Weekend Magazine*, but nobody, save for a few insiders, knew who he was. In his thoughtful, punctilious, and responsible manner, Priest set out to make his mark in America. With his first issue of *Esquire*, not only did he prove to be an accomplished, mature, and original designer, but he also created the blueprint for a new definition of the American man—a sensitive, self-aware, educated kind of a guy who until then had been called a nerd. How could a chap from London, who had never set foot in the U.S., usher in such a quintessential transition? But with magazines, success is often a question of timing. Somehow Priest did exactly what had to be done to get the man of the 1980s under way: he urbanized him. ■ His most celebrated *Esquire* layouts are complex typographic assemblies— architectural statements, in fact—facing stark, contemporary illustrations. His decorative elements—a diminutive icon, a ruled color bar, a reversed tag line—are scaled down to emphasize dramatic initial caps or tightly leaded caption blocks. Since the demise of metal type and letterpress, nobody, except perhaps Roger Black, had been able to give phototypesetting that much vibrancy. In fact, rejecting the labor-saving photo process, Priest and his staff would spend hours tracing each letter by hand to explore the visual potential of word combinations. Starting on the upper left side corner of a title page, Priest would improvise his way down, incorporating heads, subheads, bylines, tag lines, editor's notes, and captions as he went along. This feat, which would be accomplished on one pristine sheet of tracing paper, without dillydallying, required a love of discipline

reminiscent of the print shops of the past. But what made Priest such a phenomenon was his ability to combine, with this impeccable craftsmanship, a rigorous editorial approach. ■ "I had had a career in England before. . . " he says, testy, when anybody marvels at his *Esquire* performance. Indeed, he had worked at *Radio Times*, a BBC journal and one of the best read and most visually innovative publications in the U.K. There, Priest had gotten into the habit of assigning international talent, particularly Milton Glaser and Seymour Chwast, whose illustrations had a tremendous appeal to European audiences. From the States, he naturally assigned English, Australian, Canadian, French, Swiss, and German artists. He sponsored the career of more than one illustrator (Ian Pollock, Michel Guiré Vakka, Bill Sanderson, Sue Coe. . .) and soon was seen as the ultimate arbiter—invited everywhere to judge competitions. Lately he says he is disillusioned with illustrations, "simply because in general they elicit a non-reaction, and photography is so much more direct a way to communicate." A journalist, he does not sacrifice information to decoration. ■ To avoid being stale, Robert Priest always wants to be different—so much so that he wants to be different from Robert Priest. Each new magazine job is a chance to reinvent himself. After four years at *Esquire*, the longest he stayed anywhere, he went to *Newsweek* in 1983 and shed his innovator's persona for a corporate suit. Caught in a transition between two editors-in-chief, he nonetheless worked tirelessly for two years, hoping to overcome the editorial problems with fresh visual solutions. He gave up in 1985, and accepted Jann Wenner's offer at *Us* magazine. There again he shifted gears, and embraced the project without

(ABOVE) PUBLICATION: *US* MAGAZINE PHOTOGRAPHER: HERB RITTS DATE: 1985 ■ (OPPOSITE, ALL IMAGES) PUBLICATION: *GQ* ■ (TOP) DESIGNER: ALEJANDRO GONZALEZ PHOTOGRAPHER: CHRIS CALLAS DATE: 1988 ■ (CENTER) PHOTOGRAPHER: HORST ■ (BOTTOM) PHOTOGRAPHER: ANDREW ECCLES

preconceptions. He designed a new typeface, favored aqua and fuchsia in his color scheme, threw away the grid, and surprised everybody by assigning gliztsy, sexy photographs of celebrities. Priest, his critics would say, has lost it. He is now messing around with a teen magazine! ■ Although an editor at heart, Priest does not editorialize his own work. He is reluctant to pass judgment on his own performance, or the performance of people he works with. If anything, his opinions are even, informative, articulate. But don't let this fool you. This enigmatic man is in fact as inconsistent and playful as they come. I discovered this recently when I asked him a question that has had a lot of his fans puzzled since he took over *GQ* in 1988. Why do you have two uneven column widths in the front of *GQ's* book? I asked. It was indeed a touchy question. He replied with the editorial We. We did it because it works. So I tried a different tactic. Why do you like asymmetrical layouts? Because I don't like to center anything, he replied with a straight face. One last annoying question, I announced. What is your formula? He

was ready for me with a cryptic answer: I only try to have one idea per page, he said, either something consistent, or something new. Who, I queried, says what's new? I say what's new, he exclaimed, and we both laughed. ■ Priest is the only art director I know who does not seem to resent working with the marketing department. He understands that magazines are economic as well as cultural entities. He is very candid, describing *GQ* as a magazine for the "smart business person, a man of some thought, who's got a bit of mileage on him." It sounds as if he is describing himself, although with Robert Priest, one can never be sure; the pages of the magazine may show confident, well-groomed, mature individuals with a definitely European mentality; the graphic treatment may display sober styling and cropping of photographs, understated typography, rich tonality of color; all this civility is yet another camouflage. Under their good looks, the *GQ* men seem restless, inquisitive, concerned. Like Robert Priest, they are finding out that success is a handicap, unless it is constantly challenged. ■

No short-fingered
vulgarian or seltzer director-
turpentagatian is safe from this tip-sy
magazine's waspish sting

Aye *Spy*

Laurence A. Tisch, chief executive officer of CBS, to be called on Paramount..."a mindset behind entrepreneur." Forever call this, photographer, stock market king..." Father simply to reply "sometimes" and the guru of "...The Washington Post says," quick, direct and a winner: To the Sa(ca)" parish the of Minnante...

Spy magazine, New York's answer to pluck, is also up to hard hit. It is, interview and deporte, the scenery of the style and scruples, the far-ins of motion(nn). It dares to tread when other malfunctions do not, as some writ of blind factory and blazed laughter. Today off as a New single, it has maybe as one of the majors (one pagnet, for sample) matrix and cracked call boots and Goren, with such luminary as "politiligan are awashers" George Steinberg, "To every rock person," Miguel becomes "melly-polite and fearures," Gurueller Vasquez, "a very pleased employment," "Reality Afflicted" other hospital says and "freed Change"

It hardly (have very long though) says "Davis, (say of the majors of New York, should any doubt trust his. "Myabe he doesn't have a sense of humor. Maybe he doesn't mind it. Yamey Dog. For all the luck, all the fuzz, our recoveries to be very free, from people to realed to...

I don't readed "I, says of Schoenberg, whose venurality is no more nice. of a, it's yours omitted "Mr. Landore Kennedy, Entertained Man," which (The inversebetter), is and to..."to "harridess and other, tropes or guys; and to

I don't don't it," "says Warren Sieger, who pictures have copies of The New York Times, which..."

By **Ellen Stern**

THE UNHOLY TRINITY: *Spy* founders Susan E. Morrison, Kurt Andersen and E. Graydon Carter.

THE
PROM
QUEEN
FROM
HELL

By Marcia Froelke Coburn

Photograph by *Horst*

DAMN!

HAIR

By Nina Tarrkin

When the heat hits your feet, these cool summer shoes will be your best friends

Dog-Day Afternoons

FANCY FOOTWORK. *THIS PAGE. TOP:* WOVEN-LEATHER SHOES BY TO BOOT NEW YORK, ABOUT $210. *BOTTOM:* OPEN-WEAVE LEATHER LACE-UPS BY SUSAN BENNIS WARREN EDWARDS, ABOUT $525... THIS SEASON, DIRTY BUCKS DEBUT WITH DARK SOCKS. *OPPOSITE PAGE:* SUEDE BUCKS BY JOHNSTON & MURPHY, ABOUT $110. WOOL-COTTON-AND-NYLON SOCKS, POLO HOSIERY BY RALPH LAUREN, ABOUT $15. LINEN TROUSERS BY JHANE BARNES.

(ALL IMAGES, THIS SPREAD) PUBLICATION: *GQ* ■ (ABOVE) PHOTOGRAPHER: CONSTANCE HANSEN ■ (OPPOSITE, TOP LEFT) PHOTOGRAPHER: ELLEN VON UNWORTH ■ (TOP RIGHT) PHOTOGRAPHER: FABRIZIO GIANNI ■ (CENTER LEFT) PHOTOGRAPHER: NADIR ■ (CENTER RIGHT) PHOTOGRAPHER: ELLEN VON UNWORTH ■ (BOTTOM LEFT) PHOTOGRAPHER: MARIO TESTINO ■ (BOTTOM RIGHT) PHOTOGRAPHER: FABRIZIO GIANNI

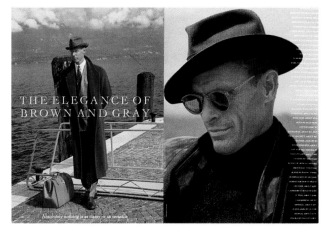

(ALL IMAGES, THIS SPREAD) PUBLICATION: *GQ* DESIGNER: ALEJANDRO GONZALEZ PHOTOGRAPHER: MATTHEW ROLSTON DATE: 1988

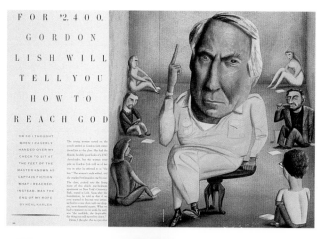

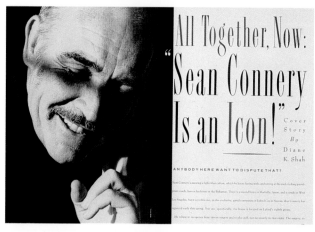

ONE
UP
ON
JAMES
BOND

THE 017 LOOKS OF 007

VERY OUTFIT JAMES
BOND WEARS HAS THE
EFFECT OF SHARKSKIN
ON HIS ENEMIES AND
ON WOMEN, BUT
EVEN THE SARTORIALLY
RESPLENDENT 007 NEEDS
A STYLE UPDATE EVERY SO
OFTEN. WE'VE OUTFITTED
THE SECRET AGENT IN THE
LATEST IN HIGH STYLE
AND, SUITABLY, HIGH-
TECH GEAR, FOR MOST
MODERN AMERICAN SPRING
MANEUVERS: DAY, NIGHT,
BUSINESS OR PLEASURE.

Bond Street wear.....
Worsted-wool suit by Christian
Dior Monsieur, about $355.
Cotton shirt by Charvet, about
$165. Silk tie by Richel, about
$50. Leather lace-ups by
Charles Jourdan, about $150.

STARRING JESSE HARRIS
(ZOLI, N.Y.C. AND
OMAR'S MEN, L.A.)
AS JAMES BOND
AND YVETTE LOZANO
(IT MODELS, L.A.)
AS POLLY MER
SPECIAL APPEARANCE
BY ANNABEL SCHOFIELD
(IT MODELS)
AS MISS MONEYPENNY
LOCATIONS AND PROPS,
YASUKO AUSTIN
PRODUCED BY
ERIC JUSSEN
EXTRAS AVAILABLE
THROUGH OMAR'S MEN
AND IT MODELS

Photographed by Mario Testino

(ALL IMAGES, THIS SPREAD) PUBLICATION: *GQ* ■ (OPPOSITE, TOP) ILLUSTRATOR: BLAIR DRAWSON ■ (CENTER)
PHOTOGRAPHER: HERB RITTS ■ (BOTTOM) PHOTOGRAPHER: ELLEN VON UNWORTH ■ (ABOVE) PHOTOGRAPHER: MARIO TESTINO

RETROSPECTIVE

RETROSPECTIVE

A significant share of this book reviews the approaches to editorial design taken by American and European magazine editors and designers of the past, from the first magazines of the mid-eighteenth century to the radical journals of the 1960s and 1970s. It is essential, however, that work reflecting and responding to current subjects, concerns, and technology also be shown. □ *The retrospective that follows is an acknowledgment of the success of a wide variety of design solutions and professional relationships in magazine design today. Included are the best examples of work by magazines and individuals that have had an impact on the industry. Skillfully synthesizing several elements—often with disparate or contrasting objectives—art director and editor strive to communicate the meaning of the magazine through typography, photography, and illustration.* □ *We are witnessing a transformation in the aesthetics and understanding of magazine publishing. Those members of the editorial design community who are fluent in the language of the new technology—including the advent of electronic publishing—and aware of the demands of their magazine's markets will be at the forefront of the profession, providing stimulus for enrichment as well as change.* ∎

(ALL IMAGES, THIS SPREAD) PUBLICATION: *LA STYLE* ART DIRECTOR: MICHAEL BROCK ■ (THIS PAGE, LEFT, AND OPPOSITE) PHOTOGRAPHER: SCOTT MORGAN DATE: 1991 ■ (RIGHT) PHOTOGRAPHER: GEORGE HOLZ DATE 1990

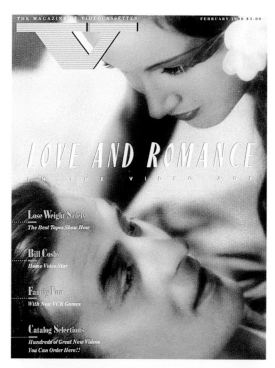

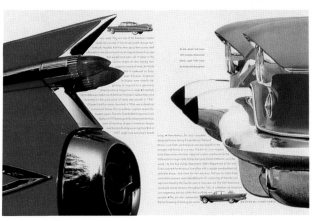

(OPPOSITE TOP) PUBLICATION: *V* ART DIRECTOR: TERRY R. KOPPEL DATE: 1988 ■ (OPPOSITE BOTTOM) PUBLICATION: *PRO-GRESSIVE ARCHITECTURE* ART DIRECTOR: DEREK BACCHUS DESIGNER: LISA M. MANGANO PHOTOGRAPHER: JOHN F. ROBBEN DATE: 1989 ■ (ABOVE) PUBLICATION: *ALMANAC* ART DIRECTOR: BRIDGET DE SOCIO PHOTOGRAPHER: HENRY WOLF DATE: 1988

(ABOVE) PUBLICATION: *WIGWAG* ART DIRECTOR: PAUL DAVIS DESIGNER: RISA ZAITSCHEK ■ (OPPOSITE, LEFT TO RIGHT IN DESCENDING ORDER) PUBLICATION: *ENTERPRISE* ART DIRECTOR: DOUGLAS WOLFE ILLUSTRATOR: MICHAEL GUIRE VAKA DATE: 1985 ■ PUBLICATION: *METROPOLITAN HOME* ART DIRECTOR: DON MORRIS DATE: 1989 ■ PUBLICATION: *PROGRESSIVE ARCHITECTURE* ART DIRECTOR: RICHELLE HUFF DESIGNER: LISA M. MANGANO PHOTOGRAPHER: STEVEN BROOKE DATE: 1988 ■ PUBLICATION: *7 DAYS* ART DIRECTOR: SCOTT MENCHIN PHOTOGRAPHER: TIMOTHY GREENFIELD SANDERS DATE: 1990 ■ PUBLICATION: *WIGWAG* ART DIRECTOR: PAUL DAVIS DATE: 1990 ■ PUBLICATION: *METROPOLITAN HOME* ART DIRECTOR: DON MORRIS DATE:1990

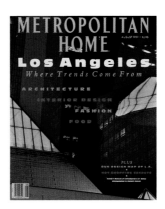

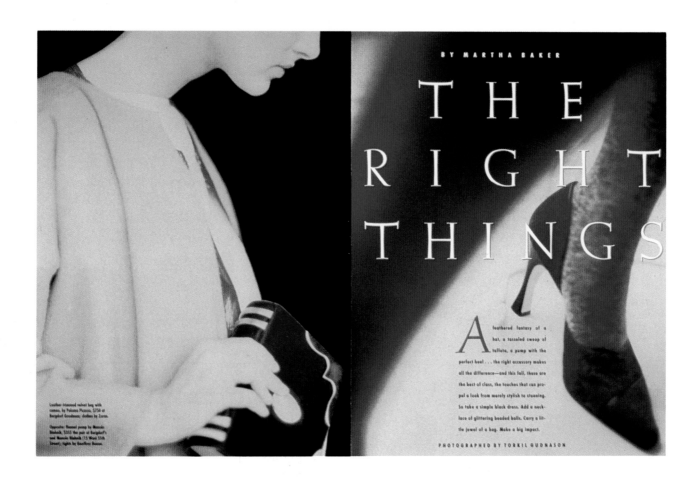

BY MARTHA BAKER

THE RIGHT THINGS

A feathered fantasy of a hat, a tasseled sweep of taffeta, a pump with the perfect heel . . . the right accessory makes all the difference—and this fall, these are the best of class, the touches that can propel a look from merely stylish to stunning. So take a simple black dress. Add a necklace of glittering beaded balls. Carry a little jewel of a bag. Make a big impact.

PHOTOGRAPHED BY TORKIL GUDNASON

Leather-trimmed velvet bag with cameo, by Paloma Picasso, $750 at Bergdorf Goodman; clothes by Zoran.

Opposite: Flannel pump by Manolo Blahnik, $355 the pair at Bergdorf's and Manolo Blahnik (15 West 55th Street; tights by Geoffrey Beene.

(ABOVE) PUBLICATION: *NEW YORK* MAGAZINE ART DIRECTOR: ROBERT BEST PHOTOGRAPHER: TORKIL GUDNASON DATE: 1990 ∎
(OPPOSITE) PUBLICATION: *VOGUE* MAGAZINE ART DIRECTOR: RAÚL MARTINEZ PHOTOGRAPHER: HERB RITTS DATE: MARCH 1992

feets of brilliance

Getting a leg up on the competition: Dolfo, Blahnik's glacé sandal with diamanté buckles, is paired with shorts covered with paillettes and jet ball fringe by Isaac Mizrahi. Shoes, about $550. Bergdorf Goodman; Manolo Blahnik, NYC; Neiman Marcus; I. Magnin. OPPOSITE: Blahnik's Pildimu mule of napa leather and suede with Dolce & Gabbana's metallic jean shorts. Shoes, about $415. Barneys New York; Manolo Blahnik, NYC; Neiman Marcus; I. Magnin. Details, see In This Issue.

315

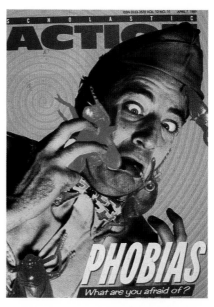
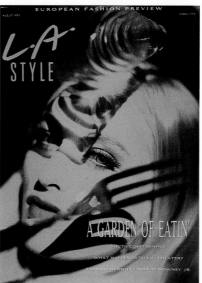

(TOP LEFT) PUBLICATION: *METROPOLIS* ART DIRECTOR: HELENE SILVERMAN DATE: 1989 ■ (TOP RIGHT) PUBLICATION: *SCHOLASTIC ACTION* ART DIRECTOR: JOAN MICHAEL DESIGNER: VIVIAN NG PHOTOGRAPHER: JIM MOORE DATE: 1989 ■ (BOTTOM LEFT) PUBLICATION: *LA STYLE* ART DIRECTOR: MICHAEL BROCK DATE 1990 ■ (BOTTOM RIGHT) PUBLICATION: *SAN FRANCISCO FOCUS* ART DIRECTOR: MATTHEW DRACE PHOTOGRAPHER: GEOF KERN DATE:1988

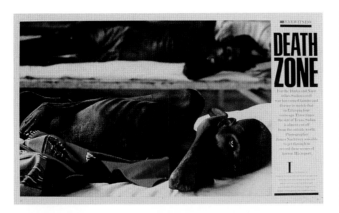

(TOP, LEFT AND RIGHT) PUBLICATION: *LIFE* ART DIRECTOR: TOM BENTKOWSKI ■ (TOP LEFT) DESIGNER: CHARLES W. PATES PHOTOGRAPHER: EUGENE RICHARDS DATE: 1989 ■ (TOP RIGHT) DESIGNER: ROBIN E. BROWN PHOTOGRAPHER: JAMES NACHTWEY ■ (CENTER LEFT) PUBLICATION: *TIME* ART DIRECTOR: RUDY HOGLUND DESIGNER: TOM BENTKOWSKI DATE: 1985 ■ (CENTER RIGHT) PUBLICATION: *MADEMOISELLE* ART DIRECTOR: KATI KORPIJAAKKO DESIGNER: WYNN DAN PHOTOGRAPHER: MAX VADUKUL DATE: 1985 ■ (BOTTOM LEFT) PUBLICATION: *CARING* ART DIRECTOR: MARK GEER DATE: 1989 ■ (BOTTOM RIGHT) PUBLICATION: *TAXI* ART DIRECTOR: DEBBIE SMITH DESIGNER: CASSANDRA MALAXA PHOTOGRAPHER: ANDREW BETTLES DATE: 1989

I may thrive on the show before the game, but when I'm on the field, I'm serious as a funeral.

(OPPOSITE) PUBLICATION: *ROLLING STONE* ART DIRECTOR: FRED WOODWARD DESIGNER: JOLENE CUYLER PHOTOGRAPHER: HERB RITTS DATE: 1988 ■ (THIS PAGE, TOP) PUBLICATION: *SAVVY* ART DIRECTOR: PAMELA BERRY PHOTOGRAPHER: GUZMAN DATE: 1989 ■ (BOTTOM) PUBLICATION: *ESQUIRE* ART DIRECTOR: TERRY R. KOPPEL DATE: 1990

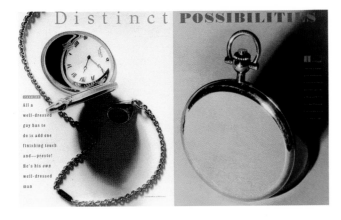 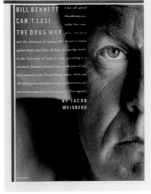 

(THIS PAGE) PUBLICATION: *INDUSTRY UPDATE* ART DIRECTOR: TERRY KOPPEL DATE: 1987 ■ (OPPOSITE) PUBLICATION: *THE BOSTON GLOBE MAGAZINE* ART DIRECTOR: LUCY BARTHOLOMAY PHOTOGRAPHER: JANET KNOTT DATE: 1989

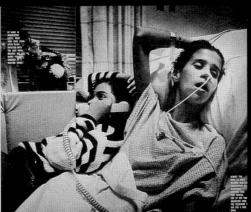

DYING AND LIVING WITH AIDS

"I'M NOT QUITE MILDRED, BUT I'M ALIVE."

STORY BY SALLY JACOBS

PHOTOGRAPHS BY
JANET KNOTT

Continued on page 42

THE ARCHITECTURE & DESIGN MAGAZINE OF

METROPOLIS

DECEMBER 1987 $3.95

The architecture of mannequins

**THE CHANGING SUBURBAN OFFICE
TECHNOLOGY AND NORMAN FOSTER
OBJECTS DESIGNED FOR THE DESK**

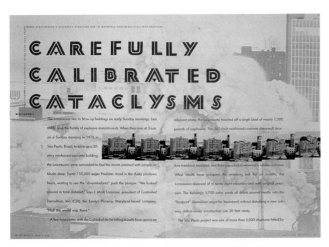

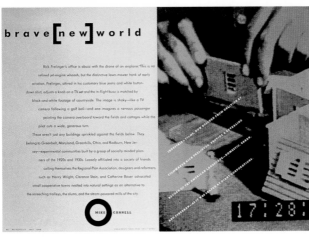

(OPPOSITE) PUBLICATION: *METROPOLIS* ART DIRECTOR: HELENE SILVERMAN DATE: 1987 ■ (ALL IMAGES, THIS PAGE) PUBLICATION: *METROPOLIS* ART DIRECTOR: HELENE SILVERMAN (TOP LEFT) PHOTOGRAPHER: MARK SULLO DATE: 1988 ■ (TOP RIGHT) DATE: 1989 ■ (BOTTOM LEFT) DATE: 1988 ■ (BOTTOM RIGHT) DESIGNER: JEFF CHRISTENSEN DATE: 1988

He hasn't **CAN** had a big hit album in years. The other Beatles are suing him. **PAUL** But with 'Flowers in the Dirt,' his strong new record, **McCARTNEY** and plans for his first world tour in more than a decade, the **GET** ex-Beatle is doing his best to toughen up his image and climb back **BACK?** to the top.

BY JAMES HENKE

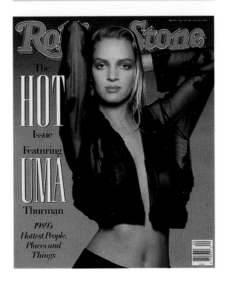

(ALL IMAGES, THIS SPREAD) PUBLICATION: *ROLLING STONE* MAGAZINE ART DIRECTOR: FRED WOODWARD ■ (OPPOSITE) PHOTO EDITOR: LAURIE KRATOCHVIL PHOTOGRAPHER: HERB RITTS DATE: 1989 ■ (THIS PAGE, TOP) PHOTOGRAPHER: MARK SELIGER DATE: 1991 ■ (CENTER) PHOTOGRAPHER: HERB RITTS DATE: 1991 ■ (BOTTOM) PHOTOGRAPHER: MATTHEW ROLSTON DATE: 1989

300 SLR

THE MERCEDES-BENZ 300 SLR racing sports car enjoyed one brief, glorious season in which it dominated every event it entered. Story by John Fitch, co-winner of the 1955 Irish Tourist Trophy and the car's sole American driver in competition. Photographs by Guy Morrison; car from the collection of the Henry Ford Museum.

(ALL IMAGES, OPPOSITE) PUBLICATION: *ELLE* PUBLICATION DIRECTOR: RÉGIS PAGNIEZ ART DIRECTOR: PHYLLIS SCHEFER DATE: 1987 ■ (TOP LEFT) PHOTOGRAPHER: GILES BENSIMON ■ (TOP RIGHT) PHOTOGRAPHER: MARC HISPARD ■ (CENTER) PHOTOGRAPHER: TOSCANI ■ (BOTTOM LEFT) PHOTOGRAPHER: MARC HISPARD ■ (BOTTOM RIGHT) DESIGNER: RÉGIS PAGNIEZ PHOTOGRAPHER: GILLES BENSIMON ■ (THIS PAGE) PUBLICATION: *MERCEDES BENZ* ART DIRECTOR: PETER MORANCE PHOTOGRAPHER: GUY MORRISON DATE: 1985

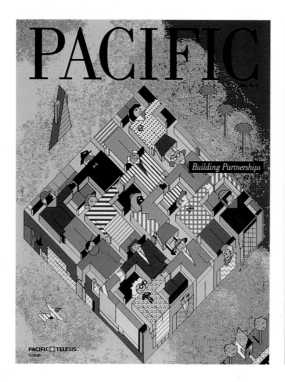

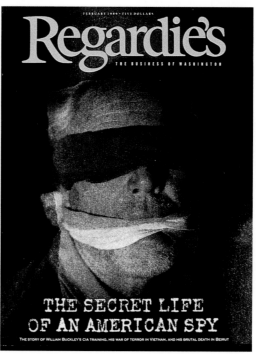

(THIS PAGE, LEFT) PUBLICATION: *PACIFIC* ART DIRECTOR: MICHAEL MABRY DATE: 1986 ■ (RIGHT) PUBLICATION: *REGARDIE'S* ART DIRECTOR: JOHN KORPIES PHOTOGRAPHER: GEOF KERN DATE: 1989 ■ (ALL IMAGES, OPPOSITE) PUBLICATION: *SPY* ■ (TOP TO BOTTOM) ART DIRECTOR: B.W. HONEYCUTT DATE: 1988 ■ ART DIRECTOR: ALEXANDER ISLEY DESIGNER: MICHAEL HOFMANN DATE: 1988 ■ ART DIRECTOR: B.W. HONEYCUTT ILLUSTRATOR: BOB ECKSTEIN DATE: 1990 ■ ART DIRECTOR: B.W HONEYCUTT DESIGNER: SCOTT FROMMERE DATE: 1988

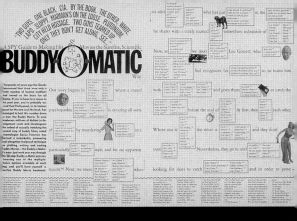

"TWO GUYS. ONE BLACK. CIA. BY THE BOOK, THE OTHER WHITE. LAPD. SLOPPY. MADMAN'S ON THE LOOSE. PLUTONIUM. CITY HELD HOSTAGE. TWO GUYS TEAMED UP. ONLY THEY DON'T GET ALONG. SEE..."

A SPY Guide to Making Hit Movies the Surefire, Scientific

BUDDY·O·MATIC
Way

MILANO! City of apartments for rents, pretty Americans pursuing modeling...

Arrivederci, Sleazeball!

I dawn on June 26, 1984, a wealthy Italian racehorse owner and professional gambler named Francesco D'Alessio propositioned his last American model of the night—and of his 40 years' earthly existence. Early-morning traffic noises from Milan's swank Corso Magenta filtered into the high-ceilinged ground-floor apartment and competed with the melody of a Cat Stevens tape. D'Alessio's own gargled playboy English and the American-civil mum...

ble of his quarry—a beautiful 26-year-old aspiring model from South Carolina named Terry Lynne Broome. □ Neither D'Alessio nor Broome was particularly steady of foot or clear of speech that morning. Several lines and a small pile of very pure cocaine were on the living-room table, and a bottle of bourbon dangled from Broome's...

HOW CHEAP ARE THE RICH? AS CHEAP AS THE REST OF US? DO THEY SCOUR THE NETHER REGIONS OF THEIR BARCALOUNGERS FOR LOOSE CHANGE? DO THEY STOCK UP WHEN THEY SEE SLOAN'S HAS A SPECIAL ON CHARMIN? WOULD THEY SUFFER THE MODERATE INCONVENIENCE INVOLVED IN DEPOSITING A CHECK FOR AN ALL-BUT-WORTHLESS SUM OF MONEY? WELL, WE CAN'T ANSWER THE FIRST TWO QUESTIONS, BUT OUR ACCOUNTANCY CORRESPONDENT, DOLORES LOWENTHAL, EXAMINED THE THIRD

every man has his PRICE
IN SOME OBSCURE CASES

A MORDIFYING SPY EXPERIMENT IN COMPARATIVE CHEAPNESS, FEATURING REAL CHECKS FOR TEENY SUMS ACTUALLY CASHED BY CANDICE BERGEN, BILL BLASS, CHER, MICHAEL DOUGLAS, HENRY KRAVIS, RUPERT MURDOCH, S. I. NEWHOUSE, DONALD TRUMP, MORT ZUCKERMAN, AND OODLES MORE

---

the 1970s

BY TONY HENDRA

I imagine a once-aspiring rock 'n' roller, now turned aspiring televangelist, searching his attic for some telltale income-tax records, when he comes across a pair of calf-high purple alligator-skin boots with two-inch soles and five-inch heels.

A teardrop forms...

Imagine Brent Junior asking Brent Senior, "What's that, Dad?" as Senior cleans out the garage to prepare for the family's move to Seattle. Without answering, Brent Senior lifts the handset from the rotting, rusted transmitter. "Breaker one-niner," he whispers into no one, "what's your handle?"

A teardrop forms...

Imagine one of San Francisco's most respected public defenders visiting New York for the first time in a decade. He passes a bar on Christopher Street as Black from the Hudson. Its storefront has been vandalized—even the FOR SALE sign is peeling. So many nights, bollied up to the bar, red bandanna in left back pocket...

A teardrop forms...

A DYNAMITE SPY BOOGIE-DOWN CELEBRATION OF THE MOST EMBARRASSING DECADE OF THE TWENTIETH CENTURY

AN EPIC STRUGGLE FOR GOLD

I

Portfolio by Sebastião Salgado
Text by Marlise Simons

WORKING A MOUNTAIN *In Serra Pelada, Brazilian laborers have gouged out 85 tons of gold in Serra Pelada.*

A HOST OF THOUSANDS *(above), near Serra Pelada, (following page).*

BACK-BREAKING *(overleaf)*

T

PANNING *In pools, Brazilian miners vainly sifter hunt the 85-pic in California.*

HAULING *Loads of muddy bags carry some 60-pound sacks.*

STEP BY STEP *workers create wide wooden ladders.*

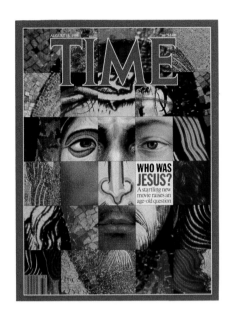

(OPPOSITE) PUBLICATION: *THE NEW YORK TIMES* ART DIRECTOR: DIANA LAGUARDIA PHOTOGRAPHER: SEBASTIAO SALGADO DATE: 1987 ■ (ALL IMAGES, THIS PAGE) PUBLICATION: *TIME* ■ (TOP LEFT) ART DIRECTOR: RUDOLPH HOGLUND DESIGNER: TOM BENTKOWSKI DATE: 1988 ■ (TOP RIGHT) ART DIRECTOR: RUDOLPH HOGLUND ILLUSTRATOR: CHRISTO PHOTOGRAPHER: GIANFRANCO GORGON DATE: 1989 ■ (BOTTOM LEFT) DATE: 1986 ■ (BOTTOM RIGHT) ART DIRECTOR: NIGEL HOLMES ILLUSTRATOR: BIRNEY LETTICK DATE: 1985

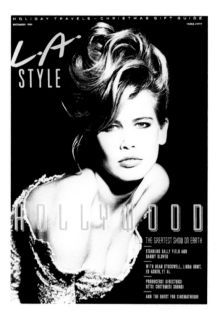

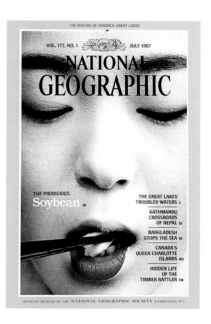

(THIS PAGE, LEFT) PUBLICATION: *LA STYLE* ART DIRECTOR: MICHAEL BROCK PHOTOGRAPHER: HERB RITTS DATE: 1989 ■ (CENTER) PUBLICATION: *7 DAYS* ART DIRECTOR: JOHN BELKNAP DESIGNERS: JEAN-CLAUDE SUARES, JOHN BELKNAP, CLAUDIA LEBENTHAL PHOTOGRAPHER: ADRIAN BOOT ILLUSTRATORS: MARC ROSENTHAL, LES KANTUREK, CHRISTOPH HITZ DATE: 1988 ■ (RIGHT) PUBLICATION: *NATIONAL GEOGRAPHIC* ART DIRECTOR: GERHARD A. VALERIO DESIGNER: WILBUR E. GARRETT PHOTOGRAPHER: CHRIS JOHNS DATE:1987 ■ (OPPOSITE) PUBLICATION: *VOGUE ITALIA* ART DIRECTOR: FABIEN BARON DATE: 1989

VOGUE

ITALIA

SET.
1989
N. 27
L. 7000

ALTA
MODA
ROMA
PARIGI

ABITO E STOLA, VALENTINO COUTURE

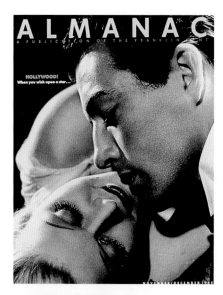

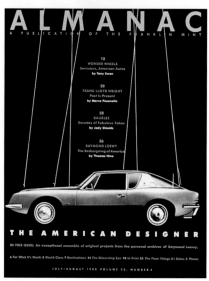

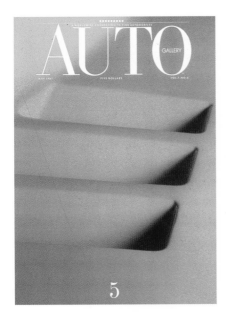 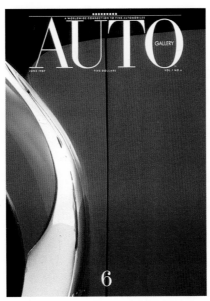 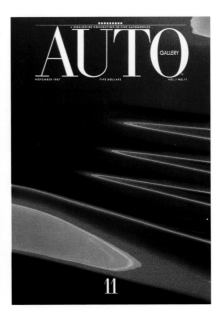

(OPPOSITE, ALL IMAGES) PUBLICATION: *ALMANAC* ART DIRECTOR: BRIDGET DE SOCIO DATE: 1988 ■ (TOP) PHOTOGRAPHERS: TED ALLEN, GEORGE HURRELL ■ (BOTTOM) ILLUSTRATOR: RAYMOND LOEWY ■ (ALL IMAGES, THIS PAGE) PUBLICATION: *AUTO GALLERY* ART DIRECTOR: MICHAEL BROCK DATE: 1987 ■ (LEFT AND CENTER) PHOTOGRAPHER: CINDY LEWIS ■ (RIGHT) PHOTOGRAPHER: BRUCE MILLER

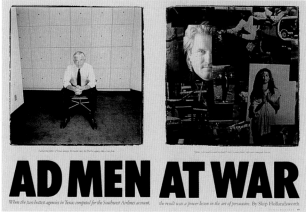

(ALL IMAGES, THIS PAGE) PUBLICATION: *TEXAS MONTHLY* ■ (TOP LEFT) ART DIRECTOR: D.J. STOUT PHOTOGRAPHER: GEOF KERN DATE: 1988 ■ (TOP RIGHT) ART DIRECTOR: D.J. STOUT PHOTOGRAPHER: WILLIAM WEGMAN DATE: 1989 ■ (BOTTOM LEFT) ART DIRECTOR: D.J. STOUT PHOTOGRAPHER: DOUG MILNER DATE: 1990 ■ (BOTTOM RIGHT) ART DIRECTOR: FRED WOODWARD DESIGNERS: FRED WOODWARD, DAVID KAMPA PHOTOGRAPHER: GEORGE KERN DATE: 1985 ■ (OPPOSITE) PUBLICATION: *THE NEW YORK TIMES MAGAZINE* ART DIRECTOR: KEN KENDRICK DESIGNER: DIANA LAGUARDIA ILLUSTRATOR: MATT MAHURIN DATE: 1985

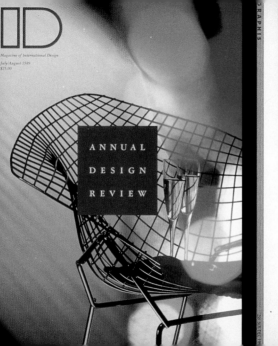

ID

Magazine of International Design

July/August 1989
$75.00

ANNUAL

DESIGN

REVIEW

een kleine keuze uit onze lettercollectie

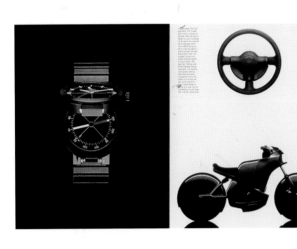

(OPPOSITE, LEFT) Publication: *ID* Art Director: GREGORY MASTRIANNI Designer: JENNIFER DOMER Photographer: FRANK MANORE Date: 1989 ■ (RIGHT) Publication: *GRAPHIS* Art Director: B. MARTIN PEDERSEN Date: 1988 ■ (THIS PAGE, TOP LEFT AND RIGHT) Publication: *GRAPHIS* Art Director: B. MARTIN PEDERSEN Photographer: PORSCHE DESIGN Date: 1988 ■ (BOTTOM LEFT AND RIGHT) Publication: *AUTO* Art Director: MICHAEL BROCK Photographer: CINDY LEWIS Date: 1987

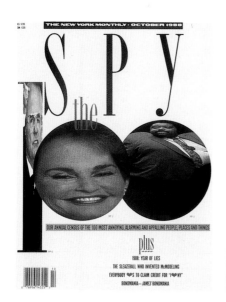
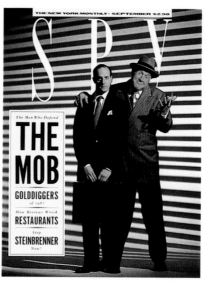

(ALL IMAGES, THIS SPREAD) PUBLICATION: *SPY* ■ (THIS PAGE, LEFT) ART DIRECTOR: B.W. HONEYCUTT PHOTOGRAPHERS: DOUGLAS KIRKLAND, SYGMA, NOLLA TULLY, RICK FRIEDMAN, BLACK STAR DATE: 1988 ■ (CENTER) ART DIRECTOR: ALEXANDER ISLEY PHOTOGRAPHER: CHRIS CALLIS DATE: 1987 ■ (RIGHT) ART DIRECTOR: ALEXANDER ISLEY DATE: 1987 ■ (OPPOSITE) ART DIRECTOR: B.W. HONEYCUTT DESIGNER: CHRISTIAN KUYPERS PHOTOGRAPHER: WILLIAM DUKE DATE: 1989

THE GOOD NEWS:

IT'S POSSIBLE TO LIVE FOREVER

THE BAD NEWS:

YOU'LL BE A SNO-KONE

WARNING: TECHNIQUES NOT FOR HOME USE

...H met the men and woman who would be frozen. He listened to their dreams

...devoid of that ancient pest, mortality. He listened to their jokes and awful poetry.

...finally got to the bottom of Walt Disney's whereabouts. And when he'd had enough of that, he

...freezers and touched a frozen dead per-

...right, he touched a *frozen dead person.* Plus

...got to look at the bobbing severed heads. Welcome to

...he entirely sincere, delightfully icky world of **cryonics**

"NO, WALT DISNEY WAS *NOT* FROZEN," the woman at Disneyland says—which means the one thing most people know about cryonics isn't true. The Disney woman angrily switches the call over to the publicity department. Paul Goldman, publicist, picks up the phone to smooth things over. He explains that the beloved creator of America's favorite rodent is interred, quite conventionally, in an urn in a filled-in hole in Forest Lawn Cemetery in Glendale, California—not, as so many of us had believed, had *hoped*, in a slab of ice somewhere beneath the Magic Kingdom. As far

PHOTOGRAPH BY WILLIAM DUKE

(ALL IMAGES, OPPOSITE) PUBLICATION: *VOGUE ITALIA* ■ (TWO UPPER) ART DIRECTOR: FABIEN BARON ■ (TWO LOWER) ART DIRECTOR: JUAN GATTI DATE: 1990 ■ (ALL IMAGES, THIS PAGE) *ART CENTER REVIEW #7* ART DIRECTOR: KIT HINRICHS DESIGNERS: KIT HINRICHS, TERRI DRISCOLL, KAREN BERNDT DATE: 1990 ■ (LEFT) PHOTOGRAPHER: STEVEN A. HELLER ■ (RIGHT TOP) PHOTOGRAPHER: STEVEN A.HELLER ILLUSTRATOR: PETER MICHELENA (RIGHT BOTTOM) PHOTOGRAPHERS: STEVEN A. HELLER, HOLLY STEWART

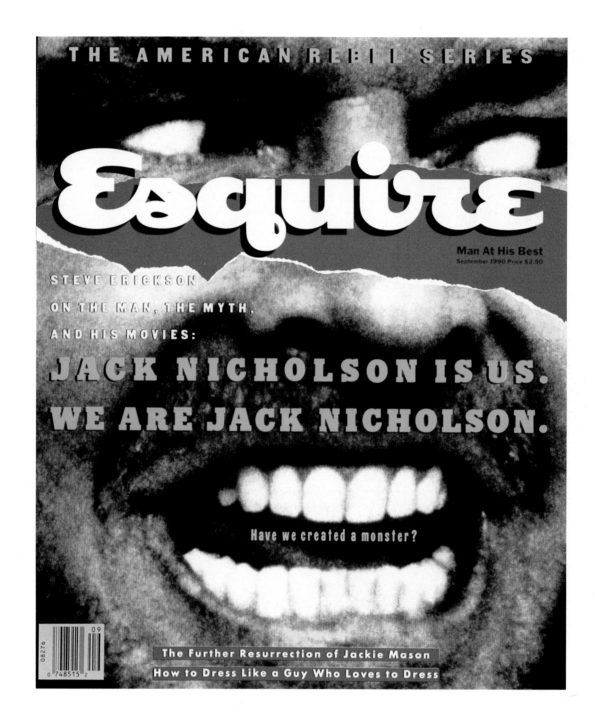

(THIS PAGE) PUBLICATION: *ESQUIRE* ART DIRECTOR: TERRY KOPPEL DATE: 1990 ■ (OPPOSITE, TOP LEFT) PUBLICATION: *LIRE* ART DIRECTOR/ILLUSTRATOR: JEAN-PIERRE CLIQUET DATE: 1985 ■ (TOP RIGHT) PUBLICATION: *LIFE* DATE: 1986 ■ (CENTER LEFT) PUBLICATION: *METROPOLIS* ART DIRECTOR: HELENE SILVERMAN DESIGNER: JEFF CHRISTENSEN DATE: 1988 ■ (CENTER RIGHT) PUBLICATION: *SPLICE* ■ (BOTTOM LEFT) PUBLICATION: *ESQUIRE* ART DIRECTOR: TERRY KOPPEL PHOTOGRAPHER: MATTHEW ROLSTON DATE: 1990 ■ (BOTTOM RIGHT) PUBLICATION: *ART CENTER REVIEW #6* ART DIRECTOR: KIT HINRICHS PHOTOGRAPHERS: STEVEN A. HELLER, RICK ESKITE DATE: 1989

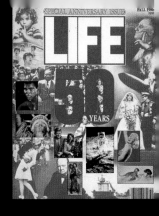

INDEX

AGHA, M.F. 14, 17

ALBRECHT, RON. 37

ANTUPIT, SAM. 185

BARDUTT-GIRON, OLIVIA. 38

BARON, FABIEN. 36
. . . . 104, 105, 106, 113, 175-183, 228, 239

BARTHOLOMAY, LUCY. 216

BAYER, HERBERT. 15

BELKNAP, JOHN. 228

BENTKOWSKI, TOM. 210, 213

BERNARD, WALTER. 19, 24-25, 62, 65, 74-75, 87, 185-189

BERRY, PAMELA. 215

BEST, ROBERT. 210

BLACK, ROGER. 47, 48, 51, 52, 155-157, 191

BROCK, MICHAEL. 42, 204, 212, 228, 231, 234

BRODOVITCH, ALEXEY. 82, 83, 103, 166

BRODY, NEVILLE. 89

BURTIN, WILL. 15

CASALIS, LAURA. 129

CLIQUET, JEAN-PIERRE. 240

DAVIS, PAUL. 62, 69, 208

DE SOCIO, BRIDGET. 206, 231

DRACE, MATTHEW. 212

ESSMAN, ROBERT N. 24

FISCHER, CARL. 30

FROUMAN, MALCOLM. 124, 125, 127

GARLAN, JUDY. 62, 69

GATTI, JUAN. 102, 106-110, 112, 113, 239

GEER, MARK. 213

GLASER, MILTON. 19, 65, 74, 86, 87, 118, 185-189, 191

HALLOCK, ROBERT. 19

HESS, CHARLES. 56

HINRICHS, KIT. 41, 239, 240

HOGLUND, RUDOLPH. 213, 227

HOLMES, NIGEL. 227

HONEYCUTT, B.W. 224, 236

HOWE, PETER. 62, 65, 66, 70, 71, 74

HUFF, RICHELLE. 208

HURLBURT, ALLEN. 18

ISLEY, ALEXANDER. 224, 236

KAELIN, ALBERT. 99

KALIWARA, RON. 137

KANE, ART. 18

KENDRICK, KEN. 232

KINGSBURY, ROBERT. 19, 155

KORPIJAAKKO, KATI. 213

KOPPEL, TERRY R. 206, 215-216, 240

KORPIES, JOHN. 224

LAGUARDIA, DIANA. 227

LANE, TERRY. 155

LEFKOWITZ, JACK 117, 119, 120

LIBERMAN, ALEXANDER 15, 18, 83, 103, 137, 138, 175, 177

LIONNI, LEO 15

LOGAN, NICK 89

LOIS, GEORGE 28, 30, 83, 86, 155, 185

LORENZ, LEE 27

LUCCHINI, FLAVIO 104

MABRY, MICHAEL 224

MARTINEZ, RAUL 138, 139, 141, 143, 210

MASTRIANNI, GREGORY 234

MENCHIN, SCOTT 208

MICHAEL, JOAN 212

MORANCE, PETER 223

MORRIS, DON 208

PAGNIEZ, RÉGIS 36, 38

PAUL, ARTHUR 18

PECK, PRISCILLA 137

PEDERSEN, B. MARTIN 234

PINELES, CIPÉ 17

POPISCHIL, HANS-GEORG 145-153

PRIEST, ROBERT 24, 25, 191-199

RICCI, FRANCO MARIA 128, 130-135

ROTHENFLUH, OTHMAR 99

RUBINSTEIN, RHONDA 48, 49, 50

SCHEFER, PHYLLIS 36, 223

SCHER, PAULA 24, 25

SHECUT, JOHN JR. 30

SCHOENING, ROGER 137

SHANAHAN, MARY 156

SHEEHAN, NORA 210

SHOSTAK, MITCH 127

SILVERMAN, HELENE 36, 212, 219, 240

SILVERSTEIN, LOU 89

SMITH, DEBBIE 213

STERMER, DUGALD 19

STOPPINI, LUCA 106

STORCH, OTTO 18

STOUT, D.J. 232

THOMPSON, BRADBURY 15, 18

UDELL, ROCHELLE 137

UNGLESS, DEREK 137, 138, 141, 143, 156

VALERIO, GERHARD A. 228

VANDERLANS, RUDY 52, 55, 56, 89

VIGNELLI, MASSIMO 42

VOLGER, JOHN 124

WOLF, HENRY 18, 65, 82, 83, 84

WOLFE, DOUGLAS 208

WOODWARD, FRED 62, 65-66, 77, 156-162, 215, 221, 232

YAMAZAKI, SANAE 30

ZACHARY, FRANK 18, 165-174

ZIMMERMAN, DICK 166

BASKERVILLE, JOHN 12

BELKNAP, JOHN 228

BENTKOWSKI, TOM 213, 227

BODONI, GIAMBATTISTA 12, 129

BRODOVITCH, ALEXEY 14, 39

BROWN, ROBIN E. .213

BULMER, WILLIAM 12

CASLON, WILLIAM 12

CHRISTENSEN, JEFF 219, 240

CAXTON, WILLIAM 12

CUYLER, JOLENE 215

DAN, WYNN 213

DIDOT, PIERRE 12

DIDOT, FIRMIN 12

DOMER, JENNIFER .235

DOYLE, STEPHEN 51

DRISCOLL, TERRI 41

FLECKHAUS, WILLY 36, 39

FROMMERE, SCOTT 224

GARAMOND, CLAUDE 12

GARRETT, WILBUR E. 228

GOLDIN, WILLIAM 15

GONZALEZ, ALEJANDRO 192, 196

GRANJON, ROBERT .12

GRIFFIN, DAVID 63

GRIFFIN, RICK 155

GROPIUS, WALTER .14

HOMER, WINSLOW .13

HURLBURT, ALLEN .39

KAMPA, DAVID 232

KEPES, GYORGY 15

KUYPERS, CHRISTIAN 236

LAGUARDIA, DIANA 232

LEBENTHAL, CLAUDIA 228

LEHMANN-HAUPT, CARL 175

LICKO, ZUZANA 55

LUBALIN, HERB 39

MALAXA, CASSANDRA 213

MANGANO, LISA M. 207, 208

MANUTIUS, ALDUS 12

MOHOLY-NAGY, LAZLO 14, 15

NAST, THOMAS 13

NG, VIVIAN 212

PAGNIEZ, RÉGIS 223

PATES, CHARLES W. 213

PEDERSEN, B. MARTIN 124, 125

PLANTIN, CHRISTOPHER 12

RAND, PAUL 15

ROCKWELL, NORMAN 18

SALISBURY, MIKE 155

SUARES, JEAN-CLAUDE 228

VAN HAMMERSFELD, JOHN 52, 57

WILLIAMS, JOHN .155

ZAITSCHEK, RISA .208

AARONS, SLIM 166
ALLEN, TED 231
ARIS, BRIAN 30
ARNO, PETER 27
ARTINI, LUIGI 134
AVEDON, RICHARD 14, 66, 104, 156

BAILEY, DAVID 105
BAILEY, RICHARD 104
BEETLES, ANDREW 213
BENSIMON, GILLES 36, 223
BERDOY, PIERRE 38
BETON, CECIL 14
BOOT, ADRIAN 228
BOTA, JUAN SUAREZ 127
BRADLEY, WILL 14
BREAKEY, JOHN 125
BROOKE, STEVEN 208
BROOKES, PETER 151

CALLIS, CHRIS 62, 64-66, 71, 74, 76, 192, 236
CARTIER-BRESSON, HENRI 14, 166
CARUGATTI, ERALDO 127
CASTALDI, ALFA 115
CHIN, WALTER 141
CHRISTO 227
CHRYWSKI, WALTER 127
CHWAST, SEYMOUR 118, 151, 188, 191
CLIQUET, JEAN-PIERRE 240
COE, SUE 191
COHEN, SERGE 152
CRUZ, JOSÉ 127
CUNNINGHAM, BILL 114

DE DIENES, ANDRÉ 17
DE LUCA, ARALDO 130, 132
DEMARCHELIER, PATRICK 138, 141, 143
DERVJINSKY 84
DRAWSON, BLAIR 198
DUKE, WILLIAM 236

ECCLES, ANDREW 192
ECKSTEIN, BOB 224
EDELMAN, HEINZ 151
EDELMANN, VALENTINE 152
ELENGA, HENK 55
ELGORT, ARTHUR 139, 141, 143
ENGLER, MICHAEL 50
ESIKITE, RICK 240

FARBIN, MARK 55
FEE, JAMES 204
FELLMAN, SANDI 234
FERRATO, DONNA 62, 63, 65, 70, 71, 74
FISCHER, CARL 66, 86
FRANCOIS, ANDRÉ 166
FREED, PETER 124
FRIEDMAN, RICK 236
FROMMERE, SCOTT 224

GIANNI, FABRIZIO 195
GILES, JEFF 159
GLASER, MILTON 189
GODARD, MAXIME 109
GOREY, EDWARD 166
GORGON, GIANFRANCO 227
GORMAN, GREG 49
GUDNASON, TORKIL 210

GUISTI, GEORGE 166
GUZMAN 215

HAAS, ERNST 177
HALLGREN, GARY 124
HANSEN, CONSTANCE 195
HANAUER, MARK 42
HELLER, STEVEN A 41, 240
HEISLER, GREGORY 189
HESS, MARK 62, 66, 74, 87, 188
HILLMANN, HANS 151
HISPARD, MARC 223
HITZ, CHRISTOPHER 228
HOFFMAN, MICHAEL 224
HOLLAND, BRAD 149
HOLZ, GEORGE 204
HOMER, WINSLOW 13
HORST 17, 192
HORVAT, FRANK 146
HOWE, PETER 65, 66, 70, 71, 74
HULING, PHIL 151
HURRELL, GEORGE 231

ILICH, MIRKO 189
JETTER, FRANCES 151
JOHNS, CHRIS 228

KANTUREK, LES 228
KENYON, SHAWN 42
KERN, GEOF 212, 232
KERN, GEORGE 232
KIESER, GÜNTHER 151
KIRK, DANIEL 124
KIRKLAND, DOUGLAS 236

KLEIN, VASDRI 50
KNOTT, JANET 216
KUNZ, ANITA 66, 160, 162

LEIBOVITZ, ANNIE 155-157
LEITER, SAUL 84
LEPAGE, JEAN FRANÇOIS 175, 182
LETTICK, BIRNEY 227
LEVINE, BARRY 156
LEVITEN, JAY 158
LEWIS, CINDY 231, 234
LINDBERGH, PETER 143, 175
LOWIT, R. 109
LYON, MARK 231

MCLEAN, WILSON 65, 70, 74, 76
MCMULLAN, JAMES 62, 66, 70, 71, 76
MACPHERSON, ANDREW .158
MAGEE, ALAN 189
MAHURIN, MATT 158, 232
MANORE, FRANK 234
MARK, MARY ELLEN 71
MARKEL, BRAD 189
MARKUS, KURT 161
MARSHALL, FRED 151
MASER, WAYNE 177
MATTELSON, MARVIN 186, 188
MATTER, HERBERT 15, 42, 123
MEISEL, STEVEN 102, 107, 109-111, 113, 175, 181, 183
MILLER, BRUCE 231
MITCHELL, JACK 24
MOON, SARAH 148
MOORE, JIM 212
MORGAN, SCOTT 204

MORIARTY, JERRY	69	SEARLE, RONALD	166
MORRISON, GUY	223	SEIDNER, D.	112
MOTT, GEORGE	130	SENNET, MARK	30
MULAS, UGO	104, 115	SELIGER, MARK	161, 221
MUNCH, EDVARD	151	SERLING, PETER	30
MUNKCASCI, MARTIN	14	SHAMES, STEPHANIE	50
		SIMPSON, GRETCHEN DOW	27
NACHTWEY, JAMES	213	SNOWDON, LORD	30
NADIR	195	SKREBNESKI, VICTOR	166
NAST, THOMAS	13	STEICHEN, EDWARD	14
NEWMAN, ARNOLD	166	STEINBERG, SAUL	27
NEWTON, HELMUT	141	
		TESTINO, MARIO	195, 198
PAGETTI, FRANCO	104	TOLOT, ALBERTO	192
PALMER, GLADYS PERNIT	114	TOSCANI	223
PARKINSON, NORMAN	166	TULLY, NOLLA	236
PENBERTHY, MARK	127	TUTTLE, JEAN	127
PENN, IRVING	14, 104, 139, 141, 210	
POLLOCK, IAN	191	VACHAROW, M. CHRISTOPHER	69
PORSCHE DESIGN	235	VADUKUL, MAX	213
		VALLHONRAT, JAVIER	104, 175, 180
RAY, MAN	14	VON GRAFFENRIED, MICHAEL	99
ROLSTON, MATTHEW	158, 196, 221, 240	VON UNWERTH, ELLEN	109, 195, 198
RICHARDS, EUGENE	213	
RITTS, HERB	25	WATSON, ALBERT	106, 159, 162
	49, 156, 160, 161, 179, 198, 215, 221, 228	WEBER, BRUCE	73, 138, 141, 162
ROMERO, JAVIER	127	WEGMAN, WILLIAM	50, 232
ROSENTHAL, MARC	228	WERNLI, RALPH	127
		WILCOX, DAVID	87
SADKOWSKI, ALEX	99	WOLF, HENRY	206
SAIKUSA, SATOSHI	182	WOLFF, TOM	224
SALGADO, SEBASTIAO	227	WYM, DAN	84
SALOMON, ERICH	15	
SANDERSON, BILL	191	ZIMMERMAN, JOHN	182

7 DAYS 208, 228

ABITARE 98
ADWEEK 186
ALMA 186
ALMANAC 206, 231
AMERICAN HERITAGE 86
AMERICAN MAGAZINE 13
APPAREL ART 15
ARCHITECTURAL RECORD 15
ART CENTER REVIEW 40–42, 239, 240
ART NEWS 15
THE ATLANTIC MONTHLY 23, 69, 186, 188
AUTO 234
AUTO GALLERY 231
AVANT-GARDE 19
AVIATION WEEK 123
AVENUE 94, 98

BASTA 98
BOSTON GLOBE 186
BOSTON GLOBE MAGAZINE 216
BULLETIN INDEX 165
BUSINESS TOKYO 186, 188
BUSINESS WEEK 24, 123–127
BUZZ 52, 56

CARING 213
CHORUS 98
CITY OF MEMPHIS 157
CLASS 98
CLOSE 95
CUE 186

DALLAS TIMES-HERALD 186
DOMUS 98

ELLE 18, 36, 37, 223
EMIGRE 53–56, 89
ENTERPRISE 208
EPOCA 95
EROS 19
ESQUIRE 18, 24, 28–30, 36
. . . . 62, 65, 71, 83, 84, 86, 175, 185, 186, 191, 215, 240

THE FACE 89, 96, 98
FACT 19

FAZ MAGAZIN 98, 145–153
FMR 95, 129, 135
FOLIO 117
FORBES 98
FOREIGN AFFAIRS 24
FORTUNE 15, 186, 188

GENERAL MAGAZINE 13, 81
THE GENTLEMAN'S MAGAZINE 13
GENTLEMAN'S QUARTERLY 24, 25,
. . . . 175, 192, 195–196, 198
GLOBE 98
GODEY'S LADY'S BOOK 13
GOOD HOUSEKEEPING 18
GRAHAM'S MAGAZINE 13
GRAPHIS 117, 165, 234, 235

HARPER'S BAZAAR 15, 18, 23, 36, 82, 83, 103, 165
HARPER'S WEEKLY 12, 13
HEALTH MAGAZINE 66
HOLIDAY 18, 165, 166
HOUSE AND GARDEN 15

ID 234
INDUSTRIAL LAUNDERER 117–121
INDUSTRY UPDATE '87 216
INTERVIEW 36, 175–177, 179

JARDIN DES MODES 18, 186

KING 98
KNOLL TABLOID 42

LADIES' HOME JOURNAL 13, 18
LANGUAGE OF VISION 15
L.A. STYLE 42, 204, 212, 228
LA VANGUARDIA 62, 75, 186
L'EUROPE 186
L'EXPRESS 186
L'EXPRESS 2: SPORT 188
LIFE 15, 39, 62, 70, 86, 185, 213, 240
LIFE, 150 YEARS OF PHOTOGRAPHY 210
LIRE 186, 187, 240
LITHOPINION 19
LOOK 10, 12, 18, 39, 157
THE LOS ANGELES TIMES 186
LUI 95